WHAT I LEARNED AS A

MORON

#1 *New York Times* Bestselling Author

MIKE EVANS

Your Road Map to Happiness

WHAT I LEARNED AS A MORON

TimeWorthy
BOOKS

P.O. BOX 30000, PHOENIX, AZ 85046

**Dedicated to those who
have been bullied as a child**

As a child, my favorite thing to do was hiding from bullies. There were so many bullies in my life that it would be impossible to name all of them.

I have a piece of pencil lead in my left hand from a bully in the fifth grade who tried to stab me in the face with his pencil. I always went to school late because I knew the bullies would beat me up. They did. I was bullied over dozens of things. I was very skinny as a kid, so I used to wear two pairs of socks and two pairs of pants to school because the kids would laugh at me and say, "You're so skinny you must have to jump around in the shower to get wet. You're so skinny that if you stuck out your tongue you would look like a zipper."

Well, I was that skinny. When I tried to get into the Army at 17 I failed the physical. I only weighed 111 pounds and was five foot, eleven inches tall. The minimum was 132 pounds. I went home and saw a sports magazine from Ryan's Sporting Goods with the picture of a muscle-bound man with his beautiful girlfriend kicking sand in the face of a skinny kid at the beach. I was the skinny kid.

The advertisement was to buy weights and build muscles. I did just that. I went down to Ryan's Sporting Goods and bought four five-pound weights and three stretch belts. I put 10 pounds near my right leg, suspended from the stretch belts, 10 pounds near my left leg, and bought a pair of boxer shorts to hide the weights.

I went back to take the physical again 30 days later. I

was walking with little steps and the sergeant said, "Boy, take a step like a man." I did and the weights clanged. I fell to my knees with tears streaming down my face.

When I got on the scale, it read 132. The sergeant said, "Isn't it amazing? I told you to go home and eat bananas. You must have eaten a lot of them because you weigh exactly 132 pounds." He laughed.

Being bullied is no laughing matter, especially when the biggest bully in your life is your father and you have nowhere to hide from him. Bullying is a cruel and terrible thing. If you're being bullied, it's not your fault. No one deserves to be bullied. Bullying happens at all ages and levels of life. Bullying is a global epidemic.

Everyone has a bullying story. Bullies come in all forms. They can be a parent, a president, or a peer. You can be bullied for the color of your skin or the style of your hair or your looks or your nationality. The bully I lived with was my father. He was relentless. The only word he ever called me besides curse words was moron. I heard the word moron thousands of times.

I sat down with my 10-year-old granddaughter recently. I told her my story of how I was struggling at the age of 10 and how she could turn her fire into fuel and her pain into power, purpose, and passion. She was facing a test called the STAR test in which she was given a low chance of passing it. She didn't simply pass it. She crushed it. I asked her, "Brooke. How did you do that?"

She smiled and said, "I turned my fire into fuel and my pain into power." I pray the same will happen with you.

CONTENTS

FOREWORD

I f ever there was a book that I believe you should read, it's *What I Learned as a Moron*. I've had the privilege of not only being a pastor but I've also had the privilege of knowing Mike Evans closer than any pastor in America for several decades now, and also being with him face to face in many meetings with world leaders. I've never met a person who had been abused and bullied more by his own father who has such astonishing confidence and has literally impacted the world.

Mike could not defend one Jew, his mother, against a Jew-hater, his father, who strangled him and left him for dead at 11 when he attempted to defend his mother from his father's abuse. His pain was turned into power, purpose, and passion. No person has done more to combat antisemitism than Mike through his Ten Boom museum in Holland, of which I served on the board, and his Friends of Zion Heritage Center in Jerusalem, and his 109 books, and thousands of events over the years, including his Facebook page that is the largest in religion globally and was created to combat antisemitism through the Jerusalem Prayer Team.

Mike Evans has ministered face to face to more than 20 million people. He was the first minister to preach the gospel in the Kremlin Palace in Moscow and the first to hold a national crusade in the Killing Fields of Cambodia. The list of lives that Mike Evans has impacted is endless. From sports figures like boxing champion

Evander Holyfield, NFL football player Deion Sanders, and NBA legend Michael Jordan, to entertainers like Steven Tyler, Jon Voight, Pat Boone, Mel Gibson, and Jay Leno, to more than 50 ambassadors throughout the world, and more world leaders and diplomats than I could even name.

Some of the leaders he has served have included President George W. Bush, President Donald Trump, Henry Kissinger, the Presidents of the Philippines, El Salvador, Guatemala, Honduras, Brazil, and Georgia, Prince Albert of Monaco, the Crown Prince of Dubai Sheikh Hamdan bin Mohammed, the Crown Prince of Saudi Arabia Mohammed bin Salman Al Saud, King Abdullah II bin Al-Hussein of Jordan, President Abdel Sisi of Egypt, and virtually all of Israel's Prime Ministers and many of Israel's Presidents.

I don't know of any minister of the gospel who has impacted more world leaders and the nation of Israel than Mike Evans has.

There is no Christian in the world closer to Prime Minister Benjamin Netanyahu and the late President of Israel Shimon Peres than Mike Evans. The revelation of living for God is not a sermon. It is a message that Mike Evans has lived out and I've had the privilege of seeing it face to face.

I pray that this book, *What I Learned as a Moron*, will transform your life the same way it transformed Mike's so that you fully understand why you were born and how you can be led and fed by the Holy Spirit to fulfill your assignment and finish strong for the glory of God.

—Pastor Mike Atkins

Mike Evans with his bicycle as a boy.

Childhood picture of Mike Evans.

Mike Evans with his mother and father
and his sisters Sherry and Sheila.

Mike Evans with his sister Sherry.

Mike and Carolyn's first daughter Michelle in front of their first home on Dream Lane.

Mike Evans (right) as a child.

Mike's mother Jean Levine.

Mike's parents Robert and Jean with his siblings Bobby, Sheila, and Jimmy.

AUTHOR'S NOTE

What I Learned as a Moron

The only word my father ever called me as a child was moron. He said it thousands of times and I believed it. I never went to high school because I thought I was a moron. Going to grade school was humiliating. I had failing grades. I even failed kindergarten.

I even failed an IQ test which only confirmed I was in fact a moron. I never read a word. I simply checked the boxes.

I picked tobacco with migrants at 13 and 14 making 20 cents an hour. I worked three jobs at the age of 15: construction from 8 a.m. to 4 p.m., bagging groceries from 6 p.m. to 9 p.m., and waxing floors Friday and Saturday nights from 11 p.m. to 7 a.m.

My mother was an Orthodox Jew. At the age of four, I was watching cartoons and after they ended, Billy Graham came on. She rushed over and shut the TV off and said, "Never watch this again. Christians hate Jews. Christians killed Jews. Billy Graham, Adolf Hitler, and the Pope are all Christians. Jesus died. Don't dig him up.

"I named you after your great grandfather, Rabbi Mikel Katznelson, who was burned to death in his synagogue with 2,000 Jews. Christians boarded up the windows and the doors of the synagogue and lit it on fire screaming, 'Christ-killers! Christ-killers!'"

As a child, I was beaten up for being a kike. I came home the first time crying, saying, "They beat me up for being a kite."

My mother said, "No, it's a Yiddish word. It means Christ's killer."

When I was young, we were very poor. We lived in the projects. I used to go to the dump for food. Most people don't know what white chocolate is. It's black chocolate that goes bad and the stores throw it out.

Years later I would push my mother's grocery cart home from the A&P grocery store on Friday nights. She didn't drive.

On the way home, professing Christians would throw eggs and tomatoes at her screaming, "Jew witch."

My father got drunk every Friday night. He would walk to the Twilight Cafe. He was an angry drunk. He'd get home between 1 a.m. and 2 a.m. Saturday mornings, and would always sit my mother down in a chair at the bottom of the stairs, screaming at her and slapping her in the face, calling her a Jewish whore and saying that I was not his son. He claimed that she had an affair with a Jewish man. She wore sunglasses a lot because of her black eyes.

I would sit on the top of the stairs crying, feeling it was my fault and wishing that I had never been born.

I felt that she was being beaten up because of me.

My father never called me son, never said l love you, and never affirmed me. The only words he called me were moron and curse words.

He began abusing me at the age of four. I ran away from home the first time only two blocks to the park with no shoes on. It was in the fall. Leaves were everywhere.

There were elderly people from a nursing home feeding pigeons. One of the nurses saw me crying and handed me bread crumbs and said, "Here little boy. Feed the pigeons."

I threw the bread crumbs down and ran off screaming, "I don't want to feed the pigeons."

My father went to church every Sunday. they called him Brother Bob. He had a big Thompson Chain Reference Bible.

At the age of eight, I found a jackknife in the snow. I was so excited that I showed it to my father. He said, "You're a liar. God hates liars."

He took me down to the basement, stripped off all my clothes, took an extension cord, and began beating me and screaming, "I will beat you to death unless you tell me the truth. God hates liars." He almost succeeded. He locked me into a dirt cellar filled with cobwebs and rats. I was covered with my own blood.

On a Monday when I was 11 the teacher told the class, "Tomorrow I want you to tell the class what you want to be when you grow up?" I showed up late hoping they would not get to me because I had a terrible stuttering problem and my only goal was to be alive at 20. I was sitting by the red bell by the door.

It was my turn just before the bell rang. I said, stuttering, "20." Everyone started laughing.

What happens to children like me with no hope. They end up dead or in prison or a mental institution or as drunks or alcoholics sleeping in the gutters. I had zero self-esteem. Hundreds of fears. I could not look a person in the eye.

Hope is the oxygen of the soul. When a child never hears I love you, or a word of affirmation, even the word son, but only curse words and moron, that child is doomed in the natural.

At the Vatican with the ninth president of the State of Israel, Shimon Peres, the international chairman of my Friends of Zion Museum, he told Pope Francis, "Michael was named after his great grandfather, Rabbi Mikel Katznelson who was burned to death in his synagogue with 2,000 Jews."

The Pope said in his broken English, "You are a Jewish man. Tell me how you came to Jesus Christ."

I shared my story with the Pope and Shimon Peres. They both began weeping. At the end, the Pope took my hand and said, "Pray for me."

This is what I shared with the Pope.

I woke up around 2 a.m. hearing my mother crying. As I sat on the top of the stairs as I had many times before, my father was calling her a Jewish whore. I got my courage up and screamed, "Stop it!"

He ran up the stairs and picked me up over his head by my throat and strangled me. As I looked into his raging, bloodshot eyes, I knew my life was over and that I'd never live to be 20.

When I became conscious after my father strangled me, I woke up in a fetal position. I had vomited all over myself. I shook my fist at God, and in anger screamed, "Why was I born?" I was angry that I was alive. My mother was getting beaten up every week because of me, I thought, and my father hated me. I should have never been born.

Suddenly, the brightest light I'd ever seen filled the room.

I thought it was my father with a spotlight coming in to finish me off, so I threw my hands up to protect my face. But it was quiet. He was never quiet.

I decided to peak through my fingers. Suddenly, I saw two nail-scarred wrists. No, the scars were not in the hands. I thought I must have gone nuts. I don't believe in Jesus. What's this? I looked up and saw the most beautiful eyes that I had ever seen.

Every color in the rainbow was in those eyes. And they were smiling eyes. You could see eternity through those eyes and angels. they were like magnets, you couldn't take your eyes off those eyes. I'd never seen a man smile until I saw the eyes of Jesus.

He looked at me with such amazing love. And he spoke and said, "Son." I'd never heard the word son. Then he said, "I love you." I'd never heard the words I love you. Then he said, "I have a great plan for your life." And he left.

But that was not the only thing that left. My speech impediment left, and my stomach ulcer left.

The only thing that didn't change was that in the morning I noticed the outline of every finger of my father's hand on my neck because he squeezed so tight that the blood went through between his fingers.

But because of hope, my pain that night was turned into power, purpose, and passion. My fire was turned into fuel.

I knew instantly why I had been born. I could not defend one Jew against a Jew-hater. I was born to defend all the Jews.

In January of this year, I was nominated for the Nobel Peace Prize for my life's work of combating antisemitism.

The first principle I learned as a moron is to. . .

1. MAJOR IN MENTORS

In 1980 I was walking through the Fairmont Hotel in Dallas Texas when a man pulled on the back of my jacket in the lobby. I had never met him before. He spoke and said, "Don't be discouraged. Peace, peace, peace. You are the seed of Abraham. I know what your father did to you, but I am your heavenly Father and have a great plan for your life. I will give you the nation of Israel. Isaiah 43:18-19."

That man was John Osteen. He became my mentor and a father figure to me. He was the first man on Earth to believe in me.

He had no idea who I was nor how discouraged I was. I was suffering from posttraumatic stress, a major neurological condition that I was told was incurable, tachycardia, and panic attacks. I thought it was over. I never told anyone the pain I was in, not even God. I loved Jesus but was scared of God because he was a Father. My only frame of reference of a father was my abusive father.

I drove home that day weeping and meditating on the promise John Osteen gave me from Isaiah 43:18-19: "Do not remember the former things, Nor consider the things of old. Behold, I will do a new thing, Now it shall spring forth; Shall we not know it? I will even make a road in the wilderness And rivers in the desert."

I sent a fax the next day to Prime Minister Begin of Israel, whom I did not know at the time, and asked him to meet with me. The Prime Minister said yes.

In the meeting, The prime minister asked me, "Why did you come?" I repeated the question because I didn't know why God had told me to come but didn't tell me why.

He talked for 10 minutes. Then he asked me again, "Why did you come?" I repeated the question, "Why did I come?"

He talked for another 10 minutes. Then he said, "Don't repeat the question." I said, "Mr. Prime Minister, I don't know why I came. I only know that God sent me."

He looked at me in astonishment and turned to his chief of staff and said " Can you believe it? He's the first man who has ever come to me and said God sent him but he doesn't know why." You have finally met an honest man shake his hand

Then the Prime Minister said Mike, do me a favor. The moment God tells you why, come back and tell me."

It was my birthday, the 30th of June 1980. Before I left I said, "I came to build a bridge."

He laughed and said, "The Brooklyn Bridge?"

I said, "No, a bridge of love between Bible-believing Christians and Bible-believing Jews."

He said, "We shall build that bridge together."

On the fourth of July, as I was praying, the Spirit of God spoke to me to go to the home of Benzion Netanyahu whose son Jonathan had been killed leading the Entebbe raid in Uganda. It was the anniversary of his death. I felt I was to comfort the family. I didn't know them. Benzion invited me in for tea. Shortly his second son arrived, Benjamin Netanyahu. He was 28 years old, grieving his brother's death. He was selling furniture for a company called RIM.

I prayed over him and said "Jonathan loved David. You loved Jonathan. Out of the ashes of your despair will come strength from God and you will be the prime minister of Israel."

He looked at me and said to his father in Hebrew, "You let a moron in the house." His father Benzion said, "Not an ordinary moron. This is the authentic moron."

I went back to Prime Minister Begin on July 5 and told him I met the Prime Minister of Israel yesterday. He said, "You are mistaken. You met me on June 30."

I said, "It's not you," and shared with him the prophecy and asked him to give Benjamin Netanyahu a job in the government. He agreed and asked Reuben Hecht his senior advisor to offer him a position.

Days later Reuben Hecht was giving a lecture on Babylonian art. At the end of the lecture, the distinguished elderly man asked if anyone had a question. I asked a question, but it was a political question. He cut me off and said, "Young man, that's not an appropriate question."

Then at the end of his lecture, he came up to me, took me by the arm, and said, "Come with me." He took me to the top floor of a big building where his office was. I had no idea who the man was. He was a senior adviser to the Prime Minister of Israel. He was a billionaire.

And he said, "Young man, that's a very good question you asked me." And he kept saying to me, "Don't call me Dr. Hecht." Since I was so young, I kept calling him Dr. Hecht. He said, "Call me by my first name, Reuben."

As we got ready to leave, I shook his hand with both of mine and I said, "It's so great to be with you today, Joseph."

He raised his voice and said, "You did that intentionally. That's not my name. It's Ruben."

I said, "I'm sorry. It's jetlag. I apologize."

"No, don't apologize. You did it intentionally. Sit down. The year was 1943. My father was a shipbuilder in Belgium. He was dying. He took my hand and his last words were, "Joseph, Joseph, the nation will be born and you will feed them bread.' And he died. No human being knows the story except my wife, Edith. You called me Joseph."

Reuben became my mentor and opened up the whole nation of Israel for me. He brought me into Menachem Begin's cabinet at a very young age. He took me to the founder of Israel intelligence Mossad who also mentored me.

Your ability to succeed is not determined by the things you know but by the things you do not know.

When you know what you don't know it creates hunger which is the fuel that ignites astonishing inventions.

When you recognize that, you'll seek mentors in your life that have wisdom and gifts that you don't have. Those who do not seek mentors are filled with pride.

Pride is the anesthesia that deadens the pain of stupidity. A man can become too big in his own eyes to be used by God but never too small.

Mentors can turn your equity into currency, and your favor into influence. Mentors give you a gift, a lifetime of wisdom that you could never obtain. The sum total of your ability to succeed is determined by the things you do not know. What you know is constant. That's why mentors are so important.

For example, when I built the Friends of Zion Heritage Center in Jerusalem, my bridge of love, I needed an international chairman.

I asked a pastor friend named Robert Morris, who founded Gateway Church, but God said, "You don't need a pastor; you need a president."

The ninth President of Israel Shimon Peres, the most beloved Jew on earth, became my international chairman and opened amazing doors. I wanted to give my Friend of Zion award to world leaders. It's been given now to more than 20 world leaders, including two U.S. presidents. It's one of the most prestigious awards given in the State of Israel.

After Shimon Peres and I met with Pope Francis, over dinner that night he said to me, "Mike, I feel like you and I are family. So I researched you. And I realized we are family we both go back to a wooden synagogue.

"Everything I've done in my life was because of my inspiration, my mentor, my hero. It was my grandfather, a cantor rabbi, and my Talmud teacher Rabbi Metzner, but he had a hero. It was the chief rabbi of the synagogue. Your great grandfather, Rabbi Mikel Katznelson. Yes, your great grandfather and my grandfather were burned to death in the same synagogue. Only God could have put us together. We are in fact family. We need to write a book together on the wooden synagogue."

The second principle I learned as a moron is to. . .

2. COMMIT YOUR LIFE TO A CAUSE GREATER THAN YOURSELF

It's the key to happiness. If I had focused on myself I would have been one of the most miserable, unhappy human beings on the planet. Instead, I am the most blessed and happiest man I've ever met. That revelation transformed me from a victim into a victor.

The two greatest days in your life are the day you are born and the day you find out why you were born. You were created to be part of a God-inspired cause greater than yourself. I have had the privilege of being part of hundreds of causes greater than myself since 11.

I had a dream of building the Friends of Zion Heritage Center. It was the bridge I described to Prime Minister Begin to be light and salt to the nation of Israel and to pastor the nation.

The Friends of Zion Heritage Center campus is a city block in Jerusalem located 600 meters from the Temple Mount. This year in Ukraine, Friends of Zion, through my son Michael's leadership, has brought Holocaust survivors to Israel and 240 metric tons of food to hungry congregations filled with refugees in the bombed cities in Ukraine. That's enough food for 500,000 hungry refugees. Friends of Zion is the brightest light in Israel comforting the house of Israel.

Many told me to "stay safe" when they heard I was going to Ukraine. I responded, "No thank you. Safety does not concern me. It's about being part of a cause greater than myself. That's the safest place on earth."

I got 18 rejections from publishers on my first book, so I published it myself and made a TV special on it. That book sold 330,000 copies between July and December in 1980 months after John Osteen give me a word of hope.

That was 18 award-winning book informercials ago. I have been told I am the pioneer of book infomercials. I don't know if that's so but I do know the 111 books I have written have helped fund my kingdom projects for decades.

The book I wrote that was rejected by 18 publishers was *Israel: America's Key to Survival*. It was endorsed by the Prime Minister of Israel.

I gave him the first copy I told him, "You can't endorse it you haven't read a page."

He said, "Don't worry about it. If they criticize me, I'm a short Prime Minister. I'll stand on the newspapers and it will make me look taller. Besides, today's news is wrapped in tomorrow's fish."

The third principle I learned as a moron is to. . .

3. PUT ALL OF YOUR FAITH IN GOD

You have two choices in life, to seek man's affirmation or God's affirmation. That can only come when you put all of your faith in God.

I received supernatural hope at 11. I've spent my life seeking that divine hope over and over again, and I have received it. No, Jesus never came back to speak with me but the voice of His words in the Bible became as real to me as his words at the age of 11.

Joseph put all his faith in God. His brothers threw him into a pit and sold him as a slave. He was falsely accused and put in prison. That was his path to the palace. Joseph went to jail to become prime minister, not Yale.

Jeremiah the suffering prophet was beaten and put in stocks and sank in the mud of an empty well and his scrolls were burned because of his words. Yet he still put all his faith in God and kept giving the word of the Lord.

Jerusalem's founding mayor Teddy Kollek knew that I liked Jeremiah. He took me to his cave. It has a different name today: Golgotha. Jeremiah's assignment was at the very spot where the blood of Christ would flow.

The fourth principle I learned as a moron is to. . .

4. CELEBRATE SUFFERING AND SACRIFICE

I am not talking about desiring suffering and sacrifice, but when it comes to see it through the eyes of your mighty God as a stepping stone and not a stumbling block.

The Bible says, "Though the fig tree does not bud and there are no grapes on the vines, though the olive crop fails and the fields produce no food, though there are no sheep in the pen and no cattle in the stalls, yet I will rejoice in the Lord, I will be joyful in God my Savior" (Habakkuk 3:17-18).

Do you want to be a victim or a victor? Do you want to be comfortable or a conqueror?

Jesus is coming back as the King of kings. If you want to be a king, you're going to have to be willing to commit yourself to sacrifice and suffering. Kings process pain and pleasure differently.

The Bible says Jesus "learned obedience by the things which He suffered" (Hebrews 5:8).

Scripture adds, "And after you have suffered a little while, the God of all grace, who has called you to his eternal glory in Christ, will himself restore, confirm, strengthen, and establish you" (1 Peter 5:10).

The apostle Paul said, "For this light momentary affliction is preparing for us an eternal weight of glory, beyond all comprehension" (2 Corinthians 4:17).

In his cell in chains he said, "I can do all things through Christ who strengthens me" (Philippians 4:13). He looked at his own death sentence and suffering for Christ and said this.

When you're lied about and betrayed and you forgive and remain silent rather than attempt to destroy the person who is slandering you, you still love them and suffer for Christ's sake. The price of admission to change the world is unspeakable evil and betrayal and when it comes you cannot play the victim.

Are the things you're living for worth Christ dying for? Are you willing to live your life in the light of eternity? The apostle Paul said that he wanted to know Christ and the fellowship of His suffering. If you truly want to change the world, then celebrate suffering and sacrifice. Seek the Jesus who shows up in the flames of fire.

It is in the quiet crucible of your personal suffering that your noblest dreams are born. God's greatest gifts are given in compensation for what you've been through. You're going to be betrayed. You're going to be rejected by those you've loved the most if you choose the narrow path.

How much rejection and pain and disappointment can you tolerate before you turn your back on the Savior? Beginning strong is not a sign of a surrendered life. Finishing strong is.

When things are going well, we see Christ as a conquering Savior. But when things go badly, do you still see Him that way?

To be an overcomer you must have something to overcome. If you don't have an opponent, you don't have a victory.

Most who celebrate with you on the mountain will not be with you in the fire. Everyone wants a theology that celebrates those who get fire protection. How about a theology that celebrates those who choose to suffer in the fire and embraces a God who walks through the fire with us?

In one week the crowds went from celebrating the Savior with their Hosannas to despising and rejecting Him. As the prophet Isaiah said, they hid their faces from Him.

Jesus never hid suffering from His followers. He told them that if you follow Me you're going to have to take up My cross. The cross was a curse word. It was a symbol of shame.

The Jesus I have found is more powerful in your suffering than in your celebrations. Sometimes He stills the storms, but most of the time He stills us in the midst of the storms. His word to you and me and this generation is to take up My cross and follow Me.

Revelations born from suffering for Christ are the engines of God that fuel His eternal purposes on Earth. It will cause you to see what He sees, hear what He hears, and do what He does.

The former Jerusalem Mayor Nir Barkat grabbed my neck and shouted in my ear after I shared my testimony of suffering as a child with the nation of Israel. "Why did you share it?"

The Christian life is not about winning and being number one. It's about Jesus being number one. If I have to protect my name at all costs, my reputation at all costs, my career at all costs, my income at all costs, and my influence at all costs, it will lead to a self-inspired narrative (S.I.N.).

The Christian life is about surrendering all of our life for His glory and His story. That's what I have learned as a moron.

The Spirit of God spoke to me to humble myself in the presence of my father. It would be the only way he would come to Christ and the only way his power over me would be broken.

I went to New Hampshire and found him in a bar trying to pick up a lady younger than my sisters, calling her a baby doll. When he saw me, he started mocking me, calling me a moron. "Hey, moron," he shouted. Then he said to everyone there, "It's a preacher, a moron preacher. Preach, preacher, preach."

I took him to his trailer in the woods and put him to bed. In the morning when he sobered up I got down on my knees and told him, "I want you to put your hands on my head and pray for me. I'm going to confess my sins in your presence."

He begged me not to do it and said when he saw me on my knees, "I've committed the unpardonable sin for what I did to you. I can never be saved."

He started weeping uncontrollably. I could feel his tears on the back of my neck I said, "You haven't committed the unpardonable sin. I forgive you. God forgives you."

Just before my father died he told me about a dream he said he had hundreds of times about black stones. He said his grandfather gave two to his father, his father gave two to him, and when he tried to give them to me he couldn't. Instead, in my hands were white stones. He said, "What does it mean?"

I said, "The black stones are generational curses. Your grandfather was an abusive drunk. Your father was an abusive drunk. You became an abusive drunk. The white stones are generational blessings. My son, his son, and his son's son will never know the black stones. The curse has been broken." He wept.

This year my son Michael David Evans II became President of the Friends of Zion Heritage Center and Museum. My grandson Michael David Evans III interned at a Jerusalem law firm this summer. He's 11. He told me, "I want to lead Friends of Zion 40 years from now." That's the power of generational blessing, and that's what I learned as a moron.

WARNING

Before you read this book, I want to make it perfectly clear to you that the person you're reading about was the most broken, bullied, abused person I had ever met: me. I was convinced that I was a moron because I had been that thousands of times by my own father, but I learned how to turn the pain into power, purpose, and passion and fire into fuel.

In the natural, I would have ended up a drug addict or alcoholic or in prison or a mental institution and for sure would have died decades ago. Please don't think highly of me, but only of my God who took such a broken life and restored my soul. Know this: If He did it for me, He can do it for you. He's an equal opportunity employer.

When my father strangled me and I became conscious I was in a rage, not because my father strangled me but because I was still alive. It made no sense that I should have been born. My mother was being abused. I thought it was because of me, because my father thought she had an affair with a Jewish man and I wasn't his son.

My father hated me. He never called me son, never said I love you, and only called me a moron. I screamed in the dark at God with my fist clenched in anger, "God, why was I born?" I'm sharing this with you because I don't want you to think for a second that I'm some amazing human being. I'm not. I was completely broken and in pain when the Lord appeared to me face to face at 11 and told me He loved me and had a great plan for my life. He healed me instantly of a speech impediment, a stomach ulcer, and delivered me from hundreds of fears.

I was gloriously saved, called, filled, and I didn't know the theology of any of it. I can tell you this, that the times where I've had the greatest favor have been the times when I've been the weakest. It was when I was broken and bleeding and could not understand the suffering. I know what it is to be under attack in my physical body, in my family and my ministry. I am a man with wounds and scars.

When I went into the ministry I was very intimidated because every preacher I met seemed to be perfect. I knew how messed up I was. I never told my wife until I was 32 years old the real story of my life and my family because I had been suffering from post-traumatic stress from the abuse of my father and it was breaking my health. I was having panic attacks. One day in prayer the Lord said to me, "I want you to know me, the fellowship of my suffering, and the power of my resurrection."

I used to hate reading the Major Prophets in the Old Testament because there was so much judgment. My father was so mean that I didn't want to hear any more about judgment. I remember saying to the Lord, "Lord, I've already suffered too much. I don't want to know you and the fellowship of Your suffering."

Then He said, "You can't know me then in the power of My resurrection."

I said to the Lord, "What's the fellowship of your suffering?"

He said, "When you can get to the place that you admit

everything that you're not." That was very painful for me because there was so much I was not. It was going to take quite a bit of time. The Lord said to me, "When you're willing to acknowledge what you're not, then you can know Me in the power of My resurrection."

I'll never forget what the Holy Spirit revealed to me. When I finally came to that place in my brokenness, in my shame, and in my pain to freely admit what I was not, the Lord said, "I'm attracted to you. And what attracts Me to you most is not what you are, it's what you're not."

The Bible says He was wounded for our transgressions. He was bruised for our iniquities, and by His stripes, we are healed. When I finally came to that place, I'll never forget what the Lord said to me. He said, "The sum total of your ability to succeed is going to be determined by the things you do not know."

I had to think about that revelation. There were so many things I did not know. How in the world would my success be determined by the things I did not know? Then it hit me. Luke 2:52. It says that Jesus increased in favor with God and with men. There were people who knew things I didn't know. If I had favor with them, I could succeed. So in essence, my inabilities, the revelation of what I was not, was an enormous key to my future success.

I'd like to give you an example of turning your fire into fuel, your pain into power, purpose, and passion. In December 1990, at the age of 44, I went to Saudi Arabia I had just come out of a hospital bed after an eight and a half hour surgery. I was in excruciating pain. Plus, the pain medicine caused me to be depressed. There's no possibility in the natural that I should have gotten on the plane and flown to Saudi Arabia. But I said to the Lord, "Lord, I'm in such pain. I can't stand what I'm seeing."

And I'll never forget what He said. "See something else. Do something great for me. It's the key to happiness, committing your life to a cause greater than yourself."

I argued with the Lord. I said, "Lord, I can't go to Saudi Arabia, I don't have a visa."

He said, "You didn't apply."

I said, "Billy Graham never got to go."

He said, "He never applied either." I flew to Saudi Arabia, in my brokenness, and in my pain. I went out on the streets of Tehran to preach. It gathered a crowd just before I started preaching. I said, we're going to sing a song. There was only one problem. I can't sing. By the way, it's against the law to preach the gospel in Saudi Arabia. Even worse, they will cut your head off for doing it on Thursdays. All of a sudden, some MPs saw me and came flying towards me. I didn't see them.

They were going to arrest me before I was beheaded. They didn't want an incident. But when one MP noticed what I had said, he stopped and started singing. He was the most beautiful baritone voice I had ever heard. I didn't know he was there and he started singing, "My eye is on the sparrow, and I know He watches me."

I cried my eyes out, because I knew God had sent him. I preached my heart out to those people. I walked back to my hotel and asked, "Lord, where do I go tomorrow?"

The Holy Spirit said, "Go to the Gulf Meridian Hotel (which was the command headquarters join operation forces) and stick out your hand to the first man coming through the revolving doors and say, 'May I go with you?'"

The first man coming through the doors was a Saudi wearing a gown. I stuck up my hand. Remember, I was a broken man. I just come out of a hospital bed. My hair was shaved on the back. I still had suture marks on my neck from the neck surgery. I was a pathetic sight to behold. But I stuck up my hand and asked, "May I go with you?"

He looked at me startled and said, "Who are you? What is your name? Where are you from?" I told him. He said, "You want to go with me?" He asked three times and I said yes three times.

He said, "Be here tomorrow morning at six o'clock, you will go with me." I arrived at 5:30 in the dark and sat in the lobby. At 6:15, 12 Jeeps drove up and the fourth Jeep was the commander of the multinational forces. He was also head of the Saudi Royal Air Force. He was the governor of the Haran and he was a prince. His name was Mohammad. He was going to the Kuwaiti border to give the invasion plans to the Egyptian third arm in the Syrian High Command. He thought I knew where he was going so he took me with them. I knew nothing. I was just a broken, hurting human being. In the midst of my brokenness, God was willing to use me because I was willing to be honest and acknowledge everything I wasn't. The surge of God's glory was the gift of faith.

On the helicopter, I started sharing Christ with him. He looked at me and laughed and he said, "You know what you're trying to do? You're trying to convert me. We cut heads off on Thursday for this."

I said, "I'm sorry, my schedule is full on Thursday. I have no time to have my head cut off." He laughed.

He said, "I like you. You're a funny guy." He took me with him as he inspected the troops. He was a sight to behold. I was inspecting the Syrian Third Army and Egyptian High Command, both enemies of Israel, and here I am a Jew who is a believer in Jesus standing next to a Muslim general and Prince inspecting the troops.

Then we went into the tent with the commanders where he gave the invasion plan. I was his guest, and he told me at the at the end, "I must introduce my guests. You have to say a few words." I said to him. I'm going to say a few words. And the words I spoke were the words of life. He was my interpreter as I shared the message of my Lord and Savior Jesus Christ, with the Syrian Third Army and Egyptian High Command leaders. When we finished, he looked at me and laughed.

He said, "I can't believe you just did that. I should cut your head off with my own sword. But I like you. What do you want to do now?"

We were in the middle of the desert. What could I possibly be doing? And then I said, "I want to preach to the 82nd airborne. They're embedded on the Kuwait border."

He said, "I can't take you there but the French Foreign Legion can." So he called to French Foreign Legion helicopters. They had no doors on them. They took me down there and the chaplain was crying when I told him who I was and why I came.

He said, "This is unbelievable. I can't believe that the Saudi Prince brought you in here."

That night, dirty and exhausted as I got back to the hotel, all the Kuwaiti princes were sitting with their worry beads in their hand in the lobby. As I started to pass them, the Spirit of God came upon me. I held my big hand up with my five fingers. I said, "Behold the five fingers of my hand. I am sent here by my Lord and Savior, the Lord Jesus Christ, to prophesy unto you, that within five days' time, you will have your country back without hardly shedding any blood."

The Kuwaiti princes looked at me and said, "If this comes to pass, then you are truly a prophet of God and we will invite you to come to Kuwait and share the message of your Jesus with the royal family."

No matter where you are today, as you're reading this book, I want to encourage you. If you're discouraged, if you're depressed, if you're fearful, I've been there. If you're weak, I've been there. If you're broke, I've been there. If you've been betrayed, I've been there.

At the age of 32, I seemed to be doing fantastic. I was written up in Time Magazine, I had preached in Arrowhead Stadium to 45,000 people, and at Giants Stadium to 60,000 people, but I was suffering unspeakable agony from post-traumatic stress from my childhood.

Few understand the pain people go through with post-traumatic stress unless they have experienced it personally. I told no one. Because of holding all of that pain I began having what's called tachycardia. My heart rate would surge and I began having panic attacks. They began when I was on TV in Atlanta at a press conference when the cameras were on me. The microphone was in my hand and I began shaking. It was terribly embarrassing.

The next six times I was preaching in churches the panic attacks happened with a microphone in my hand. Combine with the tachycardia and panic attacks, I developed a very rare neurological disease called spasmodic torticollis (also called cervical dystonia). It was from a gene among Ashkenazi Jews, which of course my background was Ashkenazi. It put the muscles in my neck into spasms 24 hours a day and my neck had terrible tremors.

When it first started happening, no one could diagnose it. Many doctors told me that I needed to go to a psychiatrist and that I obviously had some type of emotional problems as a child. Well, they were right that I did, but the spasmodic torticollis was not a mental condition. It was a neurological condition. I was in such agony that for 14 months I stopped preaching and would sit on the back steps of my ministry depressed and crying. I was ashamed that I was so weak and had let so many people down in my mind, including my darling wife and my staff at that time, which was over 35 people, along with my partners and my ministry peers.

I thought it was completely over for me. I didn't believe I could ever recover from the crisis I was facing. The stress became so severe that I started getting chest pains as if someone was stabbing me through the heart, and ended up in a cardiology ward. I'll never forget the first few days in that ward. There was a man who was screaming, terrified and fearful, yelling, "God help me!" Every couple of days the nurses would close the curtains on my room. I knew why they were doing it. Someone had died.

The man who was screaming, "God help me," wouldn't stop. Other people in the cardiology ward were screaming from their rooms for him to stop. I finally went into his room and put my hand on his arm. The moment I did he almost came out of his skin in fear. He thought God had shown up.

I told him, "I can tell you how you can get help from God." There in his room, I led him to the Lord Jesus Christ. The tears flowed down his face. Shortly thereafter he fell asleep I went back to my room.

The nurses were quite upset at me because I had disconnected from my heart monitor. They connected me back up and I fell asleep in an hour. When I woke up, I heard that same guy yelling, "Jesus help me! Jesus help me!" I started laughing till I was crying.

When I got out of the cardiology ward, I told Carolyn I needed to go to my father and ask his forgiveness. The pain and agony of his abuse were eating me alive like acid. In the natural it made no sense. My father was the one who needed to ask forgiveness, not me. But the Lord told me to manifest radical obedience and radical humility.

I drove down to New Hampshire looking for him. He was at a bar sitting next to a young lady that was younger than my own sister. He was half drunk, trying to pick her up, sweet-talking her and calling her baby. When he saw me, he turned to the other drunks in the bar and said, "Hey, my son the preacher is here. Preach, preach, preach," he chanted, and started laughing at me.

I took my father home to his trailer in the woods. I told him, "I'm going to get down on my knees and humble myself in your presence. I want to ask for your forgiveness. Then I want you to put your hands on my head and pray for me and forgive me."

My father said several times, "Don't do this," but I did. I knelt down. He started hesitating. I said, "Put your hands on my head and pray for me. I ask for your forgiveness. I humble myself."

All of a sudden, a man whose heart was like a stone started to break and I could feel hot tears flowing down my neck from his face. I heard him say, "I belong in the darkest hell for what I did to you as a child. God can never forgive me. I committed the unpardonable sin. I hated you because I saw the hand of Jesus on your life and I couldn't stand being in your presence."

That night with tears streaming down his face, I led him in the sinner's prayer. Something supernatural happened that night. The generational curse that was on his grandfather went on his father and on him. I told him that the generational curse is broken. And my son and his son will never know that curse, but only the generational blessings. He wept as I said it.

Radical forgiveness, radical humility, and radical obedience set me free and delivered me from the darkest hell of pain and agony. I was desperately trying to get man's approval through my works, which I could never get from my father. I had been working seven days a week, 14 to 16 hours a day for years on end.

The Lord spoke to me and said, "I want you to preach, plan, pray, and play. Divide your week into four quadrants. Use 25% of your time preaching, 25% of your time planning, 25% of your time praying, and 25% of your time playing."

I didn't play as a child. I started working at eight years of age when I had was laughed at because of holes in my pants and paint on my sneakers. When I told my father, he said, "Get a job and buy yourself some." I began shoveling snow, cutting grass, and delivering newspapers for a shopping center. By 15 I was working 100 hours a week for a construction company from eight to four, bagging groceries from six to nine, and waxing floors on Friday and Saturday nights.

I had never played and yet the Lord told me, "I want you to play." I'm sharing the most intimate details of my life to help you because I don't want you to think I was born with a silver spoon in my mouth and that I had the strength and the gifts to achieve what I've achieved. I want you to understand that I was the most unlikely person to be used the way God has used me. I want to encourage you to know that God did it for me and He can do it for you.

Mike and Carolyn at their wedding
November 19, 1979.

Lakewood Church Pastor
Joel Osteen and family visiting
Friends of Zion in Jerusalem.

Sheldon Adelson receiving the Friends of
Zion award with Miriam, with former
U.S. Ambassador to Israel David Friedman.

U.S. ambassadors with Donna Summers at Friends of Zion.

INTRODUCTION

Faith sees the invisible, believes the unbelievable,

and receives the impossible. [1]

As you get ready to read *What I Learned as a Moron* I want to ask you a question. What will be important in your life 100 years from now?

The answer is quite simple. Only the things that you do that echo throughout eternity. As I'm writing this I am just completing reading through the entire Bible from Genesis to Revelation in 21 days along with a 21-day Daniel fast. It feels like a spiritual IV.

I went to my dermatologist this morning. Before she met with me, her assistant came into the room. I felt the Spirit of God on me and I looked at the young lady named Ruby. "Ruby," I asked her. "Do you have peace with God?"

She said, "No, I don't. I don't know how to have peace with God."

I had the wonderful privilege over the next few minutes of leading Ruby to the Lord Jesus Christ as the tears streamed down her face that she was gloriously born again. Seconds later, the doctor walked in, who happens to also be a believer. I told her, "I'd like to introduce you to your new sister in the Lord."

The most important thing in life is being filled with the Holy Spirit and being led by the Holy Spirit. My prayer is that you will understand this revelation and find favor with God and with man from the Scripture in Luke 2:52.

On my very first trip to Israel in 1972, I was part of a tour that was having a lecture about Babylonian art. I was not interested at all in Babylonian art, but I endured that lecture. The lecture was given by a very distinguished elderly man with a white goatee by the name of Dr. Hecht. At the end of the lecture, he asked the tour group, "Do you have any questions?"

Several had questions about Babylonian art. I spoke up and said, "If Israel is weakened, will not radical Islam strike America and more specifically, New York City, and its tallest building the Empire State Building?"

He looked at me in disdain and said, "Young man, that's not an appropriate question. This is about Babylonian art." I apologized.

When the lecture ended, he came up to me and said, "Come with me." He took me up to his office and asked me questions about who I was and why I asked such a question. I kept calling him Dr. Hecht. He kept saying, "Don't call me Dr. Hecht. Call me back by my first name, Reuben."

He said, "I liked your question, but it wasn't appropriate for Babylonian art. Why did you ask that question?"

I told him that everything in the Middle East is based upon phallic symbols, and America's largest phallic symbol is New York and its tallest building. The world was pressuring Israel to give up land for peace. My concern was that Israel was the firewall keeping radical Islam from striking the West.

We had a wonderful conversation, but he kept saying to me, "Stop calling me Dr. Hecht. Call me Ruben." He was older and I was quite young and I felt it was disrespectful.

When he started to leave I reached out and shook his hand and said, "Great being with you today, Joseph."

He loudly said, "I told you my name was Reuben."

I said, "I apologize. It was a mistake. It was jet lag."

"No," he said. "It wasn't jet lag. You did it intentionally. Sit down."

I sat down and he told me a story. He said, "The year was 1943 in Belgium. My father was a shipbuilder, and he was dying. He took my hand as he breathed his last breath. He said, 'Joseph, Joseph, the nation of Israel will be born and you will feed it bread,' and he died. Joseph in the Bible fed the nation of Israel bread, so I sold the shipping business and started the granary of Israel. No human being knows this story except my wife, Edith. I have no children and I told her to tell no one. How was it possible that you knew the story of Joseph?"

I said, "I didn't know it. The Spirit of God knew."

Reuben Hecht became a spiritual mentor and father to me. He opened up the entire nation and brought me into Prime Minister Menachem Begin's cabinet. He was the senior advisor of the prime minister and a billionaire. That, without a doubt, was the favor of God.

I want to share a few more stories with you about favor to inspire you to hunger and thirst for this wonderful gift from heaven.

Living in the favor of God comes with a gift called the gift of faith. It opens incredible doors.

The Middle East peace summit took place in 1991 in Madrid, and the Spirit of the Lord told me to go there. Astonishingly, I got in as a journalist in the first seat in the first row. In the room were the most powerful leaders of the world, including Mikhail Gorbachev, President Herbert Walker Bush, and most of the Arab leaders of the world at that time.

As I was getting ready to come in, I noticed they had a huge statue being taken out of the palace and it depicted a king slaying a demon. It was a bronze statue. I asked someone, "Why are they removing it?"

They said, "Because it's not appropriate. This is a peace conference." I noticed that Prime Minister Shamir who was leading the Israeli delegation was sitting next to a very young Israeli who was his communication minister Benjamin Netanyahu. During a break, shockingly, the Egyptian ambassador came up to me and started talking to me like he and I were old friends. I had never met him before.

I said to the Egyptian ambassador, "Why don't you do what your most famous prime minister and foreign minister did?"

He said, "We have never had a prime minister who was also a foreign minister at the same time."

I said yes, "You did. His name was Joseph. And he forgave his brothers. He looked at me astonished. In seconds, the Syrian Foreign Minister walked up thinking that I must be a very close friend of the Egyptian ambassador and he began talking to me.

He said, "I want to show you a picture." He showed me a

picture of Prime Minister Shamir back in the days when Shamir was fighting the British when they were keeping Jews from coming to the country of Israel. He said, "I'm going to show this picture tomorrow at three o'clock, and accuse Shamir of being a terrorist. Spread the word around."

Benjamin Netanyahu was watching the foreign minister show me the picture. He put his hand up to his ear asking me to call him. I did.

He said, "What was he showing you?" I told him what the picture was and what the plan was. The next day was Friday, which is the day the Arabs consider the holy day. They call it Jum'ah, but all the Arabs were there.

At around two o'clock, Prime Minister Shamir stood up and said, "You know, I'm an Orthodox Jew and we need to be back in Israel before the Shabbat. I leave this meeting with my delegation and wish you all well." Then he left the room.

After he left, the foreign minister of Syria got up to speak but the only thing he could speak to was an empty chair because Shamir wasn't there. You see, it was a favor driven moment. God led me to be in the right place at the right time. The opportunity of a lifetime has to be seized in the lifetime of the opportunity, but it can only be seized if we're Spirit-led.

In 1972, the same year that I went to Israel, I met Corrie Ten Boom. It seemed by accident. I was in Texarkana, Arkansas, and I saw this elderly lady carrying her bag into a hotel. I ran up to carry it for her and she said, "It's okay young man. I'm a tramp for the Lord. But if you wish to carry it, you must have soup with me."

I had soup with Corrie Ten Boom. She asked me to tell her my story. I told her my personal testimony and she wept. Then she told me her story and I wept. I asked Corrie, "Is there any prayer you've ever prayed that hasn't been answered yet?"

She said, "Only one. That the Beje would be a witness for the Lord." The Beje was the name she used for the Ten Boom house in Holland.

When Corrie died, the Spirit of God spoke to me to go to Holland and purchase the house to answer that prayer. When I asked the owner of the house, who was an unbeliever, if he would sell it, he told me no.

I asked him, "Can I pray?"

He said, "Pray if you like."

As I prayed, all the clocks went off. It was at noon. He said to me, "Do you know what day today is?"

I answered, "No."

He said, "It's the 15th of April." That meant nothing to me. I didn't know why the date was special. Then he explained it to me.

He said, "That was the day that Corrie was born and the day she died. Yes, I will sell you the clock shop."

Not only did he sell it to me, but I purchased all of the Ten Boom articles that were in it from when she was alive from family members and turned it into a glorious witness for the Lord to answer Corrie's prayer that she shared with me that day about the Ten Boom clock shop.

The story that Corrie shared with me in Texarkana came back. She told me she was 51 and she was in a concentration camp. She was sad because it was going to be her birthday the next day. She said to the Lord, "Do you have a birthday gift for me? My father always has a big birthday party."

She said the Lord spoke to her in her spirit and said, "Yes, the last verse of the 91st Psalm."

The verse reads, "With long life shall I satisfy you."

The next day, Corrie turned 52. All the women Corrie's age were executed shortly thereafter, but Corrie was released by a clerical error. She lived 40 more years. She was 51 when the Lord gave her that birthday gift, the last verse of Psalm 91: "With long life shall I satisfy you." She lived to be 91. The birthday gift God gave her was 40 more years of life and ministry to change the world.

It's not possible to have this kind of favor in our own power. It's the favor of God. It only comes to people who are hungry and thirsty for a favor driven life.

Many years ago, God spoke to my heart to go into the third world, into war zones, into very difficult places, and share the gospel. He told me He was going to open up Africa and then said I was to go to Mexico to a certain hotel and pray. I told my wife and she looked at me kind of funny. She didn't say anything because she knows that the Holy Spirit has directed me in unusual ways. But this was very unusual. God was going to open Africa to me by me taking a trip to a certain hotel in Mexico.

I traveled to the hotel and was walking down the sidewalk in the back of the hotel one morning, praying as a couple was walking toward me. I had never met them and didn't know them. Yet the Spirit of God led me to say to the woman, "I'll help you with that African president that you are concerned about." So I said it to the woman.

The woman looked at her husband and asked, "Did you talk to him?"

He said, "No, I don't know him."

She looked at me again and asked, "You're going to help me with the African president that I'm concerned about? I say yes. She said, "My name is Maureen Reagan Revell. I'm the chairwoman of the Republican Party. My father is President Ronald Reagan. I've just met with all the key African presidents. One of them named Yoweri Museveni needs my help desperately but I can't help him. He wants to come to America and get the support of the United States but he needs a press conference in Washington, D.C., and I can't set it up. Can you?"

I said, "Absolutely." I walked up to my room and called the Executive Director of the National Religious Broadcasting Association, Ben Armstrong. I said, "Ben, my friend, would you have Ugandan President Museveni as one of the speakers on the platform the day that President Ronald Reagan speaks at the Hilton Hotel?" He said yes.

Maureen Reagan brought not only Museveni, but his entire cabinet came with them to the Hilton Hotel. I hosted them in my suite. It was an astonishing meeting. He was doing it to honor me for opening the door.

I asked President Museveni if he was a follower of the Lord Jesus Christ. He said, "No, I have no respect for Christians. Evangelists came into my country and did very wicked things."

I got on my knees and said, "I humbly ask for forgiveness."

He looked at me and said, "Why are you on your knees? It wasn't you."

I said, "Yes, if it was my brother, he was me and I want to repent."

Museveni asked, "What do I have to do to get you off your knees? Accept Jesus as my Savior?" I said yes.

I led Museveni to the Lord Jesus Christ in that room. The most astonishing thing then happened. He stood up and turned to the Anglican Archbishop and said to him, "You preach Jesus on Sundays but on Monday, Tuesday, Wednesday, Thursday, Friday, and Saturday, your people go to the witch doctors and have fetishes on their wrist and their waist and you do nothing about it. You don't stop them from going to the witch doctors. Your father is a devil. I commend you to repent and accept Jesus. Now!"

I had never heard a human being speak like this. But sure enough, the Anglican Archbishop repented, just as Museveni had said. I whispered in his ear and asked, "Isn't that a little bit too strong?"

He whispered in my ear and asked, "What would Jesus do?"

I said, "Carry on."

He went to the Roman Catholic Archbishop, shouting at him to repent, and he did.

I'm sharing these astonishing stories to get your hopes up. I am the most unlikely person that God could ever use. When you read this book, you'll understand my testimony and know that it's not because of me. It's truly God's favor. The most powerful gift in the Bible was the gift of faith. It's the gift that Jesus operated in more than any other gift. It's my prayer that the Holy Spirit will put such a hunger in your heart for a favor driven life and the gift of faith that your life will be transformed by it and you'll never be the same.

When you start experiencing the God's favor, you'll experience a divine affirmation. I experienced it this morning when I led Ruby to the Lord Jesus Christ. I'm also experiencing it right now as I'm sharing with you. May God bless you, anoint you, and transform your life. Remember, one word from God can change your life forever!

CHAPTER

....

1

"The gift of faith is not normal faith.
It's a supernatural faith that God gives you
for a special need or opportunity."

I went through the most painful crisis in my life by a dear friend who deeply hurt me more than anyone who has ever hurt me in my life since my father's strangulation. The Lord told me when He started giving me the favor of the nation of Israel and told me I would be pastoring the nation that the price of admission was going to be unspeakable evil and betrayal, and that when it came, don't play the victim. He said it was the price of admission for every prophet, priest, and king.

It came like a whirlwind and it devastated me. I was in agony over it day and night. I started a 21-day Daniel fast and read the entire Bible from Genesis to Revelation starting January 1, 2022. I was determined to go back to Bethel. In other words, I would return to the place where I first started when I saw the Lord with a pure heart.

During that season of fasting and praying and infusing the Word into my life like I've never done, the Holy Spirit came upon me with mighty power and told me to humble myself and to repent and to forgive that brother unconditionally.

It was very painful, but I obeyed God. It happened at 7:00 pm. On that Tuesday God promised me if I would do that, He would make it up to me.

I did that to my own father when he had so brutally abused me all through my childhood. When I was 31, I went to him, found him in a bar trying to pick up a woman, took him to his home, and got on my knees and started confessing my sins to him. I told him to put his hands on my head and pray for me.

He was a hard man. When he saw me humble myself like that, I could feel the hot tears running down his face and onto his neck. He said, "I deserve to be thrown into hell for what I did for you."

I said to him, "I forgive you."

✦ ✦ ✦

The night I forgave the brother who hurt me so unconditionally with tears of godly repentance, I went to sleep. When I woke up, I realized I had received a new message at 3:28 a.m. which was 11:28 a.m. in Israel. It said, "Your nomination for the Nobel Peace Prize 2022 has been successfully submitted. The Nobel Committee appreciate your effort in making this nomination."

That message I received was from Israel. Someone in Israel nominated me for a Nobel Peace Prize. Do you see what I'm saying? I humbled myself. I felt I was totally in the right. God said to give up all my rights like He did on the cross. He said that if I did that,

He would make it up to me and give me favor—and He did.

I was not aware of how I operated in the gift of faith until I had lunch one day with an evangelist, who has since passed away. He said, "I want to have lunch with you because I don't think you know how you do what you do."

He added, "I've been watching you for several years. You say you're going to go to New York City and meet with the president of Iran, Mahmoud Ahmadinejad, and it actually comes to pass. You say that you're going to go to India and preach to a million people, and it actually comes to pass. You say you're going to go preach to the Kremlin Palace in Moscow, and it comes to pass. You say you're going to speak at the 43rd General Assembly of the United Nations at the peace conference, and it comes to pass. Do you know how you do what you do?"

I said to him, "No, I don't."

He said, "It's found in 1 Corinthians 12. It's the gift of faith, verse nine. All believers have been given saving faith by God as the means of salvation. That's found in Ephesians 2:8-9. But few believers operate in the gift of faith. I don't. The Bible says to earnestly desire the best gifts. You have obviously desired this gift, and God has given to you."

Shortly thereafter, another minister came up to me by the name of Reverend Jerry Savelle. He said to me almost the identical words, "Do you know what gift you operate in?" Before I could answer he said, "It's the gift of faith. You go into places that others won't go and it puts a demand upon God and a release to the gift of faith."

Jesus said, "Very truly I tell you, whoever believes in me will do the works I have been doing, and they will do even greater things than these, because I am going to the Father. And I will do whatever you ask in my name, so that the Father may be glorified in the Son. 14 You may ask me for anything in my name, and I will do it" (John 14:12-14, NIV).

In Marks 11:23, Jesus also taught, "Truly I tell you, if anyone says to this mountain, 'Go, throw yourself into the sea,' and does not doubt in their heart but believes that what they say will happen, it will be done for them." The greatest gift Jesus operated in was a gift of faith.

One of the things I realized about the gift of faith is you don't just receive it and it stays with you. The gift of faith can come on you in an astonishing way and when it comes, you can know in your mind what you're believing for has already happened. You can't differentiate it. That's why your faith is so important. I have probably experienced the power of the gift of faith 30 or 40 times in my life. I don't believe for a second that God chose to give me the gift of faith simply because I was special. I believe that those gifts are available for all believers, but you don't hear much teaching about the gift of faith.

You hear a lot of teaching about other gifts of the Holy Spirit, but very little about the gift of faith. You also don't see people hungering and thirsting and earnestly desiring the gift of faith. You do see people earnestly hungering and desiring other gifts of the Holy Spirit but for some reason, the revelation of the gift of faith has been ignored by most believers.

I pray that God will open your eyes to it and that you will be able to truly have a purpose and favor and receive this glorious gift. In 1 Corinthians 12:4 we are told, "There are different kinds of gifts, but the same Spirit distributes them." Verses 9-10 add "to another faith by the same Spirit, to another gifts of healing by that one Spirit, to another miraculous powers, to another prophecy, to another distinguishing between spirits, to another speaking in different kinds of tongues, and to still another the interpretation of tongues."

The gift of faith is not normal faith. It's a supernatural faith that God gives you for a special need or opportunity. It's extraordinary, mountain-moving faith for supernatural results and in specific situations. Let me give you some examples. When I first began in the ministry, Carolyn and I sold our furniture. We didn't have a home at the time. We sold it for $725.

I had one service in Columbus, Indiana. It was on the Sunday of a terrible snowstorm. The pastor had gone on vacation to Florida, and there were only a couple of dozen people who showed up for the service because of the snow. We had an old car. After I preached and shared the vision God had given me to the start this ministry, I went out and the car had burned up. The wiring had shorted out. I was in a snowstorm with a young baby launching my ministry with no home and now no car.

Suddenly the Spirit of God came on me with a gift of faith and told me he was going to give me a brand new car. I had no comprehension how that was going to happen, but I sensed it deeply in my spirit. A man by the name of Gene Darnell, who had gone to the service, invited us to have lunch with him and his family. After lunch, he asked us if we could spend the night.

The next morning when I got ready to leave, his wife said, "Would you please wait? My husband's going to be here in a little while." Gene Darnell came driving up and handed me the keys to a brand new Buick Electra. He had financed that car because the Spirit of God told him to purchase the car for us.

He kept saying, "Shiloh, Shiloh. The Lord is going to use you to touch the nation of Israel and I'm supposed to plant the first seed." That was the gift of faith. We started driving in that Electra toward Texas where we were going to base our ministry and where my wife was from in Fort Worth, Texas. As we were driving through Arkansas, we I saw a sign that said Roetzel RVs. It was off of Highway 16.

I pulled up and there were motorhomes everywhere. The Spirit of God led me to walk up to one of those motorhomes and to place my hand on it and to thank the Lord for giving it, and dedicated it to the ministry. As I was doing this, the owner of the company, who was a Gideon, was having his devotional time. He looked out the window and saw me. The Spirit of God said to him, "That's a man of God. You are to give him a brand new motorhome and even pay for the hitch to connect it to his vehicle."

He came out and said, "I've never done this before but the Spirit of God just spoke to me." He told me, "You need a big car to pull it with like. . ."

I said, ". . .like a Buick Electra?"

He said, "Exactly."

I told him, "I have it." That may not seem like a big deal to most people, but it was a big deal to us in those days. When we began the ministry, we had only $725. We based the ministry in that little trailer for several years.

One Friday, a few years later, the Lord spoke to me, saying that

He had provided a home for us. We looked at a house on a street called Dream Lane. The man who owned the home wanted to sell it for $10,200. He said, "I'll carry $7,000 If you can bring me $3,200 Monday. Do you have it?"

I instantly said to him, "Yes, I have it. I'll be there Monday." When we left the driveway and headed back to our trailer, my wife Carolyn never said a word, but I knew what she was thinking. We had less than $100 in our bank account. I said, "I feel like God told me it's going to be there Monday."

That was the gift of faith. Monday morning, I went to the post office and there was only one small envelope and it was from England, Arkansas. I opened it up and it was a check for $3,200, exactly the amount I needed on exactly the day I needed it. The man's name was Charles Capps, who was a cotton farmer. That was the gift of faith.

When we begin our ministry, I saw the gift of faith providing for needs but as time went on, that gift of faith started operating in other ways. That gift of faith directed me to contact the Prime Minister of Israel Menachem Begin to ask him for a meeting on June 30, 1980.

He said yes and met with me on the June 30, even though I'd never met with him. I didn't know him. As I mentioned earlier, this meeting led to me soon praying with Benjamin Netanyahu and predicting he would become the prime minister of Israel.

That was the gift of faith in operation. I'll be sharing these stories in more detail throughout the book, but I'm trying to help you understand the significance of the gift of faith. I once told my daughter Sharon that God sent me to India to preach to a million people. When we were leaving the country, she said to me, "Dad, have you ever been to India?"

I said, "Never." And I know what she was thinking. How was it possible that there will be a million people? It was the gift of faith. The first night service in India the people were mostly Hindus. I would estimate the crowd was maybe 6,000 to 8,000 people. As I was preaching, "See Jesus," three young Hindu girls who were born blind were suddenly able to see. I didn't know until a doctor who knew the girls told us what was happening. It hit the wire services in India, and the next night, over a million people were on the beach. That was the gift of faith.

When I traveled to preach in the Kremlin Palace in Moscow, there was no way I could preach in it to the entire former Soviet Union in prime time, but it happened. That was a gift of faith. We had a warehouse full of letters from people who had come to Christ.

When I went to Saudi Arabia during the Persian Gulf War and shared Jesus with the Syrian High Command with a Saudi prince as my interpreter, that was the gift of faith. I'll never forget arriving in Saudi Arabia, because the first thing I did was go downtown and start gathering a crowd to preach to them. It's against the law to do that, and they cut your head off for that. But the gift of faith was operating.

Just before I preached, I told the crowd that there would be a song before I preach. But I can't sing. The MPs saw me and were going to arrest me but the sergeant over the MPs came up behind me. He was a phenomenal baritone assist, and a believer. When he heard me talk about a song, he started singing "My eye is on the sparrow, and I know He cares for me." The tears were streaming down my face. That was a gift of faith.

That next morning, the Spirit of God told me to go to a particular international hotel and the first man you see, stick out your hand and say, "May I go with you?"

The first man was a Saudi coming through the door. When I asked, "May I go with you?" he was offended. He asked me who I was and where I was from. I kept insisting that I wanted to go with him.

He said, "Then meet me at 6:15 p.m. tomorrow morning in the lobby and you go with me. To my amazement, the gentlemen who came was the commander of the Saudi Royal Air Force. He was the governor of Iran. He was a prince and a nephew to the king. And he was going to give the invasion plans to the Syrian High Command. He thought I knew where he was going. So he took me with him.

I shared Christ with him on his helicopter. He said, "You know what you're trying to do? You're trying to convert me. We cut heads off on Thursdays for that."

I joked, "I'm busy on Thursday. My schedule is full." He started to laugh. That was the gift of faith.

When I left Saudi Arabia, I felt led in the Spirit to go to Iraq. I preached to the Kurds one day and was prompted by the Lord to preach on Jonah and Nineveh and how the people of Nineveh repented. When I made the altar call, only one person came forward, an old man.

My Kurdish interpreter was jumping up and down crying. I asked him, "Why are you so excited?"

He said, "You preached on the king of Nineveh repenting. This is the king of Nineveh. He's the Sheikh of Nineveh. He has just believed in Jesus Christ." Because of that, the Sheikh told the president of Kurdistan that I was invited to Kurdistan on a state invitation. That was a gift of faith.

I'm sharing these stories not to brag on me, but to brag on Jesus. I want you to understand that you can live in the favor of God. The gift of faith isn't hidden from you. It's a gift of the Holy Spirit that God has made available to you if you earnestly desire it. I've realized in my life that desperation is the mother of invention. God's not going to give these gifts to content believers who are simply casual in their walk with God. These are radical, life transforming gifts, and they're for radical believers who do what God says.

I want to encourage you to begin seeking and praying, searching the Scriptures on the gift of faith. Read the stories about those who have operated in them throughout the Bible and start seeking the Lord to give you that gift, and also to give you opportunities where that gift can be manifested.

There's a picture of me presenting the Friends of Zion award to Donald Trump when he was president of the United States. But what people don't know is more than a year before I presented him with that award, I created the award up and put it on my desk with his name on it. I believed that I was going to give him that award in the Oval Office. That was the gift of faith

Jesus increased in favor with God and with man (Luke 2:52). The power of the Holy Spirit can also cause you to increase with favor with God and with people. I have put a lot of pictures in this book. The reason I did that is because I've had people say to me that there's no possibility that you could be doing the things that you're doing. They're absolutely right. There is no possibility that I could be doing it in my own power. But I'm not doing it in the natural. I'm doing it in the supernatural. I pray that the Spirit of God will put a hunger and thirst in your heart for the gift of faith and for the favor of God and that your life will never be the same.

WHAT I LEARNED AS A MORON

THOUGHT TO CONSIDER: God's strength makes you more powerful that the toughest bully you could ever face.

VERSE TO CONNECT: "Now to him who is able to do immeasurably more than all we ask or imagine, according to his power that is at work within us, to him be glory in the church and in Christ Jesus throughout all generations, for ever and ever! Amen." Ephesians 3:20-21, NIV

QUESTION TO CONTEMPLATE: Am I looking to God for strength during my times of weakness?

King Abdullah's cupbearer.

Mike Evans at the Corrie
Ten Boom Museum.

Mike Evans at the gravesite of his great grandfather's synagogue,
Rabbi Mikel Katznelson.

CHAPTER

2

Gather the riches of God's promises.
Nobody can take away from you those texts from
the Bible which you have learned by heart. [2]

Since my encounter with Jesus at the age of eleven, He has spoken to me again and again—through His Word. I've heard His still, small voice through prayer, and I've applied the four principles that define God's very DNA in my life. This is what Jesus did; He was Radically Obedient, He forgave, He humbled himself to the Father's will, and He lived a life of Radical Generosity.

Those four traits are in His DNA—the same DNA as the Father. When you magnify the image of God, you are manifesting the DNA of God in your own life. Then, and only then, can you live in the Favor of God and activate the Word of God.

What is DNA? I could give you a long, scientific explanation about deoxyribonucleic acid, the molecule that contains your genetic code, but for this book I am going to use the definition, "**D**ivine **N**ature **A**cquired." In II Corinthians, Paul wrote that,

"Anyone who belongs to Christ has become a new person. The old life is gone; a new life has begun."[3] You are given a new character, one very different from your old nature. You become a new person in Christ because of a Divine blood infusion. Paul wrote in Galatians 2:20, "It is no longer I who live, but Christ lives in me."

Not only are we created by God, it is through Him that we "live, and move, and have our being."[4] It is because of His DNA that you can have a significant life. Because He loves you, God's Spirit directs you as you walk in His favor.

I learned that lesson when, at the age of eleven, Jesus appeared to me, spoke to me, and changed my life forever. I became a new creation in Him when I saw His face and heard His voice. My birthday is June 30, and on that day in 1958 I had a stomach ulcer, a speech impediment (I stuttered), and hundreds of fears, among them the fear of looking anyone in the eye. The morning after my birthday, I walked in newness of life.

Since the age of four, my father had abused me. He broke both of my arms, locked me in the canning cellar beneath our house, and almost succeeded in strangling me to death. I had no self-esteem—not low self-esteem, but *no* self-esteem.

While my mother hated Christians, my father, a professing Christian, hated Jews. Brother Bob, as he was called, went to church regularly on Sunday morning. That was after a drinking binge on Saturday night that generally ended with him beating my mother for what he thought was her adultery.

As I mentioned earlier, as that scared, battered eleven-year-old boy, I had a life-changing encounter with Jesus Christ. I tried to intervene when my father had found yet another excuse to beat my mother. He turned his anger on me. By the time he was done using his fists on my scrawny frame, I had been dumped on the floor of my bedroom. Sometime later I awoke, my body curled into a fetal position. My face and pajamas were covered in dried vomit. Every bone and joint ached. I tried to push myself up from the floor of that dark room but fell back, the room spinning. I closed my eyes, clenched my fists in total agony, and, shaking uncontrollably, cried out to no one in particular, "Why was I born? Why?!" I saw no purpose for my life. My father hated me, and my mother suffered because of me. All I knew was my father's warped version of Christianity: Booze on Friday, beatings on Saturday, and church on Sunday. My dad's favorite Bible verse must have been Proverbs 23:14: "You shall beat him with a rod, and deliver his soul from hell." He paraphrased that as "Spare the rod, spoil the child." There were no spoiled children in his home—only abused ones. He had never given me one word of affirmation. Not once had I heard "I love you" from his lips that so tenderly and lovingly caressed a glass of amber whiskey. Jack Daniels was his "friend"; I was "moron."

"Why was I born?" As quickly as I had whispered those words, the room was flooded with a light so bright it blinded me. I thought Dad had come back to finish the job—to beat me to death, and this time I could not escape. My first thought was to crawl under the bed to protect myself. I covered my face with my hands and closed my eyes as tightly as I could squeeze them. After what seemed like an eon, I realized there was no other sound in the room. Now there was only a brilliant light. I slowly spread my fingers and eased my eyes open as imperceptibly as possible.

Instead of seeing my dad's anger-deformed face, I saw two hands reaching toward me. Above each hand and in the center of each wrist was an ugly scar. I had seen those scars in Sunday school literature. They were supposed to represent the nail scars of Jesus. Someone was playing a trick on me, but who? Did I dare look beyond the wrists to the face? Was I having a nervous breakdown? Was I going crazy?

Rather than the cold, stark fear that had filled the room earlier, I now actually felt warmth. I felt a Presence that brought both power and peace. I was being immersed in an invisible liquid love that poured over me and lodged deep within my soul. I slowly raised my head, and as my eyes followed the arms upward, I saw standing there in my bedroom the Lord Jesus Christ. He was either clothed in light or in the most brilliant white imaginable—whiter than fresh snow; whiter than the clouds that float in the sky; whiter than anything I had ever seen. Draped from His shoulder to His waist was a deep purple cloth—more purple than the heavens at sunset.

As I lifted my head to take in His face, I was instantly drawn to His loving eyes. They were smiling, happy eyes filled with every color of the rainbow. It was like looking into an illuminated bowl of the world's most highly prized jewels. I felt as if I could see through them and beyond to heaven and the promise of eternal peace. They were like magnets drawing me into their depths. Keeping His arms outstretched, He looked at me with an all-encompassing expression of love. He smiled and then said three things I had never heard before. They were like a healing salve to my wounded soul and spirit.

He said, "Son." It was the first time anyone had ever called me "Son." It was said so gently, with such love and respect for me—for me!—that I felt my heart melt. The word *son* echoed in my spirit again and again.

"I love you." Someone really did love me. What joy! I felt as if I'd just escaped a death sentence and was free. That statement alone was enough to sustain me for the rest of my life. But He continued, "I have a great plan for your life." The power and presence of Jesus were like a holy fire igniting my soul. I had a purpose! God had something for me—Michael Evans—to do. Then there was silence. I am sure only a few seconds had passed, but it felt like an eternity.

I closed my eyes, and tears slid slowly down my face. I was consumed with an inexplicable happiness. Eventually I realized that the light had departed but the overwhelming warmth remained. He was gone from my room but not from my spirit, not from my heart. I never wanted to lose that feeling of love and peace and warmth, and the unmerited Favor of God.

Despite my treatment by my father, as an adult and a Christian I knew I had to overcome my inner battles and make peace with him. He still exercised some power over me, and for a reason I failed to understand, his acceptance was important. No matter what I did, Dad withheld his approval. I could not get a word of affirmation from him to save my life, although I desperately wanted it. I didn't try to impress him with the people I had met or the places I had traveled. I knew that no matter what successes I might have in the ministry, he would never encourage me, never say, "I'm proud of you," or never call me "son." What he did call me was "bastard" because he thought I was the result of adultery on my mother's part.

For five and a half years I sent half of my paycheck to Dad to help with the house and car payments and more, yet I never heard "thank you" from him. He had to know that Jesus was real in my life. I wanted him to see that a real encounter with God could change his life forever, and I wanted to be free of his condemnation.

The day finally came when I knew I had to confront my father, but not in the way I had imagined it would be. Instead of demanding that Dad apologize to me, the Holy Spirit had prompted me to apologize to *him*. I was reminded that Exodus 20:12 says:

> "Honor your father and your mother, that your days
> may be long upon the land which the Lord your God
> is giving you."

It says nothing at all about the parent, but rather speaks directly to the child. Honoring him was not contingent upon Dad being kind, loving, good, meek, or repentant. It simply says that I, as a son, must honor my parents. So, I went looking for Dad.

After searching his regular haunts I finally found him at a local bar, working hard to entice the young woman sitting next to him to go home with him. He was holding the hand of someone about the age of one of my sisters, and calling her "Baby Doll." When he saw me, he shouted to his bar buddies that there was a preacher in the house. "Preach, preacher, preach," he laughed. He wasn't at all happy when I insisted that he take me home instead. I heard a few muttered "morons" before we were finally settled in his living room.

Obeying what I knew to be God's leading, I got on my knees and said, "Dad, God wants me to humble myself in obedience, generosity, and humility, and ask your forgiveness for any sins I've committed against you." I began to confess my failures as a son—pride, not praying for him as I should; disrespect, not to his face, but behind his back and others. Not once did I enumerate his wrongs against me. I didn't relive the beatings at his hand or the curses from his mouth. I didn't ask him why he repeatedly called me "bastard." Neither did I talk about my own successes; I even began to confess any sin I had committed since becoming a preacher, those that the Holy Spirit had revealed to me.

"Stop it!" he cried. "I can't take any more. I have committed the unpardonable sin for what I have done to you. I can never be saved! My home will be in eternal hell."

As I talked to Dad about Jesus and what He meant in my life, his hard exterior began to crack and he began to tell me of his childhood. He told me about his father's abuse and how he was made to work in the fields from the time he was five or six years old. He confessed that he could barely read or write. Then he leaned forward in his seat and gripped my hands so hard his knuckles turned white. "Son," he cried, "I should have been put in prison for what I done to you."

He wrapped his arms around me, and at that moment I felt his tears running down my neck. As he began to weep, he told me he had not cried even when his father died. Instead he had said, "I'm glad the old fool's dead."

God's grace and mercy filled me. My heart overflowed with compassion for the man I thought I could never forgive much less love, and I led him to Christ there in his living room. That was the beginning of a healing process that lasted until the day he died.

In the last weeks of Dad's life, he willed everything he owned to me. God's favor on my life has been so abundant that in turn I was able to give his entire estate to my six brothers and sisters. I spoke at his funeral and talked about his record as a war hero and how much he loved his mother. Sadly, those were the only good things I could say about him. His funeral was the conduit for the Favor of God to once again explode in my life

FINDING GOD'S FAVOR

THOUGHT TO CONSIDER: God loves you and His Spirit leads you despite the bullies or situations you will face in life.

VERSE TO CONNECT: "Anyone who belongs to Christ has become a new person. The old life is gone; a new life has begun." 2 Corinthians 5:17, NLT

QUESTION TO CONTEMPLATE: What is keeping you from following God's direction for your life today?

Mike Evans with Benjamin Netanyahu
on July 4, 1980.

Mayor of Jerusalem Moshe Lion
and the *Jerusalem Post* presenting Mike
with the Lion of Jerusalem award.

Ambassador Friedman, Mike Evans, and the Mayor of
Jerusalem at the Friends of Zion headquarters in Jerusalem.

Mike Evans with his peers, America's leading evangelical leaders, presenting
Donald Trump with the Friends of Zion award—given to over 20 world leaders.

Mike Evans presents the Friends of Zion award to
Vice President Mike Pence at the Friends of Zion Museum
in Jerusalem.

CHAPTER

3

Give the best you have, and it will never be enough.

Give your best anyway. [6]

Wnat is the secret to activating the Word of God in *your* life? First, you must understand the revelation of the image of God, and the four components of living in the Favor of God: Radical Obedience, Radical Forgiveness, Radical Humility, and Radical Generosity. These things allow His image to be magnified in your life, to be lifted up.

As a young seminary student I once admitted to one of my professors that I didn't really like church. I asked the question: "What's it for? I can buy a tape and listen as I fish. I can send my offerings in the mail. I just don't like going to church." He had no answer for me, but God in His infinite mercy showed me that church is the place where His mind and energy meet to bless His children. That's when I fell in love with church. I wanted to be where God's people were.

In 2003 my desire to be with the people of God would lead me to visit my good friend David Wilkerson at Times Square Church in New York City. Several months before, God had prompted me to write a book, *Beyond Iraq: The Next Move—Ancient Prophecy and Modern Day Conspiracy Collide*. I closeted myself in my study and quickly completed the first draft. After the book was published and released, I was able to secure only one commitment from a Christian network program to discuss its contents, and then it was cancelled. But I knew that the Favor of God went before me and His Word had been activated in my life.

After I ended the phone call with the network executive who had cancelled my interview, I left my study for my prayer room and fell on my knees before God. I reminded Him that the book was done at His prompting. It was His idea—and I had done my best. As I lay on the floor before God, the Word from Psalm 1:1–3 flooded my mind:

> Blessed is the man who walks not in the counsel of the ungodly, nor stands in the path of sinners, nor sits in the seat of the scornful; but his delight is in the law of the Lord, and in His law he meditates day and night. He shall be like a tree planted by the rivers of water, that brings forth its fruit in its season, whose leaf also shall not wither; and whatever he does shall prosper.

I arose from the floor, called my daughter Rachel, and asked her if she would go with me to New York City to promote the book. She readily accepted, and the next morning we boarded a flight for the Big Apple. As soon as we checked in to our hotel, we each took a stack of books and began to make the rounds of the various television studios. I told Rachel, "If Jesus doesn't do it, I will sink. But I'd rather sink knowing I had faith in the Lord instead of flesh." I felt we were living on the brink of a huge miracle.

On Sunday, Rachel and I attended Times Square Church. After the service, David Wilkerson graciously met with us to pray about the launch of the book. I deeply appreciated his prayer, and as a result, we decided to stay one more night.

The next morning my phone rang. I was stunned when the woman on the other end identified herself as a producer for Neil Cavuto on Fox News Channel. That was only the beginning. Over the next several months, I scheduled appearances on sixty-one programs—television and radio. By June, *Beyond Iraq* had sold 53,000 copies, and in July it hit the *New York Times* bestseller list in the top ten. I had discovered the secret to activating the Word of God and receiving the Favor of God. It was showered on me because of my Radical Obedience to His leadership.

It was perhaps the disciple John the Baptist who was the first to discover the secret to activating the Word of God in his life. It was the realization that the image of God had to be reflected in everything he did. John wrote, "He must increase, but I *must* decrease." [7]

Later Jesus, in trying to prepare His disciples for His coming crucifixion, said to them: "And I, if I be lifted up from the earth, will draw all men unto me." [8]

As Jesus increases in your life through obedience, forgiveness, humility, and generosity, the promises of God are activated. The Scripture is very clear on these four qualities in the life of a Believer. The apostle Paul wrote to the Romans about obedience:

Don't you know that when you offer yourselves to someone as obedient slaves, you are slaves of the one you obey—whether you are slaves to sin, which leads to death, or to obedience, which leads to righteousness?[9]

Jesus taught the disciples the value of forgiveness:

> "And whenever you stand praying, if you have anything against anyone, forgive him, that your Father in heaven may also forgive you your trespasses."[10]

Regarding humility, Jesus said:

> "But the greatest among you shall be your servant. Whoever exalts himself shall be humbled; and whoever humbles himself shall be exalted."[11]

And what of generosity? Its importance was highlighted in Luke chapter 6. Jesus exhorted His listeners:

> "Give, and it will be given to you. A good measure, pressed down, shaken together and running over, will be poured into your lap. For with the measure you use, it will be measured to you."[12]

I had never heard a sermon preached about how Radical Obedience, Radical Forgiveness, Radical Humility, and Radical Generosity can bring the Favor of God into a life, but I've lived my life proving it to be true. Since I fully committed my life to Jesus, I've been living in His favor. It means that God is hidden from my natural vision, but His plan and purpose for my life are not. They can be revealed through His Word and through the Holy Spirit.

The times in my life and career when I've needed God's direction, it has often come from both sources but is always confirmed by the written Word.

In Luke 2:52, the Bible gives us a rare glimpse into the early life of Jesus. It says, "And Jesus increased in wisdom and stature, and in favour with God and man." I have met a lot of people in my life who are not *increasing* in stature; they are *decreasing*. Do you have favor with Man? God said we could. How do we increase in favor with God and Man? How do we keep from decreasing—becoming a minus rather than a plus?

Now, you might also ask the question of the Bible: What is its value? The reality is that every word in it is a Spirit word, spoken by many prophets, priests, and kings and activated by every succeeding generation. If we activate God's Word in our lives, we will increase in favor with both God and man.

How can we activate the Word in order to gain the Favor of God? In Genesis 1:26–27 God says, "'Let us make man in our image. . . .' In the image of God created he him; male and female created he him." How are we made in His image, and what is the purpose of that? We are both physical and spiritual beings. God has personhood! God sees, hears, and feels. So do you! How can you activate the image of God and ignite His Word in your life? I am going to answer that question by exploring Radical Obedience, Radical Forgiveness, Radical Humility, and Radical Generosity in the lives of men and women such as David, Moses, Isaiah, Esther, Abraham, Joseph, and others in the Bible.

FINDING GOD'S FAVOR

THOUGHT TO CONSIDER: Give the best you have, and it will never be enough. Give your best anyway, despite the bullies or difficulties you will face.

VERSE TO CONNECT: "Blessed is the man who walks not in the counsel of the ungodly, nor stands in the path of sinners, nor sits in the seat of the scornful; but his delight is in the law of the Lord, and in His law he meditates day and night." Psalm 1:1-2, NIV 1984

QUESTION TO CONTEMPLATE: What is keeping you from living by the power of God's truth in your life today?

President Donald Trump signing an executive order against antisemitism on American college campuses. He presented Mike Evans with the pen.

Mike Evans with Secretary of State Mike Pompeo.

Mike Evans with former Israeli Prime Minister Benjamin Netanyahu in Israel.

Mike Evans with Ambassador David Friedman and his wife
Tammy Friedman and Prime Minister Benjamin Netanyahu
with his wife Sara Netanyahu

Carolyn Evans with
Michael David Evans III at the
Jerusalem Prayer Team
Holocaust community center.

Mike Evans with international chairman of
Friends of Zion, Israeli President Shimon Peres.

CHAPTER

4

If you find serenity and happiness,
some may be jealous. Be happy anyway. [13]

Carolyn and I are the proud parents of three beautiful daughters, and in 1984 God gave us another gift—a son. Carolyn said to me, "Honey, I want to name him Michael David Evans II after you." There was only one problem with that: I didn't have a middle name. Her response was, "Well, that's your problem." My next stop was the courthouse where I had my legal name changed to Michael David Evans. When the judge asked me why I wanted to change my name, I told him I wanted to be named after my son.

Now Michael and I share the middle name of one of Israel's greatest kings: David. We are blessed because King David is a perfect example of all four components necessary to activate the Favor of God in our lives.

In I Chronicles, the second chapter, the lineage of David is preserved for posterity. The chronicler wrote: "And Boaz begat Obed, and Obed begat Jesse." David was Jesse's youngest son, the runt of the litter, the sheepherder. Samuel was the high priest in Jesse's day. It was a rare thing for the man who held that position to be out in the field searching for a candidate to be king. Saul had been king, and yet God had rejected him because of disobedience. Not only did God reject Saul, He repented of having chosen him to rule over His people, Israel. Now He had sent Samuel on a mission to find the man who would be king:

> The Lord said to Samuel, "How long will you grieve over Saul, since I have rejected him from being king over Israel? Fill your horn with oil, and go. I will send you to Jesse the Bethlehemite, for I have provided for myself a king among his sons." [14]

Samuel was dispatched to the house of Jesse to anoint one of his sons. As each stood before the high priest, Jesse wondered: Would it be the tall, handsome one? Would it be the most skillful one? Would it be the son considered to be a warrior? Surely Samuel would know when the right man was paraded before him; but as Jesse watched silently, he realized none would do. God rejected each of them for the role of king. He did not reject the man—no, not at all! Each one was loved by God. It was simply that not one of Jesse's older boys was God's choice to rule over Israel: I Samuel 16, verse 10 notes:

> Jesse tried to present each son to Samuel in his best light, but without success. Finally, Samuel said to Jesse, "The Lord has not chosen these."

Disappointed, Samuel turned to Jesse and asked, "Is that all?"

Jesse thought of his youngest son who was out in the field keeping the sheep. Jesse was certain he had known which of his sons would be best to be king, but there was no one left—except the youngster.

Jesse must have thought: *He's just a kid. He lives alone—well, just him and the sheep. How in the world could he be God's choice? He's not qualified. Surely Samuel doesn't intend to anoint David! He's just my harp-playing, psalm-singing son, occupied with sticks and stones and a slingshot. He just watches the sheep—a woman's job.* But Jesse obeyed Samuel and sent someone to fetch David. Samuel was determined that the gathering would not eat until the last son had stood before him and God.

David was stunned when someone showed up to take his place in the sheepfold. He had been called home with no preparation, no indication of what the problem might be. Maybe he stopped by a stream to wash the smell of the sheep off his hands. Perhaps he just ran straight home; we don't know. What we do know is that the moment Samuel saw this handsome young man with the beautiful eyes, he said, "He is the one! I will anoint him." Just as Jesus said years later, "The last shall be first." [15] Regardless of what Jesse or Samuel thought, God had chosen David. He had equipped His choice in the Judean foothills; He had seen the heart of a servant in David; and He had watched as the young shepherd developed the skills to protect his father's flocks that had been entrusted to him. Now the youngest was to become king:

> Then Samuel took the horn of oil and anointed him
> [David] in the midst of his brothers; and the Spirit of
> The Lord came upon David from that day forward. [16]

As Jesse's offspring, David was to be a key ancestor of Jesus Christ:

> There shall come forth a shoot from the stump of
> Jesse, and a branch shall grow out of his roots. . . .
> In that day the root of Jesse shall stand as an ensign
> to the peoples; him shall the nations seek, and his
> dwellings shall be glorious. [17]

David's life would never be the same. When he was called home from his duties as a shepherd, he could have hesitated. And yet he displayed Radical Obedience—to his father, to his king, and to his God. That Radical Obedience placed him in the forefront of Jewish history, and on the throne that would one day be occupied by the Messiah.

David spent years of his life running from King Saul, the man he was anointed to replace. He was rejected by the one whom he served as armor bearer. He was ridiculed by his brothers, and in Psalm 27, David says, "[Even] my father and mother forsake me." [18] Perhaps you, like me, have been rejected by a mother or father, a sibling, or a beloved child. We can learn one valuable lesson from David: Rejection does not determine our anointing—only God can!

David practiced Radical Humility. He willingly served his father as a shepherd. It had not been his lot to be the eldest with the greatest inheritance, or the warrior who served under the king. No, it was his job to rise early in the morning to tend the sheep, to spend lonely days and nights finding food and water for his charges, protecting them from the marauders that attacked. It was his place to submit to the will of his father, Jesse, to follow his instructions, even if it meant being the laughingstock of his siblings.

I can sympathize with David. In my own life, after Jesus appeared to me, I kept it to myself. Dad would have thought I was lying, and that always meant a beating. Mom would have been horrified that I had given my life to Jesus. I didn't tell my brothers and sisters because I knew, like David knew, that I would be mocked and criticized.

After David's anointing by Samuel, there came a morning that Jesse ordered his youngest son to take supplies to his brothers who were battling the Philistines in the Valley of Elah. Upon his arrival, he saw the imposing figure of Goliath and heard the challenge being hurled across the valley to his quaking audience on the other side. David was incensed that no one in Saul's army had the courage to face the giant. They all stood on the sidelines, intimidated by the ferocity of the giant warrior. But David was not foolhardy; he knew beyond a doubt that only through the power of God could anyone defeat this adversary. He asked those around him what would be the reward for the one who slayed the enemy. David's brothers were angered by his question and began to ridicule him. He then marched before Saul and offered to fight the giant.

When Saul questioned both his youth and ability, David replied:

> "I have been taking care of my father's sheep and goats. . . . When a lion or a bear comes to steal a lamb from the flock, I go after it with a club and rescue the lamb from its mouth. If the animal turns on me, I catch it by the jaw and club it to death. I have

done this to both lions and bears, and I'll do it to this pagan Philistine, too, for he has defied the armies of the living God! The Lord who rescued me from the claws of the lion and the bear will rescue me from this Philistine!" [19]

David was radically humble; he knew that he was unable to do anything except through the power of God. He declined to accept any commendation for his feats; he gave God the credit. He boldly assured Saul that God would stand with the man who dared go forth in His name; God would give him the victory. In humility, David offered himself to be an instrument in his Father's hands.

King Saul offered David his personal armor for the battle with Goliath. After having tried it on, the young man realized that the covering made by mortal hands was insufficient for the task. Like the apostle Paul, David understood he was only safe when covered with the full armor of God. He would be vulnerable in Saul's armor; he would be invincible wrapped in the presence of Jehovah-Sabaoth—the Lord our Protector.

In this modern-day "me first" society, instead of doing it "God's way," we've done it "our way." James 1:17 (NKJV) says, "Every good gift and every perfect gift is from above, and comes down from the Father of lights. . ." We need to acknowledge God's provision and offer the praise due Him. He is the Source of every good thing—life, health, opportunity, talent, and blessing. God is Jehovah-Jireh, our Provider.

David had learned that lesson as a shepherd. God had miraculously provided protection for him and for his flock. When he faced the giant, he was prepared. Crossing the brook, David selected five smooth stones and dropped them in his shepherd's bag. As he approached the valley of Elah, Goliath began to fling insults:

He said to David, "Am I a dog, that you come at me with sticks?" And the Philistine cursed David by his gods. "Come here," he said, "and I'll give your flesh to the birds and the wild animals!" [20]

David's battle cry was simply, "I come against you in the name of the Lord Almighty, the God of the armies of Israel, whom you have defied." [21]

God had proven to be strong in battle, present during trials, a Light in the darkness, springs of Living Water in the desert, David's Provider. That was the basis for his humility, knowing that he himself could do nothing, but that he could do anything through God if his faith was rooted and grounded in Him. Yes, David was a perfect example of Radical Humility. It identified him as a wise leader, not an egotistical power monger.

In the end, Goliath lay on the ground—a stone embedded deeply in his forehead. David used the giant's own weapon to lop off his head and give Israel the victory—not by might, nor by power, but by the Spirit of the Lord of hosts. [22] David had long known that with God on his side, he was in the majority.

From David you can learn that operating in humility does not mean you renounce your own self-esteem. While some would view a humble man or woman as a submissive doormat, the truth is that through God the individual possesses power—controlled by strength and self-control.

The shepherd boy who became king also practiced Radical Forgiveness. When his brothers belittled him in front of the entire army of Israel, David forgave them. When his father didn't think him worthy to be introduced to Samuel, David forgave him. David spent his early years running and hiding from Saul. He was stalked like a criminal because of Saul's jealousy. David hid in caves, took refuge in enemy territory, rejected opportunities to kill his adversary, and loved Saul's son, Jonathan. In the end, David forgave the man that God had chosen to be the first king over Israel.

As an example of Radical Forgiveness, David forgave his son Absalom, who tried to wrest the kingdom of Judah from his father. Filled with pride and egotism, blinded by his own good looks, proud of his long, luxuriant mane of hair, besotted with power, this son of David and Maacah decided he was above the law. Exiled to his mother's homeland of Geshur, he languished there for three years while nurturing a hatred for David. When Absalom was allowed to return, his loathing was aggravated by the rumors that God had chosen Solomon, his half brother as David's successor. So strong was his abhorrence that he determined to unseat his father and set a plan in action to do so. Once he had accomplished his aim of driving David from Jerusalem and wresting the kingdom from him, Absalom was counseled to do something so odious that it should have ensured David's lifetime loathing—he was advised to openly lie with David's concubines who had been left behind to watch over the king's house.

In II Samuel 19, David was finally able to return to Jerusalem after Absalom's death. Betrayed by his son, banished from the throne, expelled from Jerusalem, still David mourned the loss of his son more than his kingship. When troops loyal to David gathered in battle against the army of Absalom, David waited anxiously for word of his son's safety. Like the father of the prodigal son, he longed for the return and repentance of his son; but unlike that father, David's desire was not to be granted. A messenger arrived from the battlefront to inform the exiled king that while fleeing the skirmish, Absalom's hair became entangled in the branches of a tree. Held captive by his tresses, the presumptuous young man was hacked to death by his pursuers.

David was heartbroken and fell into deep and bitter mourning, and in his grief, he forgave:

The king was overcome with emotion. He went up to the room over the gateway and burst into tears. And as he went, he cried, "O my son Absalom! My son, my son Absalom! If only I had died instead of you! O Absalom, my son, my son." [23]

Isn't that a perfect picture of God's Radical Forgiveness? As Jesus hung on the cross, He cried, "Father, forgive them." As His blood-bought children, we have been invited to "Come and dine" at His table. Because of grace and Radical Forgiveness, He has promised to restore that which the enemy has stolen from us—sevenfold. [24]

Near the end of his life, David was the picture of Radical Generosity. It was his desire to build a permanent home for God in Jerusalem—a temple worthy of the King of the Universe. He shared this desire with the prophet Nathan. In a dream, God advised the prophet that David's successor, Solomon, would be the one to build the Temple. David was crushed. He could have gone off in a huff, angry with God for not honoring his request. Not David; he amassed a large quantity of precious metals—gold and silver— and precious stones with which to build and adorn the Temple.

By today's standards, this totaled three thousand tons of gold and thirty thousand tons of silver. He gathered and stockpiled other materials his son Solomon would need to erect the house of God:

> David gave orders to gather together the aliens who were residing in the land of Israel, and he set stone-cutters to prepare dressed stones for building the house of God. David also provided great stores of iron for nails for the doors of the gates and for clamps, as well as bronze in quantities beyond weighing, and cedar logs without number—for the Sidonians and Tyrians brought great quantities of cedar to David. [25]

David didn't let disappointment stand in the way of generosity. Don't allow the Enemy to rob you of a blessing. Solomon wrote:

> If your enemy is hungry, give him bread to eat; and if he is thirsty, give him water to drink; for so you will heap coals of fire on his head, and the Lord will reward you. [26]

David gave radically, although he did not live to see the fruits of his labor. The Temple was built and lavishly furnished due to his sacrificial offering.

In the midst of unrelenting opposition, David was able to accomplish great things for his King, because he practiced Radical Obedience, Radical Forgiveness, Radical Humility, and Radical Generosity. He stayed small in his own eyes, and knew that the key to success was to obey Jehovah.

WHAT I LEARNED AS A MORON

THOUGHT TO CONSIDER: Bullies and enemies will be jealous when you choose to be joyful and find peace. Be happy anyway.

VERSE TO CONNECT: "Do not consider his appearance or his height, for I have rejected him. The LORD does not look at the things people look at. People look at the outward appearance, but the LORD looks at the heart." 1 Samuel 16:7, NIV

QUESTION TO CONTEMPLATE: What would happen today if you focused on pleasing God rather than focusing on what others think?

Mike Evans with the Prime Minister of Monaco
at the Friends of Zion Heritage Center in Jerusalem.

Mike Evans with actor Jon Voight.

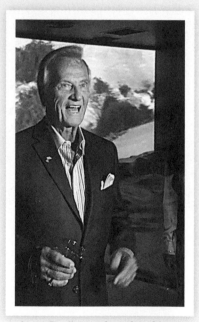

Actor Pat Boone, longtime friend
of Mike at the Friends of Zion
Heritage Center in Jerusalem.

Mike Evans speaking with former
U.K. Prime Minister Tony Blair.

Mike Evans with Jason Greenblatt,
former White House Middle East Envoy,
and former U.S. Ambassador
to Israel David Friedman.

@EITAN_ASRAF

Mike Evans overlooking the
Temple Mount.

Mike Evans in a meeting with former Iranian
President Mahmoud Ahmadinejad.

PART ONE:
WHAT I LEARNED
AS A MORON

MAJOR IN
MENTORS

Former U.S. Secretary of Treasury
Steve Mnuchin with Mike Evans.

Ivanka Trump, Jared Kushner, Trump attorney Jay
Sekulow, Mike Evans, and Ambassador David Friedman.

Mike Evans speaking with world leaders.

CHAPTER

5

*Faith sees the invisible, believes the unbelievable,
and receives the impossible.* [27]

In 1991 i underwent nine hours of intensive surgery to correct
a neurological problem to my neck. For one week I endured
taunting from the Enemy that God would never be able to use me
again. Finally I began to pray. God's answer to the jabs from Satan
was not at all what I expected to hear. I expected sympathy; I
thought God would comfort me while I complained. Instead, God
very plainly said to me, "So, the Enemy is doing exactly what he is
supposed to do. It's time for you to take control of the situation."

When I asked God what He wanted me to do, I was speechless!
He instructed me to go to Saudi Arabia to the staging area for the
Persian Gulf War and preach the Word to the troops amassed there.
Was that Radical Obedience—or a suicide mission?

My response was typical—I think: "Excuse me, God. First, don't
You know I had surgery a little over a week ago? Secondly, don't You
know that I'm Jewish, and the Saudis don't like Jews? Thirdly, I'm

a preacher—and they don't really like preachers over there, either. And last but not least, I read in the newspaper a few days ago that no visas are being issued for that country. Just how do You expect me to go?"

That still, small voice whispered, "Apply for a visa."

So I trudged down to the passport office and skeptically applied for a visa, never for one moment thinking it would come through. One week later, I held the visa in my hand. I was delighted at God's miraculous intervention, right? Hardly! I set about to tell God my other problem: I had no invitation, no reason to go. It wasn't like there was a Christian church on every corner clamoring for me to come preach. I didn't know a soul in that dry and forsaken country. God was surprisingly silent. It was then I knew beyond question that I had to obey Him.

Flight arrangements were made and I climbed aboard for a twenty-plus-hour flight. When the plane finally landed, I was exhausted. I was just two weeks post-op and still experiencing pain from the surgical procedure. Radical Obedience sometimes comes with a price—pain.

After I cleared customs I went in search of a hotel. I checked in to a room, sat down on the side of the bed, and prayed, "Father, here I am. Now what?"

I opened my eyes, picked up the Saudi telephone book, and opened it randomly. I couldn't read a word of Arabic, but there before me was an advertisement with the words *Dhahran Hotel* in English. That's when God said, "Go."

I ran into the bathroom, splashed water on my face, ran a comb through my hair (what hadn't been shaved for the surgery), and raced downstairs to the concierge. A taxi was hired to take me to the hotel, and was I ever happy when I arrived! (If you've never ridden in a taxi in a Middle Eastern country, you've missed a thrill.) Over the front of the hotel fluttered a banner that read, "Joint Operation Command." Inside the hotel was also the headquarters for the various television networks that were transmitting live broadcasts.

When I left my hotel room, I had tucked my Bible under my arm. I walked right into the Dhahran Hotel with it in my hand. I stopped the first official-looking person I met, stuck out my hand, and said, "How are you?"

The man looked at me with horror etched on his face. "Who are you? And what on earth are you doing here with that Bible?" I replied that I was an evangelist from the United States.

"You can't be!"

I had no idea that chaplains assigned to the forces in the Muslim nation were not allowed to wear crosses. They were called "Recreational and Motivational Coordinators."

The official was really encouraging. "You're going to jail."

I was perplexed by his pronouncement. "Why?"

"You're a Christian! It's impossible. How did you get here?"

"British Airlines," I smiled. "There are flights in three times a week."

His next direction stunned me. "Go back to your hotel, pack your belongings, and be out of here within forty-eight hours. If you aren't, you will go to jail."

I began to think maybe he was right—maybe I would go to jail. Perhaps God's will was for me was to preach in prison like Paul.

After I climbed into the cab, I began to pray. I gave the taxi driver directions but had no idea where we were going. When I called out to him to stop, we sat in front of the headquarters for the 82nd Airborne stationed at the McDonald Douglas aircraft plant. I got out of the taxi, paid the driver, and walked over to the gate.

"I need to speak to the chaplain," I said to the guard.

"Who are you?"

"I'm Mike Evans, an evangelist from Dallas."

"How did you get here?" That question was rapidly becoming repetitive.

"British Airways," I again replied.

"You, sir, are going to jail."

"I've already been told that. Now, may I please speak to the chaplain?"

Eventually, I was allowed to pass and given directions to the chaplain's office. His response was much like everyone else's: "I don't know how in the world you got here. What do you want?"

"I want to preach to the troops."

He shook his head in astonishment. "Well, I'll call them together, and then I'm leaving."

Radical Obedience won me both the Favor of God and the honor of preaching to our troops every day until I left the country. It was both humbling and encouraging to know that God was using me to minister to our men and women so far from home and in such precarious circumstances.

While in Saudi Arabia, God spoke to me to go to Iraq to comfort the suffering refugees: *Take food and medicine to the Kurdish people who have been targeted by Saddam Hussein.* In the middle of a field,

I preached to the refugees day and night for a week. Finally my strength was gone, and I was almost too hoarse to speak. I didn't realize I was in the perfect place to be blessed by God.

Gathering all the strength I had left, I tried to think of a topic for one more sermon before my departure. All I really wanted to do was find a comfortable bed, take a shower, and crawl under the covers. Radical Obedience was the last of my worries. Then I heard that still, small voice instructing me to preach one last sermon on Jonah and Nineveh. I did the best I could, telling how Jonah rebelled against God but finally went to Nineveh. I told of the king's repentance and the revival that broke out because of Jonah's obedience. When I asked if anyone wanted to come to Christ, only one person responded—an old man in a dusty robe. I was as disappointed as Jonah had been. My interpreter was concerned about my reaction and asked, "Why aren't you rejoicing?"

"I'm happy for one soul," I said, "but I was hoping for more."

"My dear brother," the interpreter said, "the one soul who just found Jesus is the current king of Nineveh! He is the Kurdish sheik of sixteen provinces, and the capital is the site of ancient Nineveh. He has accepted Jesus and has invited you to go to Nineveh, because he believes if you will preach, they will repent."

I learned yet again that "to obey is better than sacrifice." [28] God blesses Radical Obedience.

WHAT I LEARNED AS A MORON

THOUGHT TO CONSIDER: God blesses radical obedience, even when we don't know what will happen.

VERSE TO CONNECT: "Has the Lord as great delight in burnt offerings and sacrifices, As in obeying the voice of the Lord? Behold, to obey is better than sacrifice, And to heed than the fat of rams." 1 Samuel 15:22, NKJV

QUESTION TO CONTEMPLATE: What radical step of obedience is the Lord calling you to take next?

Mike Evans with his grandson Ethan and the former Prime Minister of Israel Ehud Olmert.

Mark Levin and David Friedman at the Friends of Zion Museum in Jerusalem.

Mike Evans with comedian Jay Leno in Israel.

Award-winning musical artist Michael W. Smith visits Friends of Zion Museum in Jerusalem.

Mike Evans with the Crown Prince of Saudi Arabia
Mohammed bin Salman Al Saud.

Mike Evans talking with actor and director Mel Gibson.
Gibson directed one of the world's top-selling films on the
life of Jesus called "The Passion of the Christ" in 2004.

Former U.S. Secretary of State Mike Pompeo visits
the Friends of Zion Museum in Jerusalem.

CHAPTER

6

There are two kinds of people: those who say to God, "Thy will be done," and those to whom God says, "All right, then, have it your way." [29]

Throughout my ministry there have been times when my life has been in danger because I choose to radically obey God's instructions. I have been targeted by terrorists while driving from Beirut to the Israeli border and threatened by a white supremacist in the United States. During every major conflict in Israel, missiles have flown over my head, and yet God has spared my life. God is sovereign, and it is He who determines the number of our days. Abel's life was but a vapor, but his story of Radical Obedience is told often.

Radical Obedience is defined as "the act or practice of obeying; dutiful or submissive compliance." It goes the extra mile, and one of the earliest examples of obedience to God's command was that of Abel, the second son of Adam and Eve. In Hebrew, Abel means "breath, or vapor," perhaps an indication of the shortness of his life. James wrote: "Your life is like the morning fog—it's here a little while, then it's gone." [30] Most of us are familiar with the first murder recorded in the Bible. Cain, the older brother, was a tiller of the ground—a farmer; Abel was a keeper of sheep. Genesis does not tell us exactly how the two brothers knew what was considered a proper sacrifice to the most Holy God, but clearly they did. Perhaps Jehovah had given them instructions when He offered a blood sacrifice for the sin of Adam and Eve in the Garden.

As soon as the first couple realized the significance of their choice to defy God, they recognized that they were naked. In an attempt to hide their sin, the two covered themselves with fig leaves. (Couldn't they find anything else?) It was their way of handling their nakedness—the do-it-yourself way. However, God had a different plan. He killed an innocent animal—Genesis doesn't say what the animal was—and with the skin made "coats of skins" and clothed them. The lives of innocent animals were taken in order to cover the sin of Adam and Eve. It is a perfect picture of the Radical Obedience of Christ who would give His life to cover the sins of the world.

The story of God's grace to their parents must have been told over and over to the two sons, Cain and Abel. Both worshipped God and brought their sacrifices to present to Him, but each brought a different offering. Genesis 4:3 says that "Cain brought the fruit of the ground." He approached the altar of sacrifice with whatever came to hand. His gift was one of convenience—for show, one given not in faith, but in haste, a last-minute effort. Though he gave lip service to Jehovah, he was not a godly man; instead, he was quick to anger, self-indulgent, and jealous. Cain's wrathful response when

God rejected his spur-of-the-moment offering was indicative of his character:

> But he did not accept Cain and his gift. This made Cain very angry, and he looked dejected.
>
> "Why are you so angry?" the Lord asked Cain. "Why do you look so dejected?" [31]

Cain was angry that God dared reject his sacrifice. So indignant was he that he stood boldly at the altar and argued with the Creator of the universe. His anger and terrible attitude could not mask his knowledge that the requirements had not been met—and he knew that God knew. Even before Christ offered grace to everyone through His death on the cross, God offered Cain a second chance:

> "You will be accepted if you do what is right. But if you refuse to do what is right, then watch out! Sin is crouching at the door, eager to control you. But you must subdue it and be its master." [32]

Cain could have reviewed the requirements for an acceptable offering, humbled himself before God, and returned with a proper sacrifice. Instead, he chose to stomp away with Jehovah's warning ringing in his ears. Sin became his master and he responded accordingly.

Abel—both Matthew and the writer of Hebrews refer to him as "righteous"—had made preparation for his offering. He had chosen a firstborn from the flock. His offering was not a skinny, lame, marred sheep; it was the best he had to offer. Abel approached the altar humbly and penitently, bowed low in the presence of Almighty

God, and presented his gift in faith that his obedience would be honored—his gift accepted.

Abel's offering of a sheep was his way of acknowledging what God had done in the Garden when He wrapped Adam and Eve in animal skins. He presented an animal from his flock in both a thank offering and a sin offering. In essence, he was saying, "I want to be obedient. I am thanking You for showing grace to my parents, and I am asking You to show the same grace to me."

The two brothers walked away from the altar with totally different countenances. Abel's was radiant with God's love and approval; Cain's was dark, his face infused with rage, his heart filled with jealousy.

Solomon, the wise king, defined the effects of jealousy:

> Jealousy is cruel as the grave. Its flashes are flashes of fire. [33]

Abel's hands were raised in praise to Jehovah; Cain's fists were clenched in fury. He was so filled with resentment that he lured Abel into the field and murdered him.

Suddenly God called to Cain, "Where is Abel, your brother?"

A sullen Cain replied, "I don't have any idea. Why are you asking me, anyway? Am I my brother's keeper?" [34]

The punishment for Cain's crime was swift and severe. God stripped him of the land that he had tilled and banished him from His presence. He was consigned to be a vagrant and wanderer. And God warned:

> "Therefore, whoever kills Cain, vengeance shall be

taken on him sevenfold." And the Lord set a mark on Cain, lest anyone finding him should kill him. [35]

When the horror of Cain's sin gripped him, he cried, "My punishment *is* greater than I can bear!" [36]

Of the lives of Cain and Abel, noted Christian minister and author John MacArthur wrote:

> Abel's sacrifice was accepted because he knew what God wanted and obeyed. Cain's was rejected because he knew what God wanted, yet disobeyed. To obey is righteous; to disobey is evil. Abel was of God; Cain was of Satan (1 John 3:12). . . Abel offered a better sacrifice because it represented the obedience of faith. He willingly brought God what He asked, and he brought the very best that he had. In Abel's sacrifice, the way of the cross was first [foreshadowed.] The first sacrifice was Abel's lamb—one lamb for one person. Later came the Passover—with one lamb for one family. Then came the Day of Atonement—with one lamb for one nation. Finally came Good Friday— one Lamb for the whole world. [37]

Radical Obedience cost Abel his life but won him a place in the Bible's Hall of Heroes:

> By faith Abel brought God a better offering than Cain did. By faith he was commended as righteous, when God spoke well of his offerings. And by faith Abel still speaks, even though he is dead. [38]

Abel responded to the call of God. His decision to obey regardless of the circumstances or the outcome led to his death, but it also produced great faith and an even greater reward. When you live in obedience, you are doing well, for it is the highest level of devotion you can present to God. You live in the Favor of God when you overcome sin through obedience.

WHAT I LEARNED AS A MORON

THOUGHT TO CONSIDER: Radical obedience can lead to danger, but you're always safest in the hands of God.

VERSE TO CONNECT: "By faith Abel brought God a better offering than Cain did. By faith he was commended as righteous, when God spoke well of his offerings. And by faith Abel still speaks, even though he is dead." Hebrews 11:4, NIV

QUESTION TO CONTEMPLATE: What act of faith will you take that will outlive your life?

Mike Evans with former Canadian
Prime Minister Stephen Harper.

Mike Evans with his dear
friends President Abdel
Fattah Al-Sisi and General
Abbas of Egypt.

Mike Evans with Jared Kushner and key leaders at the United Nations.

Mike Evans in Hollywood receiving an award.

Mike Evans at a bombed Israeli home during the 2020 Gaza War.

Mike Evans with attorney Alan Dershowitz and Israeli ambassador to the U.S. Ron Dermer at the White House.

Mike Evans being Bar Mitzvahed by terrorist survivor Rabbi Yisroel Goldstein of the Poway Synagogue.

CHAPTER

7

The good you do today, will often be forgotten.

Do good anyway. [39]

God's plan for my life included sharing His Word in places few would dare to go and preach the Gospel—places like war-torn Lebanon, Mogadishu, and Somalia during the week of the al-Qaeda attack on the Blackhawk helicopter troops; Russia, Cuba, and the Congo during the week of the Rwanda massacre; and Cambodia. Like the apostle Paul, I heard the "Macedonian call" [40] and could not refuse to answer. Amazingly, I was again hearing the voice of God through His Word, and mysteriously activating that Word.

How did I know it was God directing me to go to the uttermost parts of the earth to preach? I had heard His voice as a child of eleven. I have trusted Him with my life and my ministry. I have learned that sometimes He speaks through His Word, some-times through godly men and women, and sometimes through circumstances. And then there are the times He speaks directly into your spirit.

It was no surprise when the call to go to Cambodia came during prayer one evening: *"Go to the Killing Fields."* I hurriedly put together a crusade team and flew to Cambodia for a meeting with a group of the country's leaders to ask permission to hold a crusade.

Permission was granted, and God encouraged me to preach boldly to the heads of that communistic, totalitarian government. Miraculously, the leaders of the country, still in the shadow of the murderous Khmer Rouge government, approved the crusade. Tens of thousands of Buddhists and Khmer Rouge murderers gathered as we proclaimed the message of Jesus Christ—crucified, resurrected, and coming again. It was the largest harvest of souls in the history of that nation.

Cambodia was a dark and tormented country overshadowed by the slaughter of more than two million people between 1975 and 1979. God had been forgotten by the majority; only a minority was left to intercede for the souls of the Cambodian people.

It must have been reminiscent of the plight of the world during Noah's time as told at length in Genesis 6:

The Lord saw how great man's wickedness on the earth had become, and that every inclination of the thoughts of his heart was only evil all the time. The Lord was grieved that he had made man on the earth, and His heart was filled with pain. [41]

Everywhere the Creator looked, evil reigned. Verse seven says God repented that He had made Man—one of the few times in the Scriptures where He did so (see chapter three) God could see that Mankind was limited only by his imagination. All seemed to be lost, the only thing left was to destroy it all. But wait! There *was* one righteous man among the unrighteous. His name was Noah, and he found favor in God's eyes.

The Statler Brothers told the story of Noah in their bestselling song "Noah Found Grace in the Eyes of the Lord":

> So the Lord came down to look around a spell
> And there He found Noah behavin' mighty well
> And that is the reason the Scriptures record
> Noah found grace in the eyes of the Lord. [42]

One day as Noah was going about his business, God spoke to him. He warned Noah that He was about to intervene. Was that righteous man as grieved about the lawlessness on earth as God was? Had Noah spent time in fellowship with the Creator, seeking His face and His will? No matter the reason, Noah had captured God's attention. Because of Noah's righteousness, God determined not to just wipe the slate clean and start over with a new creation.

God had a plan, and it involved obedience. He began to share with Noah that he had been appointed to complete a special assignment—building an ark. Now, Noah probably had no idea what an "ark" was, and yet he was willing to follow God's directions. Then the Master Architect gave His builder the blueprint for the ark: It was to be 300 cubits long by 50 cubits wide by 30 cubits high. (That translates to about 450 feet long by 75 feet wide by 45 feet high.) The ark would have three floors to house the creatures that God commanded would be loaded in the structure. Upon its completion, it was to be coated within and without with pitch.

In the Hebrew language, the word pitch means "to cover over, to atone for sin." The ark was designed to cover Noah and his family. God's judgment was rampant over the face of the earth, but inside the ark, the family was safe. When Christ died on the cross, He provided the pitch, the blood that covers our sin. The Believer who is coated by the blood of Christ—pitch—is safe from the wrath of God.

Noah's obedience would ensure him, his wife, his three sons—Shem, Ham, and Japheth, and their wives—a place of safety. They would be spared the destruction that was about to rain down—literally—upon the earth. As he worked on the vessel, Noah preached righteousness to any who would listen. The response: ridicule, derision, mockery, and scorn.

Bible scholars tell us that before the time of Noah, it had not rained on the earth. The faithless were unable to accept by faith that God would fulfill His declaration—whether or not they knew what "rain" was. They had the choice to believe or reject—and the overwhelming majority chose unbelief and rejection.

Noah and his family obeyed the voice of God, the direction to enter the ark and be saved. Noah must have been quite an example to his sons who worked alongside their father to fulfill God's directive. He obeyed despite the harassment. He had followed the instructions to gather the animals as outlined and see them safely inside. He had gathered food for the preservation of his family, all the while warning of the impending disaster. He was an obedient servant of Jehovah—the characteristic of a true servant of God.

Simply stated: Noah believed God—and like Abraham after him—it was "counted it to him for righteousness." [43] And God blessed him abundantly. Because of his faith and obedience, Noah received a rich reward from the Creator. He enjoyed intimacy with Jehovah. They walked and talked together. God laid out the plan and Noah followed it to the letter. Faith coupled with obedience cannot be undervalued. These are qualities that must infuse the spiritual life of a Christian in order to enjoy the Favor of God.

Noah and his sons labored one hundred years on the ark. He obeyed when God warned him of "things not yet seen." God hadn't given Noah a preview of what "rain" was. Noah hadn't seen anything that remotely resembled a flood. And yet, "By faith Noah. . .in reverence prepared an ark for the salvation of his household." [44]

The King James Version says, he was "moved with fear." You might say, "Aha, that's why he did it. God held a big stick over him and said, 'You'd better do this or I'll let you have it.'" Not that at all. Noah reverenced God, and thus he obeyed God's instructions.

When God gave the blueprint for the ark, it contained only one door set in the side of the structure. It hung open, ready and waiting to receive any who desired to enter in and be saved from God's judgment. The ark was another foreshadow of the life of Jesus Christ. Jesus said:

> I am the door. If anyone enters by Me, he will be saved, and will go in and out and find pasture. [45]

Just as there was only one door into the ark, and Noah by his obedience was allowed to enter in, so there is one Door into the presence of God. Again, Jesus said He was the "way, the truth, and the life" and "No one comes to the Father except through Me." [46] The door to the ark was left open until the last possible moment.

After 120 years of preaching, of warning people of the judgment of God upon all the earth, of obedience in building the boat, not one person chose to board the ark! Then Noah and his seven family members entered in. . .and GOD SHUT THE DOOR! [47]

Why was it important that God shut the door? It was symbolic of His authority, and of Man's accountability. As the sound of the door being slammed shut echoed throughout the surrounding area, the first drops of rain began to fall. Now it was too late—no one else was allowed to enter the ark. Judgment was falling from the cloud-laden sky. Lightning flashed and thunder rattled as torrents of water poured down. From beneath the earth, underground waters erupted and raced across the landscape. The ark began to rock and then rise to float on the flood waters. Noah and his sons had faithfully and obediently executed God's command to construct the ark and to enter it, and thus they were spared.

In writing about the life of Noah, Rev. Greg Pratt made a list entitled "All I will ever need to know I learned from Noah." In his list he included:

1. Don't miss the boat.

2. Remember that we are all in the same boat.

3. Plan ahead. It wasn't raining when Noah built the Ark.

4. Stay fit. When you're 600 years old someone may ask you to do something really big.

5. Don't listen to critics; just get on with the job that needs to be done.

6. Build your future on high ground.

7. Speed isn't everything; the snails were onboard with the cheetahs.

8. When you're stressed, float awhile.

9. Remember the Ark was built by amateurs, the Titanic by professionals.

10. No matter what the storm, when you are with God there's always a rainbow waiting. [48]

Noah exercised Radical Obedience in following God's plan for his life. He wasn't popular with the crowd; his only affirmation came from God. His job was long, hard, tedious, and tiring, but he continued to move forward each day. But Noah found favor in the eyes of the Lord—and he and his family landed high and dry! Because of his obedience, God made a promise and sealed it with a rainbow:

> "I establish My covenant with you and with your descendants after you. . . Never again shall all flesh be cut off by the waters of the flood; never again shall there be a flood to destroy the earth." And God said: "This is the sign of the covenant which I make between Me and you. . . I set My rainbow in the cloud, and it shall be for the sign of the covenant between Me and the earth. . . . and I will remember My covenant which is between Me and you and every living creature of all flesh; the waters shall never again become a flood to destroy all flesh. [49]

God's covenant was a covenant of hope. It was a covenant of love. After all, Noah and his family had just seen the entire earth wiped clean of life except for that which resided in the ark. So God made a promise and sealed it with a sign—a rainbow. The rainbow wasn't for Noah—no, it was for God. He said to Noah:

> When *I* see the rainbow in the clouds, *I* will remember the eternal covenant between God and every living creature on earth."[50]

This doesn't mean that God is forgetful; it simply means that when God sees the rainbow, He is reminded to act on His covenant promise. When Jehovah remembered the children of Israel, He sent His servant Moses to lead them to safety. When He remembered the estate of sinful Man, He sent His Son to redeem Mankind. From a rainbow in the clouds to a covenant written in blood, God's love for His Creation is evident. When we respond to Him in Radical Obedience, He showers His favor on us.

WHAT I LEARNED AS A MORON

THOUGHT TO CONSIDER: God has a plan for your life, and it includes your obedience to Him.

VERSE TO CONNECT: "By faith Noah, when warned about things not yet seen, in holy fear built an ark to save his family. By his faith he condemned the world and became heir of the righteousness that is in keeping with faith." Hebrews 11:7, NIV

QUESTION TO CONTEMPLATE: Is there an area where you are hesitant to radically obey God's call in your life?

Mike Evans with former Israeli Prime Minister Benjamin Netanyahu and his wife Sara Netanyahu at the opening of the U.S. Embassy in Jerusalem.

Mike Evans with Friends of Zion international chairman and President Shimon Peres.

Carolyn Evans presenting Ruth Graham with a Christian Woman of the Year award.

Israel Defense Forces visiting Friends of Zion Heritage Center in Jerusalem.

CHAPTER

8

Obedience means marching right on
whether we feel like it or not.
Many times we go against our feelings.
Faith is one thing, feeling is another. [51]

When radical obedience is one of the controlling factors in your life, you move when God says, "Go." I can empathize with Abraham. One month after Carolyn and I were married, God gave me a scripture, and based upon His Word and the leading of the Holy Spirit, we felt directed to go to North Little Rock, Arkansas. We had received a call from Dwayne Duck, a pastor in the area. He told us about a barber, Troy Collier, who was diligently working to start a Teen Challenge Center. Troy was looking for a couple to oversee the work. When we arrived we found a table piled high with bills and a backlog of letters from people who needed a safe place to detoxify. When arrested on drug charges, offenders could either go to Tucker Prison, Cummings Prison, or Teen Challenge. We soon had twenty-one individuals who had committed to our program. So many young people were led to Christ that we needed a discipleship center in the countryside—away from the temptations of drug addiction and city life—to train them in the Word. Because of the faithfulness of God and His people, we soon had the facility we needed.

Aware of God's law of sowing and reaping, we planted the largest seed we had in order to begin this ministry. The outlook was bleak. There was no money, and Carolyn and I had only one room all our own the first year of our marriage, but it was a joyous, glorious year. We did everything we could possibly do for the young people God had entrusted to us. Lives were radically transformed. (I remember that Carolyn and I had only one argument that first year. Her poodle chewed the cover off my *Thompson Chain-Reference* Bible. I was not a happy camper.)

At the end of that year in Arkansas, we moved to Chicago to begin our second work. It was there that we eventually founded our current ministry. This was the first time I would share the vision that God had placed on my heart to help the nation of Israel. The nation would become the abused mother I had always wanted to defend—and couldn't.

When God called Abraham, he became the father of the Chosen People. When the two words *radical* and *obedience* are combined, do you think immediately of Abram who obeyed God's instruction to leave his homeland and set out for an unknown destination? Or is it the Abraham who was instructed to offer his only son to God on an altar of sacrifice? Would you—could you—have done that?

We first read of him in Genesis chapter 11, but his name there is "Abram." Jewish tradition tells us he was born in the 1,948th year after the creation of the world or 1800 BC. (It is interesting that in 1948 AD the nation of Israel was reborn.) Abram's father, Terah, a seller of idols, was a descendant of Shem. Apparently the story of God's grace and mercy in saving Noah and his family from extinction had not reached down through the years to Terah.

Abram, according to that same tradition, worked for his idol-worshipping father but as a young man began to doubt the value of worshipping gods made of wood and stone. He began to believe that the world had been made by one Creator. He tried to share his beliefs with Terah, but to no avail. One day, in his father's absence, Abram took a hammer and smashed all his father's idols except the largest one. In the hands of the stone god, he placed the hammer used to wreak havoc to his father's stock. When he was questioned by a distraught Terah, Abram replied that the largest of the statues had destroyed the others. Terah cried: "Don't be ridiculous. These idols have no life or power. They can't do anything." Abram replied, "Then why do you worship them?"[52]

One day as Abram was going about his usual activities, God called to him:

> "Go from your country, your people and your father's
> household to the land I will show you. I will make you
> into a great nation, and I will bless you; I will make
> your name great, and you will be a blessing. I will
> bless those who bless you, and whoever curses you
> I will curse; and all peoples on earth will be blessed
> through you."[53]

Abram was living in Ur of the Chaldeans when God called him forth. Shortly after his very first conversation with the Creator, his father gathered the family together—Abram, Sarai, and Lot, his grandson—and started out for Canaan. When they reached Haran, however, the family settled. Sometime after his father's death, Abram gathered his family and crossed the Euphrates River, making their way down to Canaan.

As you read about Abram and Sarai, you see lapses in their faith. Isn't it refreshing to know that even those who are held up as examples often struggled with faith issues? Old Testament men and women were as human as you and I. The truth is that God gave Abram the opportunity to learn about the benefits of Radical Obedience—and he did. But not until after Abram and Sarai had been denied a child year after year; not until his nephew Lot departed and claimed the most watered area in all the land as his own, and not until Sarai grew tired of waiting on God to provide a son. Her tactics brought into the world the strife and turmoil that plagues the Middle East even today.

Sarai's desperate anguish over her barrenness drove her to devise a plan to provide Abram with an heir. Now, this was not God's plan. He had already promised Abram a son from whom would descend a people that numbered as many as the stars:

> But Abram said, "Lord God, what will You give me, seeing I go childless, and the heir of my house is Eliezer of Damascus [a servant]?" Then Abram said, "Look, You have given me no offspring; indeed one born in my house is my heir!" And behold, the word of

the Lord came to him, saying, "This one shall not be your heir, but one who will come from your own body shall be your heir." Then He brought him outside and said, "Look now toward heaven, and count the stars if you are able to number them." And He said to him, "So shall your descendants be." [54]

Sarai couldn't wait for God to act. Now, if you've ever longed for a child, you know this desire can become all-consuming. Think of the story of Hannah, the mother of Samuel. So distraught was she as her prayers for a child were offered, the high priest thought she was drunk. The desire to hold a babe in her arms takes the foremost place in the thoughts of a woman who longs for a child. Such was Sarai—to the point that she began to plot her own course, and that of Abram.

It was her desperation that propelled her to offer Hagar, her Egyptian handmaiden, to Abram as a surrogate. Yet, despite Sarai's interference, there is a lesson to be learned. In her misery, Sarai turned from faith in God, from dependence on Jehovah, to works—dependence on self. She had a plan and nothing was going to deter her from seeing it come to fruition. Hagar represents works—man or, in this instance, woman—taking matters into their own hands. Abram could have said, "No." He could have reminded Sarai that God had made a promise to him and he would continue to believe God. That didn't happen. When presented with a pretty little doe-eyed handmaiden, Abram capitulated.

By the time Hagar was heavy with child, Sarai was consumed with jealousy and Abram was forced to endure the contentious atmosphere he had helped create within the camp. It continued to roil within him even after the babe was born and named Ishmael. And then God fulfilled his promise to Abram and Sarai. He said to Abram (loosely translated), "It's time for you to step up to the plate and walk uprightly before me. No more delayed obedience. I want your undivided attention." God then made another stipulation:

> "No longer shall your name be called Abram, but your name shall be Abraham [father of a multitude]; for I have made you a father of many nations. . . . As for Sarai your wife, you shall not call her name Sarai, but Sarah [noblewoman] shall be her name. And I will bless her and also give you a son by her." [55]

Soon Abraham reached the age of ninety-nine and Sarah eighty-nine, both obviously well past normal childbearing age. Then came the day when Sarah awoke to find that she was pregnant in her old age. She who had laughed at the pronouncement that she would bear a child—she who had intervened and proposed her own plan for an heir—Sarah was now carrying Isaac, the son of promise. Not only had God taken away her barrenness, He provided the strength to carry the child to term and to bring it forth.

Then the trouble with Hagar and Ishmael became increasingly apparent. Eight days after Isaac was born, he was circumcised, and after the babe was weaned, Abraham hosted a huge celebration for the son born to Sarah. One day Sarah spied Ishmael mocking Isaac. At that moment, her anger reached volcanic level and she exploded. Sarah demanded that Abraham literally drive Hagar and her son from the encampment with only what bread and water they could carry. Abraham had to bear the pain, heartache, and tragedy of losing Ishmael as he complied with Sarah's demands.

God had fulfilled his vow, and the child of promise had finally arrived. Abraham set about to teach God's covenant promises to his son. And then horror descended into Abraham's life:

> Then [God] said, "Take now your son, your only son Isaac, whom you love, and go to the land of Moriah, and offer him there as a burnt offering on one of the mountains of which I shall tell you." [56]

We often underestimate just how outrageous, how despicable this must have seemed to Abraham. It seems impossible to believe that he didn't question God's directive, but the narrative doesn't suggest that. (Neither is there any mention of whether he told Sarah of God's command.) You and I have read the rest of the story and know the outcome—Abraham knew only what God had demanded of him. Yet verse 3 says:

> So Abraham rose early in the morning and saddled his donkey, and took two of his young men with him, and Isaac his son; and he split the wood for the burnt offering, and arose and went to the place of which God had told him. [57]

This time Abraham did not argue nor did he hesitate to obey God's directions. He didn't bargain with God; he didn't ask for anything in return for his obedience. Instead, he immediately made arrangements for the three-day journey to Mount Moriah.

I believe his heart was so heavy it was difficult for him to place one foot in front of the other. I believe he was puzzled about God's plan. Abraham was not some Superman—a spiritual hero with mystical powers, he was "everyman" and he was about to offer the child of promise. How would you feel if you knew you were about to lose a beloved son or daughter? Abraham was surely no different.

So off they set on a three-day hike across the desert terrain—a journey of some sixty miles—to the place designated by God. When they arrived, Abraham asked the servants to wait while, "the lad and I will go yonder and worship." Then he added what might well be a hint to the strength of his faith, "and we will come back to you." [58]

After three days of spiritual wrestling with God, Abraham was assured that God would provide. As he unloaded the wood from the donkey and laid it on Isaac's back, the lad asked, "Look, the fire and the wood, but where is the lamb for a burnt offering?" [59] And in verse 8 with great conviction and complete assurance, his father replied, "My son, God will provide for Himself the lamb for a burnt offering." Abraham had not figured out just how God would provide—a lamb wandering by, Isaac raised from the dead, a last-minute stay of execution—but he was convinced that provide God would!

I have a mental picture of father and son slowly trudging their way up the mountain to the place where God finally says, "Here; this is it." When they arrived, Abraham and Isaac set about gathering stones to erect an altar to Jehovah. Abraham carefully laid the wood and knelt before his son. He gently bound Isaac's hands and feet, and laid him on the altar. Now, Isaac was old enough to run for his life. Not only did Abraham display Radical Obedience, so did his beloved son, Isaac.

Just as Abraham raises the knife to plunge it into Isaac's heart, an angel of the Lord cries, "STOP! Don't hurt the boy."

And He said, "Do not lay your hand on the lad, or do anything to him; for now I know that you fear God, since you have not withheld your son, your only son, from Me." [60]

I believe Abraham heard something rustling in a bush near the altar. He looked around and there, held fast, was a ram caught by its horns. With unparalleled gratitude, Abraham untied his son, bound the ram, and laid it on the altar as a sacrifice to his faithful Jehovah-Jireh, his provider. The angel then goes one step further; he reiterates the pact God made with Abraham:

> "By Myself I have sworn, says the Lord, because you
> have done this thing, and have not withheld your son,
> your only son—blessing I will bless you, and multiply-
> ing I will multiply your descendants as the stars of
> the heaven and as the sand which is on the seashore;
> and your descendants shall possess the gate of their
> enemies. In your seed all the nations of the earth shall
> be blessed, because you have obeyed My voice." [61]

Obedience and faith go hand in hand. One cannot exist without the other. Strong faith produces Radical Obedience, which touches the heart of God, moves the hand of God, and releases the blessings of God. This extraordinary happening took place about two thousand years before Christ was born, and yet it's a perfect picture of God's offering of a substitute for our sins. He would offer up His own son for our redemption.

Just as God was faithful to Abraham, so He is committed to His children today. He lovingly gives us just what we need—not what we want. In so doing, He fulfills His will in our lives—to redeem us unto Himself. Because of Abraham's radical obedience, he knew well what it meant to live in God's favor, and he received perhaps the ultimate honor:

> "Abraham believed God, and it was accounted to him for righteousness." And he was called the friend of God. [62]

That great orator and preacher Charles Spurgeon said of obedience:

> Having once discerned the voice of God, obey without question. If you have to stand alone and nobody will befriend you, stand alone and God will befriend you. [63]

Abraham's obedience proved to be unflinching at the command of God. Isaac, the son of sacrifice, was a foreshadow of the One who also bore the wood upon His back—His own cross. [64] Christ became the sacrifice who shed His blood for the salvation of mankind.

WHAT I LEARNED AS A MORON

THOUGHT TO CONSIDER: Faith involves obeying the eternal facts of God over the temporary feelings of self.

VERSE TO CONNECT: "By faith Abraham, when called to go to a place he would later receive as his inheritance, obeyed and went, even though he did not know where he was going." Hebrews 11:8, NIV

QUESTION TO CONTEMPLATE: Will you choose faith over feelings when tested to choose the way that is most comfortable today?

Mike Evans being interviewed by Governor Mike Huckabee in Israel.

Mike Evans at an event caring
for orphans in Israel.

Texas Gov. Greg Abbott receives
the Friends of Zion award.

CHAPTER

9

The beginning of greatness is to be little;
the increase of greatness is to be less;
the perfection of greatness is to be nothing. [65]

In 1978 after I was invited to go with the late Jamie Bucking-ham, international author and columnist, on what had become for him a regular trek through the Sinai, I was traveling through my own desert place and looking forward to leaving my ministry cares behind to hike and fellowship with Jamie and his group of friends for eleven days. As with other paths down which God has led me, this too would be an unforgettable life experience. It seemed that God's wonderful plan for my life also included sand, heat, scorpions, and flies.

As our group followed in the footsteps of Moses, I began to draw some comparisons between his life and mine. We had both been abandoned as children—Moses out of love and a desire to be protected; me out of hatred and the abuse that followed. Eventually,

Moses was rescued and protected by Pharaoh's daughter; I, too, was rescued by the assurances of Jesus that He had a great plan for my life. Even so, the feelings of worthlessness and fear that I could not have a successful ministry plagued me during the trek across the sands of the Sinai.

After returning home, I was sitting on my back steps one day when I finally reached the end of my rope. Dropping my head into my hands, I prayed, "God, my life is in Your hands. I surrender to You. If You want me to go, I'll go. If You want me to stay, I'll stay. I want only to be in Your will. You told me You loved me and had a great plan for my life. Please, Lord, speak to me again. I desperately need to hear Your voice once again."

The next day, I flew to preach for a minister friend of mine. As I sat in the confining seat in coach, I began to pray. *Lord, I have no joy, no peace. As soon as I've preached tomorrow, that's it. I'm so ashamed; I've failed You. I don't know what else to do but quit.* I turned my face to the window as tears slid down my cheeks. It was at that moment—the lowest of my ministry—that God spoke His Word into my spirit. That still, small voice said, *"Isaiah 43:18–19. Pray it in faith!"* I was again hearing His voice through His Word! I had no idea how big this discovery was, and that it would be as powerful as Jesus speaking to me face-to-face just as He had when I was eleven.

I had no idea that the boy from the Projects would eventually claim Menachem Begin as his mentor and I would have the privilege of partnering with him to found the current Christian Zionism movement. Nor did I know that I would prophesy over a depressed twenty-eight-year-old salesman whose brother had been shot in the back in Entebbe, Uganda, during the rescue of Israeli hostages. I had no idea I would tell him that he would be prime minister of Israel twice, or that I would relate the story the following day to Prime Minister Begin, who would offer him a government position.

I reached for my Bible and opened it to read God's words of assurance:

> "Do not remember the former things, nor consider the things of old. Behold, I will do a new thing, now it shall spring forth; shall you not know it? I will even make a road in the wilderness and rivers in the desert." [66]

I had thought God was through with me; now He promised to do a new thing. I would soon find out that it would take Radical Obedience to see God's plan come to pass.

Just as God promised to do a new thing in my life, so He began, through Moses, to do a new thing in the lives of the Children of Israel, held captive in Egypt.

Moses' story of Radical Obedience must begin with his mother, Jacobed, who hid him from the Egyptian people for three months after his birth. Because of the explosive birth rate among the Israelites, Pharaoh had issued a decree that every Hebrew male child was to be slaughtered. He instructed the midwives to kill every child as soon as he emerged from the womb. Instead, they united to save as many children as possible, one of them being Moses. When Jacobed's son became too old to hide, she took reeds and wove a basket. She waterproofed it and set it among the bulrushes on the bank of the Nile. Moses' sister, Mariam, was posted at a distance to watch over the child.

Miracle number one: The child was not consumed by the crocodiles that inhabit the Nile. Miracle number two: Pharaoh's daughter came down to the water's edge to bathe and spotted the basket with the child inside floating on the water. She sent one of her handmaidens to fetch it, and recognized immediately that it was a Hebrew child. Mariam crept from her hiding place and tremblingly approached the princess. She timidly offered the services of her mother, Jacobed, as a wet nurse for the baby. Miracle number three: So it was that the mother of Moses was able to nurse her own son. Her obedience brought the Favor of God and His protection over her son:

> And the child grew, and [Jacobed] brought him to Pharaoh's daughter, and he became her son. So she called his name Moses, saying, "Because I drew him out of the water." [67]

So Moses was reared in the household of Pharaoh, a house of wealth and privilege. Nothing else is recorded of Moses' life until he was a young man. As suddenly as he disappeared from the pages of the Bible, he reappeared. Moses was out walking one day when he happened upon an Egyptian taskmaster beating a Jewish slave. So incensed was Moses that he killed the Egyptian and hid the body. The following day, he saw two Hebrew men fighting. He adopted the role of intermediary, but one of the men challenged him:

> "Who made you a prince and a judge over us? Do you intend to kill me as you killed the Egyptian?" So Moses feared and said, "Surely this thing is known!" [68]

Immediately Moses realized that his relationship to an Egyptian princess would not spare him the wrath of Pharaoh. He had murdered a man who was carrying out a direct order from the king. Moses, having heard that Pharaoh had placed a price on his head, packed his knapsack and headed for the backside of the desert.

He was seeking a place of refuge and solitude but instead walked right into the middle of a dispute between Midianite shepherds and the seven daughters of Reuel (also known as Jethro), a Midianite priest. The male shepherds were determined to keep the sisters from drawing water for their sheep. Moses (who likely didn't look at all like Charlton Heston) stepped into the fray, drove the shepherds away, and watered the flocks.

Three separate incidents marked Moses' early life, yet in all three he exhibited an almost compulsive need to combat wickedness. His intervention was limited to the underdog: he championed the Hebrew slave; he intervened when two Jews were fighting, and again when a group of gentiles were oppressing another like group.

Moses had no idea he would meet his future wife at the watering trough. Reuel offered Moses the job of sheepherder as well as the hand of his daughter, Zipporah, in marriage. Now Moses was content. He had a job, a wife, and soon a child, Gershom. He didn't know that he was about to face the challenge of a lifetime—greater than leaving home and family, greater than the daily grind of taking care of the sheep. God was about to intervene in Moses' life in a unique way.

One day as he led the sheep to the far reaches of Mount Horeb, he stumbled upon a bush that burned brightly but was not consumed. This was totally against the laws of nature, and Moses turned aside to see this phenomenon. He must have been stunned when from the midst of the bush the Lord spoke to him:

> "Do not come any closer," God said. "Take off your sandals, for the place where you are standing is holy ground." Then he said, "I am the God of your father, the God of Abraham, the God of Isaac and the God of Jacob." At this, Moses hid his face, because he was afraid to look at God. The Lord said, "I have indeed seen the misery of my people in Egypt. I have heard them crying out because of their slave drivers, and I am concerned about their suffering. So I have come down to rescue them from the hand of the Egyptians and to bring them up out of that land into a good and spacious land, a land flowing with milk and honey— the home of the Canaanites, Hittites, Amorites, Perizzites, Hivites and Jebusites. And now the cry of the Israelites has reached me, and I have seen the way the Egyptians are oppressing them. So now, go. I am sending you to Pharaoh to bring my people the Israelites out of Egypt." [69]

Was Moses shocked that though he had killed a man in Egypt, he was about to be sent back to the scene of the crime with instructions to confront Pharaoh? Now, the king from whom Moses fled had died. Moses could have let fear rule his life, and while he did argue about his ability to sway both Pharaoh and the Children of Israel, he ultimately chose to obey the call of God upon his life. God had captured his attention and dealt with Moses' concerns—he was to find his older brother, Aaron, and demand that Pharaoh "Let my people go!"

> "You shall speak all that I command you. And Aaron your brother shall tell Pharaoh to send the children of Israel out of his land. . . . And the Egyptians shall know that I *am* the Lord, when I stretch out My hand on Egypt and bring out the children of Israel from among them." [70]

In essence, God was telling Moses that his obedience would bring deliverance to the entire Hebrew nation in bondage in Egypt. Obedience would bring triumph over Pharaoh's army; submission to God would defeat the enemy. Moses and Aaron willingly complied with God's directives; they did just as He had instructed. Together, they went before the king and demanded that he release the Children of Israel to go into the desert and worship Jehovah God.

Despite his trepidation, Moses obeyed, and like Abraham, his obedience won him a place in the Hall of Faith in Hebrews chapter eleven, and showered the Favor of God upon his life. However, his obedience to the Creator did not end with the crossing of the Red Sea and the defeat of Pharaoh's army. Even though Moses had led the Israelites out of Egypt and into the wilderness, he had been assigned the responsibility of leading them to the Promised Land. Yet God equipped him for the task.

Moses was called by God to the heights of the mountaintop to personally receive the Ten Commandments—the only man to have seen God's glory and lived. He chose a young man from among the Israelites, Joshua, to accompany him halfway up the mountain.

Once on the mountaintop, Moses received these instructions:

> "There is a place near me where you may stand on
> a rock. When my glory passes by, I will put you in a
> cleft in the rock and cover you with my hand until I
> have passed by. Then I will remove my hand and you
> will see my back; but my face must not be seen. [71]

After Moses received the Ten Commandments written on the stone tablets by the very finger of God, he returned to the camp to deliver them to the people waiting at the base of Mount Sinai. But what did he find when he descended out of the cloud? He found a people reveling in rebellion and delighting in disobedience. Having grown weary of Moses' absence, the Israelites prevailed upon Aaron to make them a god of gold—a calf. "Come on," they said, "we don't know what has happened to Moses. We need a god that will lead us out of the wilderness." The psalmist David wrote of those who worshipped other gods. It was a description of idol worshippers of that time, but resonates with similar people of our time:

> But their idols are silver and gold, made by human
> hands. They have mouths, but cannot speak, eyes, but
> cannot see. They have ears, but cannot hear, noses,
> but cannot smell. They have hands, but cannot feel,
> feet, but cannot walk, nor can they utter a sound
> with their throats. Those who make them will be like
> them, and so will all who trust in them. [72]

While the people danced before the golden calf, God warned Moses of trouble in the camp, and threatened to destroy the people

Moses had led out of Egypt. Moses interceded for the rebellious Israelites, and God heeded his plea to spare them. As Joshua and Moses reached the bottom of Mount Sinai, they were stunned by the sight that met their eyes:

> When Moses approached the camp and saw the calf and the dancing, his anger burned and he threw the tablets out of his hands, breaking them to pieces at the foot of the mountain. And he took the calf the people had made and burned it in the fire; then he ground it to powder, scattered it on the water and made the Israelites drink it. [73]

Moses must have turned to Aaron and asked, "What were you thinking?!" Aaron's answer would have won an Oscar for his response and his lame excuse. Can you picture him with arms upraised and a shrug of his shoulders?

"Do not be angry, my lord," Aaron answered. "You know how prone these people are to evil. They said to me, 'Make us gods who will go before us. As for this fellow Moses who brought us up out of Egypt, we don't know what has happened to him.' So I told them, 'Whoever has any gold jewelry, take it off.' Then they gave me the gold, and I threw it into the fire, and *out came this calf*!"

Aaron didn't bow in contrition and take responsibility for his actions. He tried to justify going along with the crowd. How often does that happen—drifting into disobedience instead of taking a stand? We chuckle at Aaron's ingenuous reply, but haven't we been guilty of the same? We excuse our own behavior while pointing a finger at someone else's fall into sin.

So distraught was Moses that he literally drew a line in the sand:

> So he stood at the entrance to the camp and shouted, "All of you who are on the Lord's side, come here and join me." And all the Levites gathered around him. Moses told them, "This is what the Lord, the God of Israel, says: Each of you, take your swords and go back and forth from one end of the camp to the other. Kill everyone—even your brothers, friends, and neighbors." The Levites obeyed Moses' command, and about 3,000 people died that day. [74]

From the time of Adam and Eve's sin in the garden to Christ's death on the cross, the wages of sin has always been the same: death. [75] Although it must have grieved Moses to issue God's order, he was obedient. Radical Obedience is not easy. It requires laying aside Self and clinging to God's promises.

God would later call Moses to the top of the mountain to give the law again. This time Moses had to carve the stone tablets out of the rock. When he descended the mountain the second time, he didn't stop with just reading what God had dictated, he called upon the Children of Israel to be faithful to keep the laws they had been given. Moses was intent that his followers be not just hearers of the word but doers as well. As Samuel the prophet would later say to King Saul, "Obedience is better than sacrifice, and submission is better than offering the fat of rams." [76]

The Israelites were encouraged to obey the Word of God, to pass it on to their children:

> "You shall teach them diligently to your children, and shall talk of them when you sit in your house, when you walk by the way, when you lie down, and when you rise up."[77]

Moses wanted God's chosen ones to understand just what He expected from them. He wanted a people set apart from the wickedness, the depravity, and the worship of idols made by Man. They needed to specifically understand the importance of:

> "You shall have no other gods before me. You shall not make for yourself an image in the form of anything in heaven above or on the earth beneath or in the waters below. You shall not bow down to them or worship them; for I, the Lord your God, am a jealous God. . ."[78]

During the years of wandering through the desert, Moses was obedient to the Divine instructions given him. Not only did he display Radical Obedience but extraordinary patience. He led a company of people that continually grumbled, complained, and mutinied. It was not surprising that eventually Moses' patience reached its breaking point, and in anger, he failed to follow God's instructions (Numbers 20). He disobeyed God at that one crucial juncture and his punishment was that he was not allowed to enter into the Promised Land. That honor would belong to his successor, Joshua. However, God *did* take Moses to the top of the mountain and allow him to see the other side—the land that flowed with milk and honey. Then Moses died and the Lord buried him. No man knows his burial site even today.[79]

Despite missteps, Moses' life was characterized by Radical Obedience. He led a nation of rebellious, dissatisfied, disobedient, quarrelsome, and complaining people through the wilderness to the banks of the Jordan River. Through all the ups and downs, the years of wandering in the desert, Moses held high the name of Jehovah-Nissi—God our banner. It was a banner of encouragement "to give you a future and a hope." [80]

Moses was able to defeat the forces of the enemy because he was submissive to God's will, and so can you. He delivered his people from the chains of darkness and degradation because he complied with Jehovah's instructions. Just as Moses' Radical Obedience won him the unfailing Favor of God, so it will open the door to the Favor of God in your life.

WHAT I LEARNED AS A MORON

THOUGHT TO CONSIDER: Moses was able to defeat the forces of the enemy because he was submissive to God's will, and so can you.

VERSE TO CONNECT: "Do not remember the former things, Nor consider the things of old. Behold, I will do a new thing, Now it shall spring forth; Shall you not know it? I will even make a road in the wilderness And rivers in the desert." Isaiah 43:18-19, NKJV

QUESTION TO CONTEMPLATE: What area of life do you need to change to more closely align with the will of God today?

Mike Evans with Egypt's President Sisi.

Mike Evans with the former
President of Honduras.

Mike Evans with former Israeli
Prime Minister Menachem Begin.

Mike Evans presenting his Friends of Zion
award to the President of Georgia.

CHAPTER

10

*If you are successful, you will win some unfaithful friends
and some genuine enemies. Succeed anyway.* [81]

My own "for such a time as this" moment occurred in 1981, when my ministry was threatened with disaster because of lies. I was more in need than ever of God's favor. Being prodded by the Spirit of God to request a meeting with Prime Minister Menachem Begin, I flew to New York en route to Israel and took a room at the Plaza Hotel to pray. The following morning as I sat in the hotel, reading my Bible, God again gave me the same scripture He had given me in the past:

> But those who wait on the Lord shall renew *their*
> strength; they shall mount up with wings like eagles,
> they shall run and not be weary, they shall walk and
> not faint. [82]

I sent a wire to the prime minister's office requesting a meeting and advising him of where I would be staying. I didn't know if he would see me, but I was going to do what God had directed me to do.

Now, I had never met Menachem Begin and had no idea why he would ever want to meet with me, an unknown Christian minister. I wasn't a Rev. Billy Graham or a noted politician—just a guy from the other side of the tracks determined to obey the call of God.

Several days later, I set off for the airport and the encounter that was to provide the focus of my life and ministry. After a long and tiring flight, I checked in to a hotel in Jerusalem and began to pray. For a week I prayed and fasted in my hotel room.

One morning the phone rang shrilly. A voice on the other end said, "Mike Evans? This is Yehiel Kadashai, Prime Minister Begin's personal secretary. The prime minister has agreed to meet with you. Are you available this afternoon?"

My heart stood still. I stammered, "Yes, what time should I come?"

Mr. Kadashai confirmed a time, and I dropped the handset back in the cradle. My knees turned to jelly and I sank down on the bed. I was going to meet the prime minister of Israel! God had honored His promise to me. It was the beginning of a friendship that lasted until Mr. Begin died, and opened door after door for me in the nation of Israel. God's favor is most often apparent when we are in a place of brokenness, as was Esther, and as was I. It is then that the hand of God reaches out to us in grace to lift us up.

Esther's story would compare with a modern fairy tale: A beautiful young Jewish girl torn from her homeland and taken as a captive to Persia; a tyrannical ruler who banished his queen from her royal position and initiated a search for her successor; and of course, an evil villain, Haman, who desired to perpetrate genocide against the Jews.

Ahasuerus (also known as Xerxes), wealthy ruler of Persia, decided to share his great treasure with his subjects. After seven days of banqueting, the king summoned his beautiful queen, Vashti, to the party. She refused the king's request and was immediately banished from Ahasuerus' presence. The king was crushed to lose his lovely queen but felt he had no choice in the matter. Her disobedience could not be tolerated, as it would be seen as a weakness in the king's leadership ability.

The king's advisors decided that Ahasuerus needed something to take his mind off Vashti and issued a decree:

"Let beautiful young virgins be sought for the king." [83]

Enter Esther, whose Hebrew name was Hadassah, which is derived from the word for "myrtle." She was aptly named, for the myrtle tree has leaves whose fragrance is only released when they are crushed. She was a Hebrew orphan who lived with her Uncle Mordecai. Esther and her people had been in captivity for over one hundred years when she was carried off to the palace in Shushan against her will and placed in the house of the women under the care of the eunuch, Hegai. Esther could have wailed and pouted and bemoaned her circumstances, but she retained a quiet and humble spirit. Hegai was so captivated that he took exceptional care of her, even going so far as to give her a special place in the harem. It was from there that, after twelve months of beauty treatments, Esther was selected to spend a night with the king. When she was summoned, Hegai took care to advise her on how to capture Ahasuerus' attention. She was obedient to Hegai's suggestions and so captured the king's notice that she gained favor and was chosen as queen to replace Vashti.

Esther and Ahasuerus were not the only characters necessary to the plot; now we are introduced to Haman. He was the highest official in the kingdom—the personification of pride and lust for power. When Esther's uncle had refused to bow down to Haman, the egotistical official determined that the entire Jewish race would suffer his vengeance. What he didn't know was that the king owed Mordecai a great debt of gratitude for having once saved his life, which had not been repaid. Mordecai had overheard a plot to kill the king and duly reported it. His actions were recorded in the chronicles of the king.

Haman was unaware of Mordecai's deed; he knew only that the Jew failed to bow in his presence. Thus began the plot to destroy an entire people.

> Then Haman said to King [Ahasuerus], "There is a certain people dispersed and scattered among the peoples in all the provinces of your kingdom whose customs are different from those of all other people and who do not obey the king's laws; it is not in the king's best interest to tolerate them." [84]

The king, unaware of Haman's true intent, agreed to the plan and issued a proclamation to that effect. The news of the scheme soon reached Mordecai, who carried the information to his niece.

Esther's uncle challenged the queen to approach Ahasuerus (a move that could be punishable by death) and ask for the salvation of her people. In encouraging her to do so, Mordecai confronted

Esther with these timeless words:

> "For if you remain silent at this time, relief and deliverance for the Jews will arise from another place, but you and your father's family will perish. And who knows but that you have come to your royal position for such a time as this?" [85]

Esther reminded Mordecai that to approach the king without being summoned could cost the queen her life. She had not yet revealed to Ahasuerus that she was a Jewess; that knowledge could also have meant instant death, and yet she chose to obey her uncle. She was willing to sacrifice her life to save her people. Her only request was that the Jews gather together to fast and pray with her and her handmaidens. Her response to Mordecai was magnificent, the epitome of Radical Obedience:

"Go, gather together all the Jews who are in Susa, and fast for me. Do not eat or drink for three days, night or day. I and my attendants will fast as you do. When this is done, I will go to the king, even though it is against the law. And if I perish, I perish." [86]

On the third day, Esther dressed in her most beautiful gown, wrapped herself with royal robes, and then with confidence stepped into the throne room. Seeing his beautiful queen slip into the hall pleased Ahasuerus and he extended his golden scepter in her direction. She stepped forward with assurance and touched the staff to obtain the pardon it offered her. The king asked, "What do you desire? I will give you up to half my kingdom."

Rather than respond directly to Ahasuerus' offer, Esther instead invited him and Haman to join her in her quarters for a banquet. When the day arrived, the king again offered Esther up to half his kingdom. Again she requested their presence at a second banquet. She informed the king that she would then make her request known to him.

Ahasuerus must have been a bit baffled, but so engaging was Esther that he complied. Haman's ego was so inflated at having been given special attention by the queen that he set off home in a cloud of self-aggrandizement. As he left the palace, he saw Mordecai sitting at the gate. Haman's entire evening must have been ruined when once again, the Jew failed to bow down at his passing. He was enraged because he had not received the honor he thought due him.

While Haman pouted and plotted against the Jews, the king discovered that Mordecai had never been rewarded for having saved his life. To determine how best to honor Mordecai, Ahasuerus asked Haman:

> "What shall be done for the man whom the king delights to honor?" [87]

Haman's internal and self-centered response was:

> "Whom would the king delight to honor more than me?" [88]

Certain that he would be granted all the things on his personal bucket list—fame, power, and wealth—Haman continued:

> "If the king wishes to honor someone, he should bring out one of the king's own royal robes, as well as a

horse that the king himself has ridden—one with a royal emblem on its head. Let the robes and the horse be handed over to one of the king's most noble officials. And let him see that the man whom the king wishes to honor is dressed in the king's robes and led through the city square on the king's horse. Have the official shout as they go, 'This is what the king does for someone he wishes to honor!'" [89]

With chest puffed out, Haman waited for the king to announce that he was the one to be acclaimed. Imagine his fury when Ahasuerus calmly announced that the man to be honored was none other than Mordecai. Delighted with Haman's answer, the king shouted:

"Quick! Take the robes and my horse, and do just as you have said for Mordecai the Jew, who sits at the gate of the palace. Leave out nothing you have suggested!" [90]

Haman was humiliated! After doing the king's bidding, he crept off home to his family and friends for a big pity party. They did not have long to console him, for soon after his arrival the queen's footmen arrived to carry him to the second banquet.

As Esther wined and dined her guests, the king asked the nature of her request and again offered her up to half of his kingdom. This time she did not hesitate:

"If I have found favor with you, Your Majesty, and if it pleases you, grant me my life—this is my petition. And spare my people—this is my request. For I and my people have been sold to be destroyed, killed and annihilated. If we had merely been sold as male and female slaves, I would have kept quiet, because no such distress would justify disturbing the king." [91]

Ahasuerus was stunned! Who would dare threaten the queen? Esther promptly pointed a finger at the culprit and confirmed it was:

"An adversary and enemy! This vile Haman!" [92]

The king was enraged. He rose from the banquet table and stalked out into the palace garden. Haman, in fear for his life, threw himself on the couch on which Esther reclined and began to plead with her. At that moment the king returned to the hall, and seeing Haman on the couch screamed, "Will he even molest the queen while she is with me in the house?" [93]

Now, Haman had ordered a long pole about 75 feet high erected near his house for the express purpose of impaling Mordecai. One of the queen's eunuchs informed the king of the pole and its purpose. Ahasuerus immediately ordered that Haman be impaled on the pole meant for Mordecai. The grisly sentence was carried out forthwith.

Esther had then turned to the king and informed him of Haman's evil plot to destroy the Jews, her people. Unfortunately, the king could not rescind the original order, but he issued a second set of orders that permitted the Jews to fight for their lives against their enemies. A royal celebration was held in Susa; Mordecai was honored by the king; and Esther was given all of Haman's properties and wealth.

If we could, we might ask Esther if Radical Obedience garners the Favor of God. She came to the king in mortal fear and left with supernatural favor. She came in despair and left rejoicing. She came representing a people who were marked for destruction and left the king's presence with a pardon.

Esther obeyed at the risk of her own life so that the Jews might be spared the edge of the sword. Her Radical Obedience brought the Favor of God not only into her life, but the lives of her people, the Jews. Still today, the feast of Purim is celebrated in honor of the deliverance of the Jews in Persia.

Under the tutelage of Mordecai and then Hegai, Esther accepted instruction with a spirit that was both godly and teachable. She exhibited amazing strength and Radical Obedience. Her humility was so striking that she easily won the respect of others, and ultimately became queen. With Haman's wicked plot and evil plans, we see why God chose this beautiful, obedient woman as His instrument. It was these attributes—obedience, humility, and determination—that saved her people from destruction and won the Favor of God. Esther had learned Radical Obedience and had, indeed, come to the kingdom for just such a time.

You, too, can live in the fwhen you approach the King of Kings in Radical Obedience and humbly submit yourself to Him.

WHAT I LEARNED AS A MORON

THOUGHT TO CONSIDER: Obedience can bring the favor of God on your life and the lives of others.

VERSE TO CONNECT: "But those who wait on the LORD Shall renew their strength; They shall mount up with wings like eagles, They shall run and not be weary, They shall walk and not faint." Isaiah 40:31, NKJV

QUESTION TO CONTEMPLATE: What is one area of your life you need to humble before the Lord to experience His favor upon you and those you will impact?

Friends of Zion Heritage Center campus, aerial image.

Mike Evans with son Michael Evans at the dedication of Friends of Zion Museum.

Michael Evans with his father on a state invitation in Iraq, hosted by President Barzani in Kurdistan.

Israeli Defense Forces visiting Friends of Zion in Jerusalem.

Mike Evans with Israeli Prime Minister and longtime friend Benjamin Netanyahu.

Mike Evans speaking with Dallas Cowboys superstar Deion Sanders.

Mike Evans at a Hanukah party with President Donald Trump at the White House.

CHAPTER

11

All of God's people are ordinary people who
have been made extraordinary by the purpose
he has given them. [94]

When god began to direct me to a worldwide ministry, I opened my Bible and began to read and seek His direction. One day as I prayed, the Spirit of God told me that He wanted me to preach in several Third World countries. I reminded Him that I would need funds for travel and crusade expenses.

"How much do you need?"

"About one hundred thousand dollars," I whispered.

"Is that all?"

"Excuse me, Lord. I really haven't put pencil to paper. Make it two hundred and fifty thousand—that should be enough."

"Is that all you will need?"

"Well, half a million."

"Is that all?"

"Okay, let's round it off and make it a million."

I had circled Philippians 4:19 and dated it years ago, and at that moment I felt a supernatural upsurge of faith. It was as if God had activated that scripture.

"All right, so be it. But don't reveal this to anyone. Don't ask for it and don't tell anybody the need. That is the condition for getting a million dollars for those Third World crusades."

Soon after that, I walked into my office. My secretary said a woman was on hold on the phone and wanted me to pray for her. The Holy Spirit impressed that I was to pray with this lady. So I prayed for her. The following week, the caller, Madeline Chaffin, phoned again to ask if my wife and I would have dinner with her. The Holy Ghost whispered, *"Say yes,"* so I obeyed, although I had no idea who this lady was. But I had a promise from God, "And my God shall supply all your need according to His riches in glory by Christ Jesus."[95] I felt in my spirit that God was about to activate yet another of His promises. We met her at one of Dallas' most distinguished hotels. She escorted us to the top floor.

As we sat down, she smiled and said, "This is a blessed day for you. I know you must wonder why I asked you here for dinner—and especially since we've never met. My husband is a very wealthy man. He has presented me with millions of dollars that I have to give away. The Spirit of God told me to call some ministries and ask the head of each two questions: One, 'Will you pray with me?' and two, 'Will you share a meal with me?'

"So I picked up the phone and called a very large ministry, but I couldn't get through to the leader. But when I called your office, you prayed for me. When I called back later and asked, 'Will you have a meal with me?' you said you would. So I'm going to give you a million dollars."

I sat there in stunned silence. God whispered, *"It pays to listen to the voice of the Spirit. Now you have the funds for the overseas crusades."* God had called me to do what seemed impossible, just as He asked the same of Gideon, and Daniel, and the Three Hebrew Children.

After having been a recipient of a God-given land, the Israelites disobeyed Him time after time, resulting in one mess after another. Judges were appointed by God to deliver His people from the persecution they faced because of their bad choices. The first judge appointed was Othniel; the last was Samuel.

About one hundred years before Samuel, there was a judge named Gideon. When he was called, the Israelites were in subjugation to the Midianites, a warrior tribe descended from Abraham through one of his wives, Keturah. [96] Under the thumb of the Midianites, the Israelites lived not in houses in the Promised Land, but in caves and crevices in the rocks. Plenty had been replaced with paucity, with hunger and lack.

Each year during the harvest, the Midianites would descend like locusts upon the country and destroy the fields. After seven long years of being preyed upon, the Israelites began to pray for deliverance. One day, as Gideon was threshing wheat in a secluded spot, an angel of the Lord suddenly stood before him:

> And the Angel of the Lord. . .said to him, "The Lord is with you, you mighty man of valor!" Gideon said to Him, "O my lord, if the Lord is with us, why then

has all this happened to us? And where are all His miracles which our fathers told us about, saying, 'Did not the Lord bring us up from Egypt?' But now the Lord has forsaken us and delivered us into the hands of the Midianites." [97]

Gideon had yet to learn it is we who turn our backs on Him, the Giver of Life and Peace, Jehovah-Shalom. He was about to discover that God does not forsake His own, that Radical Obedience brings the Favor of God.

Gideon had been chosen by God to engage the entire Midianite army in battle. Gideon's first reaction to God's instructions was one of disbelief. He was no valiant warrior; he was in hiding from the enemy while threshing wheat. Not a very courageous beginning for a deliverer. Gideon was from the tribe of Manasseh, from its most inconsequential family. He was the youngest son, and in his own words, "the least in my father's house." [98] He could not comprehend that God wanted *him* for the task at hand. He was not some superhero—he was a simple man with little to commend him as a soldier. He had two things in his favor—willingness and obedience.

Hudson Taylor, the great pioneer missionary to China, might well have described Gideon's life when he said, "I have found that there are three stages in every great work of God: first, it is impossible, then it is difficult, then it is done." [99]

To confirm the call on his life, Gideon asked for a sign. God acquiesced to his request and gave him not one, but several signs:

> "Take the meat and the unleavened bread and lay
> them on this rock, and pour out the broth." And he

did so. Then the Angel of the Lord put out the end of the staff that was in His hand, and touched the meat and the unleavened bread; and fire rose out of the rock and consumed the meat and the unleavened bread. And the Angel of the Lord departed out of his sight. [100]

After the offering was instantaneously and miraculously consumed by fire, Gideon was given his first test of obedience. Would he pass or fail? Israel's deliverance depended on his decision, and it wasn't an easy one. It would pit Gideon against his father and friends:

> "Take the second bull from your father's herd, the one that is seven years old. Pull down your father's altar to Baal, and cut down the Asherah pole [used in the worship of the fertility goddess] standing beside it." [101]

So concerned was Gideon that he chose to obey God, but not during the daylight hours; it was in the middle of the night. He was astounded when he discovered that his father, Joash, stood with him when Gideon's actions were challenged by Baal worshippers. In essence, Joash said, "If Baal's upset, let Baal handle it." This was another assurance that Gideon's radical obedience had won him the Favor of God.

Gideon then issued the call for the people to gather. He was amazed when 32,000 assembled. He was overwhelmed at the response but still needed reassurance from God that he was doing the right thing. Gideon asked for another confirmation—not once, but twice:

"Look, I shall put a fleece of wool on the threshing floor; if there is dew on the fleece only, and it is dry on all the ground, then I shall know that You will save Israel by my hand, as You have said." (Judges 6:37 NKJV)

The following morning, Gideon took up the fleece and wrung water from it onto the dry ground that surrounded the fleece. Still not totally convinced, Gideon asked God to reverse the process, and God complied. The next morning, the ground was wet, and the fleece was dry. Finally Gideon got the message: This was his job to do.

He looked around at the number of people and must have been stunned by the size of the crowd. But God had other plans! He told Gideon that the group was too large and needed to be pared down. Why? God didn't want the people to think they had won the battle on their own merit; He wanted it known far and wide that the God of Abraham, Isaac, and Jacob fought for His people. Gideon was advised to send home all who were fearful. That cut the ranks by two-thirds—down to only 10,000 men. Still, God deemed there were too many. He devised one further test:

"Everyone who laps from the water with his tongue, as a dog laps, you shall set apart by himself; likewise everyone who gets down on his knees to drink." And the number of those who lapped, putting their hand to their mouth, was three hundred men; but all the rest of the people got down on their knees to drink water. Then the Lord said to Gideon, "By the three hundred men who lapped I will save you, and deliver the Midianites into your hand."[102]

Three hundred men! That was Gideon's army. The Midianite army was said to be "without number."[103] Yet Gideon obeyed God's specific instructions. Each man was to carry a trumpet and a pitcher with a torch inside. The men were divided into three companies of one hundred each and disbursed around the perimeter of the Midianite camp. At the appointed time, they were to blow the trumpets, smash the lamps and yell, "The sword of the Lord and of Gideon."[104]

Total pandemonium seized the enemy camp. The mighty Midianite army fled before the army of the Lord. Gideon pursued the enemy until it was vanquished:

> Thus Midian was subdued before the children of Israel, so that they lifted their heads no more. And the country was quiet for forty years in the days of Gideon.[105]

Gideon could have walked away from God's plan at any time. In the natural, it must have seemed totally impossible to win Israel's freedom from the marauding, murderous Midianites. However, Gideon chose Radical Obedience to the call of God.

When you, like Gideon, surrender your own preconceived ideas of how to win the battle, it will bring the Favor of God, victory, deliverance, and peace.

WHAT I LEARNED AS A MORON

THOUGHT TO CONSIDER: When God is on your side in battle, victory is guaranteed.

VERSE TO CONNECT: "And my God will meet all your needs according to the riches of his glory in Christ Jesus." Philippians 4:19, NIV

QUESTION TO CONTEMPLATE: What attitude would God have you change to better trust in Him to overcome the problems you face?

Mike Evans hosting the U.S. Embassy dedication gala in Jerusalem with senior advisors to the president Jared Kushner and Ivanka Trump, Secretary of State Steve Mnuchin, Senators Lindsey Graham and Ted Cruz, U.S. Ambassador to Israel David Friedman, and other VIPs.

Mike Evan's hosting Trump Evangelical Advisers in Israel.

Ambassador David Friedman, Tammy Friedman, Carolyn Evans,
Sara Netanyahu, Mike Evans, and Prime Minister Benjamin Netanyahu.

Mike Evans with Israeli Prime
Minister Naftali Bennett.

Mike Evans with Benny Hinn.

Carolyn Evans with Michelle, Shira, and Rachel.

CHAPTER

12

What you spend years creating,
others could destroy overnight.
Create anyway. [106]

The fiery dart that launched my own persecution and "lion's den" experience was flung by none other than Ruth Carter Stapleton, the sister of President Jimmy Carter. Ruth and I had both spoken at a rally in Giants Stadium in New Jersey. She was there to encourage people to join her on a tour to Israel. As a lead-in to that, Ruth said excitedly, "I am going to announce today that I am going to visit Mike Evans' headquarters at Stoneybrook on Long Island to tell Jews about Jesus."

Several Jewish organizations were upset about Ruth's announcement. They lobbied the president to stop her by asking Prime Minister Menachem Begin to call Mr. Carter and protest her participation in the Long Island event. It was truly like being in the midst of a den of hungry lions, and the night had not yet passed.

Before the trip to Long Island materialized, Ruth had flown to New York City and strongly denounced me as a cult leader akin to Reverend Moon, the leader of the Moonies. She said I had deceived her, and summarily cancelled her appearance with me. Her publicist, Mack, tried to bolster my shattered spirit. "It's politics, Mike! Don't take it personally." The next fourteen months were a living hell. I began to get death threats. The Long Island Council of Churches turned against me. My denomination turned against me.

The Enemy seemed determined to stop me in any way possible. Sometime later, I decided to purchase a pickup truck at an auction in Connecticut. As I headed home to Long Island on I-91 in a terrible rainstorm, a semi came speeding up behind me at what seemed to be eighty or ninety miles per hour. I had the cruise control on the truck set on 65. I realized if I didn't move over, the driver would run over me. I couldn't change lanes, however, because a car was too close for me to make the lane change safely, so I tapped my brakes. That move enraged the semi driver and he accelerated. I quickly jerked the wheel to move over a lane as the semi raced up behind me. My pickup did a 360-degree turn, barely missing the semi. I was able to regain control but suddenly realized the driver was still chasing me down the interstate. I believe he was attempting to kill me. The only thing that saved me was the tollbooth ahead. I aimed my truck for one lane but quickly changed at the last minute while the semi slid by in an adjacent lane.

As I praised God for deliverance, I realized it was just another of God's amazing providential actions in my life. Each time He delivers me, I am reminded through His Word of all the promises that are mine. By applying the four principles—Radical Obedience,

Generosity, Humility, and Forgiveness—and by magnifying the image of God, the Word of God is activated in me through the Divine assignments God sends my way.

In Scripture, the lives of Daniel, Shadrach, Meshach, and Abednego reflect Radical Obedience at every turn—from birth and captivity until death. Submission to Jehovah was far from easy, but it was preferable to giving obeisance to the gods of the Babylonians. When we study the book of Daniel we see it as a treatise on the End Times; however, it is also an in-depth study on obedience.

Daniel and his three companions were among the scores carried off to Babylon by Nebuchadnezzar's armies. They were snatched from their homes and families. We are not told if their relatives survived the battle and ransacking of Jerusalem. The young men were marched to a foreign land to endure whatever trials and degradation that faced them. Despite the circumstances surrounding these four young men, they did not relinquish their faith in Jehovah.

These Hebrew boys from noble, nurturing families had been accustomed to being in a warm and caring atmosphere. They were homesick and unsettled, and things would only get worse. Their familial protection had been stripped from them, and they were at the mercy of a pagan king and his minions. Yet God had not forsaken them; their training had not abandoned them; their faith in Jehovah was secure. They would be faced with trials and demands that would challenge their beliefs—would they remain faithful?

One of the first tests Daniel and his friends would be subjected to was over the food provided to them. The king had ordered that they be fed from his table:

Then the king ordered Ashpenaz, chief of his court officials, to bring into the king's service some of the Israelites from the royal family and the nobility—young men without any physical defect, handsome, showing aptitude for every kind of learning, well informed, quick to understand, and qualified to serve in the king's palace. He was to teach them the language and literature of the Babylonians. The king assigned them a daily amount of food and wine from the king's table. They were to be trained for three years, and after that they were to enter the king's service. Among those who were chosen were some from Judah: Daniel, Hananiah, Mishael and Azariah. The chief official gave them new names: to Daniel, the name Belteshazzar; to Hananiah, Shadrach; to Mishael, Meshach; and to Azariah, Abednego. [107]

Daniel, Shadrach, Meshach, and Abednego were determined not to eat the food offered to idols and petitioned the Babylonian official to allow them to eat only vegetables and water. With reluctance, the keeper agreed. The resolve of the young men and their obedience to God's law won them the respect of Nebuchadnezzar and the official, and the Favor of God. They had passed the first test with flying colors, but another, more difficult test lurked around the corner. How would they handle a life-threatening situation?

Nebuchadnezzar was not unlike many politicians today: He began to believe his own public relations stories. As his ego grew, so did his desire to erect a statue in accordance with his wealth and power. The artisans loosely based the design of the image on a dream that Nebuchadnezzar had experienced, the meaning of which Daniel had interpreted. The king opened the doors to his vast storehouses of golden treasure to provide the materials from which the idol was to be made. It is entirely possible that some of the golden vessels taken from the Temple in Jerusalem were included in those melted and used to fashion the graven image.

The Chaldeans worshipped a number of heathen deities, but nothing as brilliant and magnificent as the statue that rose up from the plain of Dura. It was ninety feet tall and nine feet wide—probably with an appearance much like an obelisk. Nebuchadnezzar was elated with the statue when it was completed and issued an edict to the people of Babylon. The image was to be dedicated as an object of worship, and all would display their consummate devotion by bowing down before the image:

> "As soon as you hear the sound of the horn, flute, zither, lyre, harp, pipe and all kinds of music, you must fall down and worship the image of gold that King Nebuchadnezzar has set up. Whoever does not fall down and worship will immediately be thrown into a blazing furnace." [108]

Now, Daniel and his friends had cut their teeth on the laws of God, specifically the Ten Commandments. Moses had instructed the children of Israel in Deuteronomy 11:19 that the Word of Jehovah was to be taught to the children "when you sit in your house, when you walk by the way, when you lie down, and when you rise up." The tenets and precepts of God's law were ingrained in the minds and spirit of those young men.

The first and second commandments are very specific:

> "You shall have no other gods before me. You shall not make for yourself an image in the form of anything in heaven above or on the earth beneath or in the waters below. You shall not bow down to them or worship them. . ."[109]

The day appointed by Nebuchadnezzar arrived accompanied by great pomp and ceremony. Off to one side of the dais from which the king held court was a reminder of the punishment for disobedience: the ovens into which those who refused to bow would be thrown. (In retrospect, perhaps Adolf Hitler took a page from Nebuchadnezzar's book in building the ovens used during the Holocaust.) On the plain surrounding the image, the people gathered awaiting the strains of the musical instruments that were to signal the moment to fall on their faces and worship the golden statue.

The powers of darkness danced in anticipation of the destruction of the trio of Hebrews in the king's court—who were likely to refuse the order to bow. Satan probably waited with sulfurous breath to see the defeat of God's chosen people. The king had decreed compliance with his edict; God declared a different scenario. When Nebuchadnezzar looked out over the prostrate participants, he saw three young men standing tall—Shadrach, Meshach, and Abednego. They had determined not to disgrace the God of heaven. Jehovah was their Lord and King—they would bow to no other.

Their detractors—those jealous of the honors that had been bestowed on Daniel and his companions—could not wait to advise the king that three of his subjects had dared to flagrantly defy his order:

> "But there are some Jews whom you have set over the affairs of the province of Babylon—Shadrach, Meshach and Abednego—who pay no attention to you, Your Majesty. They neither serve your gods nor worship the image of gold you have set up." [110]

Nebuchadnezzar's anger boiled. How dare they not obey his commandment! He ordered the men brought to stand in his presence. He demanded, "Is it true? Did you not bow down before the golden image as I ordered? Don't you know the punishment that awaits you if you refuse to bow?"

Shadrach, Meshach, and Abednego quietly explained to the king that they could not bow to any image because of their fidelity to Jehovah God. Nebuchadnezzar's visage grew darker as he pointed toward the ovens burning brightly in the distance. He ordered the instruments to play again in order to give these three young men a second chance to adhere to his instructions. Again they refused. As they stood before the king, the three Hebrew men replied:

> "King Nebuchadnezzar, we do not need to defend ourselves before you in this matter. If we are thrown into the blazing furnace, the God we serve is able to deliver us from it, and He will deliver us from Your Majesty's hand. But even if He does not, we want you

to know, Your Majesty, that we will not serve your gods or worship the image of gold you have set up." [111]

The king was infuriated by their answer. He ordered the ovens stoked seven times hotter. He then commanded the mightiest men in his army to bind the three men and toss them into the furnace. So hot was the fire that the men who marched Shadrach, Meshach, and Abednego to the furnace were killed. "But God"—(don't you love those two words)—But God had not overlooked the Radical Obedience of his children. As the men who stood strong in His Name landed in the midst of the fire, He poured out His favor upon them and joined them there. As the fire lapped up the bindings of His servants, Jehovah tamed the flames—they lost the ability to devour.

From his royal perch high above the furnace, the king watched in anticipation of seeing the three defiant Hebrews totally destroyed. Suddenly, his triumph turned to fear. He grew pale as he lurched from the throne and pointed toward the all-consuming flames. He stuttered, "Did we not cast three men bound into the midst of the fire? . . . Look!. . .I see four men loose, walking in the midst of the fire; and they are not hurt, and the form of the fourth is like the Son of God." [112]

Arthur Smith wrote a rousing spiritual about the experiences of the Three Hebrew Children titled "The Fourth Man." The chorus reads:

> They wouldn't bend. They held onto
>   the will of God so we are told.
> They wouldn't bow. They would not bow their

knees to the idol made of gold.
They wouldn't burn. They were protected by the
    fourth man in the fire.
They wouldn't bend, they wouldn't
    bow, they wouldn't burn. [113]

In amazement, the king abandoned his throne and strode across the plain. He crept as close to the fire as he safely could and cried:

> "Shadrach, Meshach and Abed-Nego, servants of the Most High God, come out, and come here." Then Shadrach, Meshach, and Abed-Nego came from the midst of the fire. And the satraps, administrators, governors, and the king's counselors gathered together, and they saw these men on whose bodies the fire had no power; the hair of their head was not singed nor were their garments affected, and the smell of fire was not on them. [114]

Nebuchadnezzar was overwhelmed by the miracle that accompanied their obedience to the Most High God. He decreed:

> "Blessed be the God of Shadrach, Meshach, and Abed-Nego, who sent His Angel and delivered His servants who trusted in Him, and they have frustrated the king's word, and yielded their bodies, that they should not serve nor worship any god except their own God! Therefore I make a decree that any people, nation, or language which speaks anything

amiss against the God of Shadrach, Meshach, and Abed-Nego shall be cut in pieces, and their houses shall be made an ash heap; because there is no other God who can deliver like this." Then the king promoted Shadrach, Meshach, and Abed-Nego in the province of Babylon. [115]

Radical Obedience won the favor of the king, but more importantly, it captured the Favor of God. He honored their faithfulness.

There would be another test of obedience for Daniel just as life-threatening as the one for his friends. In Chapter 5 of Daniel, Babylon fell to the Medes and Persians. They took the entire kingdom without having launched an arrow or raised a lance. The prophet Isaiah cried, "Babylon is fallen, is fallen! And all the carved images of her gods He has broken to the ground." [116] Nebuchadnezzar's golden idols had been crushed into dust.

The amazing thing about the bloodless coup was how little it affected Daniel in the king's court. He survived the upheaval, and at the beginning of the chapter Daniel was appointed as one of three governors over the kingdom. The new king was Darius, who ruled contemporaneously with Cyrus.

One thing is clear throughout Daniel chapter 6: God rules! Nations rise and nations fall, but God's plan will go forward according to His timetable. That should give us great hope as we see Daniel exactly where God has placed him. We will also see that God is unfettered by Man's pronouncements. Darius, the new leader, was a man of power and organization; he had great skill and intellect. He held no loyalty to the God of Israel, and yet as we read in the sixth chapter, we find that he has knowledge of Daniel's Jehovah.

Daniel was no longer a young man. It is likely that he was nearing ninety years of age. Through all the intervening years, he had remained faithful to God and was a committed witness. Far from being "on the shelf," his experience was utilized both by Darius and by God. We can see from his longevity in the Babylonian and then the Medo-Persian Empire that Daniel was a man of wisdom, a dynamic leader, and a capable administrator. Added to those traits was a close relationship to Jehovah, which afforded him the ability to interpret dreams and visions. He was God's man for that time and in that place. The "king's heart is in the hand of the Lord. . .He turns it wherever He wishes." [117] God turned the heart of Darius toward a Hebrew man and placed him in a strategic place of authority.

Often when Believers are set in a place of authority, it is not long before the Enemy raises his ugly head, determined to target the faithful—and Daniel was no exception. Soon others in the court were plotting:

> So the governors and satraps sought to find some charge against Daniel concerning the kingdom; but they could find no charge or fault, because he was faithful; nor was there any error or fault found in him. Then these men said, "We shall not find any charge against this Daniel unless we find it against him concerning the law of his God." [118]

There were no charges of adultery; no Watergate break-ins, no Iran-Contra Affairs, no hidden bodies in the attic. The accusers could find no fault in Daniel; his life was exemplary. He was a target in good standing of the Fellowship of the Offended. They had to resort to subterfuge in order to trap their rival. Daniel was known abroad for his custom of praying with his face toward Jerusalem three times each day. The pattern had been established. So his adversaries took advantage of Daniel's routine and approached the king:

> "King Darius, live forever! All the governors of the kingdom, the administrators and satraps, the counselors and advisors, have consulted together to establish a royal statute and to make a firm decree, that whoever petitions any god or man for thirty days, except you, O king, shall be cast into the den of lions. Now, O king, establish the decree and sign the writing, so that it cannot be changed, according to the law of the Medes and Persians, which does not alter." [119]

Sneaky, weren't they? And, of course, the king was flattered by all this attention. Who wouldn't want to be God for a month! Obviously, Darius wanted all the accolades and adoration, so he succumbed to the temptation and signed the decree. He was swept away on a tide of ego and pressed his signet ring into the wax on a document that would become a law, which could not be changed. The thing was done—bow to any God except Darius and become lion fodder.

When Daniel heard of the new law that had been imposed, what do you suppose he did—wring his hands and cry, "Why me, God?" Did he begin to look for a secret place to pray? No! Verse 10 says:

Now when Daniel knew that the writing was signed, he went home. And in his upper room, with his windows open toward Jerusalem, he knelt down on his knees three times that day, and prayed and gave thanks before his God, as was his custom since early days.[120]

Fear did not reign in Daniel's life. God had been faithful to him and to his friends. He had no reason to doubt. Either he would be preserved in the lion's den, or he would not, but he was committed to doing the will of God. He failed to compromise his beliefs to gain the favor of the king.

The obvious happened: The men who had lain in wait for Daniel to make a misstep were overjoyed. When they saw Daniel kneeling in his window with his face toward the Holy City, they gleefully ran to the king:

"Have you not signed a decree that every man who petitions any god or man within thirty days, except you, O king, shall be cast into the den of lions? . . . That Daniel, who is one of the captives from Judah, does not show due regard for you, O king, or for the decree that you have signed, but makes his petition three times a day."[121]

Darius likely felt like he had been hit right in the solar plexus! He was stunned by this turn of events: A man he greatly admired was now in dire straits because of Darius' egotism.

Daniel's detractors were shouting, "That Hebrew, that foreigner, refused to obey the king! Now you must obey the decree you have signed and toss him to the lions." Let me assure you that these were not lion cubs, nor were there only one or two in the den, as we often see in illustrations. There were a sufficient number of lions to rip Daniel to shreds and devour him in a matter of minutes.

Daniel was summarily arrested and led to the lair where the lions were penned. He was cast inside and a stone was brought to seal the mouth of the den. King Darius then sealed it with his signet ring and returned to the palace. So distressed was the king that he spent the night silently fasting. In other words, in his sleepless-ness he didn't call for the musicians, or the dancing girls, or other diversions. The Bible says, "And he could not sleep." I can believe he spent the night pacing in his bedchamber. At the earliest opportu-nity, he burst forth from his room and went in search of an answer:

> At the first light of dawn, the king got up and hur-ried to the lions' den. When he came near the den, he called to Daniel in an anguished voice, "Daniel, servant of the living God, has your God, whom you serve continually, been able to rescue you from the lions?" Daniel answered, "May the king live forever! My God sent his angel and he shut the mouths of the lions. They have not hurt me, because I was found innocent in his sight. Nor have I ever done any wrong before you, Your Majesty." [122]

Doesn't it seem a bit late for Darius to question whether or not Daniel was safe? It seems that every seed Daniel had sown into the king's life erupted at the mouth of the lion's den in the words, "Daniel, servant of the living God, has your God, whom you serve. . ." He wanted to know if everything Daniel had said to him was true. Could the living God deliver, do the miraculous, save the endangered? Darius had his answer as soon as he heard the words, "My God sent His angel, and he shut the mouths of the lions."

There is no record that Daniel offered any argument to the king before he was led away to the lion's den; only after God had vindicated him and saved him from the jaws of the ferocious beasts did he offer any defense. He knew he had been innocent of anything other than obedience to Jehovah-Shammah, the Lord who was present in the lion's den. Daniel had sought the kingdom of God and had been rewarded. Daniel's Radical Obedience won him the favor of the king, but more importantly, it won him the continued Favor of God.

WHAT I LEARNED AS A MORON

THOUGHT TO CONSIDER: Your obedience during impossible situations can lead to God working in miraculous ways.

VERSE TO CONNECT: "If we are thrown into the blazing furnace, the God we serve is able to deliver us from it, and he will deliver us from Your Majesty's hand. But even if he does not, we want you to know, Your Majesty, that we will not serve your gods or worship the image of gold you have set up." Daniel 3:17-18, NIV

QUESTION TO CONTEMPLATE: What impossible situation do you face that requires God's power to succeed?

Mike Evans with Ivanka Trump, Jared Kushner, and the Chief Rabbi of Israel.

Mike Evans presents the Friends of Zion award to Ambassador
David Friedman, senior adviser to President Trump Jared Kushner,
and Middle East Envoy Jason Greenblatt.

Mike Evans preaching in Manilla, Philippines.

Mike Evans speaking to more than two million people in Sao Paulo, Brazil.

Mike Evans speaks to tens of thousands during an outdoor evangelistic event.

Mike Evans chairing "A Night to Honor Israel" at the Alabama Governor's Mansion in 1980.

Mike Evans speaking to over one million people in Madras, India.

PART TWO:
WHAT I LEARNED
AS A MORON

**COMMIT YOUR
LIFE TO A CAUSE
GREATER THAN
YOURSELF**

Mike Evans, Benzion Netanyahu, Benjamin Netanyahu, and Carolyn Evans.

Prime Minister Benjamin Netanyahu and
Prime Minister Yitzhak Shamir at the
Madrid Peace Conference.

Mike Evans, Prime Minister Benjamin Netanyahu,
and Minister of Jerusalem Affairs Ze'ev Elkin.

CHAPTER

13

*To be a Christian means to forgive the inexcusable,
because God has forgiven the inexcusable in you.*[123]

Healing in my own life has been an ongoing work, and
with God's help I have learned not to listen to the lies of
the Enemy. I have replaced negative talk with what God's word says
about *me* as His child. I have learned at His feet that God values *me*.

After my father's estate was settled and I was named sole
heir to his earthly possessions, I wrote a letter to my siblings. It
simply said:

> To my beloved brothers and sisters:
>
> The probate hearing is over and the judge has ruled.
> This is to inform you I have instructed the attorney
> that I will not accept the will and have withdrawn my
> name from it. Therefore, Dad's estate in its entirety
> will be divided between the six of you.

I will absorb personal expenses incurred while assisting Dad the last few months of his life and for the funeral service. You will not be billed for anything. For years, Dad attempted to give me the estate and I refused. I wish you God's richest blessings.

Your loving brother,
Michael

Over the years, I've learned that Radical Forgiveness can give us the spiritual, physical, emotional, and financial prosperity we seek. How? These four things magnify the image of God, activate the Word of God, and bring the Favor of God.

Forgiveness is a gift. When we choose to forgive, we are giving an unearned and undeserved reward. It is the legacy given to us by Jesus at Calvary! An old song says, "He paid a debt He did not owe; I owed a debt I could not pay."[124] Jesus did not owe salvation; He gave His life freely for all. We only have to accept His gift.

Affirmation is another factor at work in seeking the Favor of God. We cannot activate the Word of God while living in discouragement and defeat. The problem is that without the revelation of God, we will waste time seeking approval from other sources. Men often depend on their jobs, their wives, their toys—boats, cars, electronic gadgets—or on their friends for affirmation. The truth is: There is a God-sized vacuum in the spirit of Man and nothing can fill it except the Creator.

When we seek to grow in the image and Favor of God, we do not require Man's affirmation. We have the Word, and through it God speaks to us again and again. We are not limited to one singular encounter when we are in the depths of despair; the Word gives light and life day by day, moment by moment. It gives direction, empowerment, affirmation, mercy, and grace.

We must first activate His voice through His Word. Daniel wrote: "Yet I heard the [voice] of his words; and while I heard the sound of his words I was in a deep sleep on my face, with my face to the ground." [125] Some have never heard the "voice" of the Word through which we can have Radical Obedience, Radical Generosity, Radical Humility, and Radical Forgiveness.

Before my father died, I was able to give him the gift of Radical Forgiveness. None of my siblings were able to do that. They were united by a single thread—hatred for our father. It has all but destroyed them. They have been cruel to others, violent, drug users, and more. All was blamed on their abusive childhood. Hearts and lives have been made bitter and become broken because of a refusal to seek the image and Favor of God—because of the lack of desire to forgive.

My friend, God is crazy about you! He can give you all the affirmation you will ever need. Without affirmation from the Father, we may compromise our integrity, lie, cheat, steal, or lower our standards; but His affirmation is all we need.

You and I live in a less than perfect world, and because of that Jesus said:

> "Woe to the world because of offenses! For offenses must come, but woe to that man by whom the offense comes!" [126]

Rest assured, dear friend, that you will be offended—it *will* come. The ideal response is to greet the offense with love and forgiveness. Radical Forgiveness begins with God. His is the supreme pardon. It is impossible to forgive radically without God, but the Bible tells us that with God, "all things are possible." [127]

"One of the secret causes of stress plaguing millions of people is unforgiveness," says Dr. Don Colbert, MD. [128] You and I must determine to avoid unforgiveness at any cost. Just as a virus strikes a computer and destroys it from within, so unforgiveness can attack the body and cause a multitude of health problems. It is believed that stress levels rise when unforgiveness is harbored in one's soul. A person who embraces unforgiveness is the one partaking of a deadly poison, all the while wishing ill-will toward the offender. Refuse to lift and sip from the glass of poison. Choose instead to offer Radical Forgiveness. It will result in total healing of body, soul, and spirit.

Radical Forgiveness pardons and moves on—it doesn't constantly rehearse the wrong done. Radical Forgiveness doesn't hold on to past hurts and offenses. It doesn't hold pity parties or "poor little me" memorials. That only gives more life to the past. I love what the apostle Paul said:

> "No, dear brothers and sisters, I have not achieved it,
> but I focus on this one thing: Forgetting the past and
> looking forward to what lies ahead. . ." [129]

Unforgiveness is like walking the path with a one-hundred-pound weight on your back. We should "lay aside every weight," and that includes unforgiveness, in order to experience the Favor of God in our lives daily.

The subject of Radical Forgiveness cannot be complete without talking about forgiving yourself. You will never be able to move forward to a life of love and grace until you are able to forgive past mistakes. When allowed to fester, infection sets in and can eventually destroy you. The Enemy uses unforgiveness as a stepping-stone to eat away at our faith in God's mercy and forgiveness. It is essential that you learn to forgive yourself for the sake of your spiritual health. Forgiving oneself is perhaps the hardest kind of Radical Forgiveness, but we must remember that Nehemiah wrote, "You are a God ready to forgive, gracious and merciful." [130]

God has bestowed Radical Forgiveness upon His children. He forgives totally, and with no hesitation. Today, make the decision to give the gift of Radical Forgiveness—not only to those who have wronged you, but also to yourself. Let go of your past mistakes and failures; lay them at the feet of Jesus, the Author and Finisher of your faith.

In the next few chapters we are going to look at some biblical examples of men who chose Radical Forgiveness and thereby won the Favor of God.

WHAT I LEARNED AS A MORON

THOUGHT TO CONSIDER: Radical forgiveness will magnify the image of God, activate the Word of God, and bring the blessing of God in your life.

VERSE TO CONNECT: "No, dear brothers and sisters, I have not achieved it, but I focus on this one thing: Forgetting the past and looking forward to what lies ahead." Philippians 3:13, NLT

QUESTION TO CONTEMPLATE: Who or what do you need to forgive in your life today?

Mike Evans speaking at a White House dinner with President Donald Trump, Franklin Graham, and evangelical leaders.

Mike Evans with NFL players at Friends of Zion Museum in Jerusalem.

Israeli Defense Force officers
visiting Friends of Zion.

Brazil President Jair Bolsonaro
receives the Friends of Zion award.

Mike Evans with MLB baseball star
Darryl Strawberry and his wife Tracy.

Fellowship Church pastor
Ed Young, Jr. and his wife
Lisa at Friends of Zion.

CHAPTER

14

"If you want God to bless you and use you greatly, you must be willing to walk with a limp [as did Jacob] the rest of your life, because God uses weak people."[131]

The story of jacob and esau is one of family forgiveness; however, there are times when that forgiveness must be offered to our extended church family. One Sunday morning at church, a man approached me and introduced himself. His name was Ray. After we had chatted for a few minutes Ray, who seemed like a very godly man, said the Lord had impressed him to ask me for help. He needed to borrow $32,500 for one week. He offered to give me a post-dated check, which I was to deposit at the specified time. Wanting to help a brother in need and not taking time to pray about it, I agreed to help him. The next day Ray accompanied me to the bank, where I secured a cashier's check in the amount he needed. In turn, he handed me the post-dated check. Ray skipped town with our money and left me holding a worthless piece of paper.

I was devastated! Jesus kept admonishing me to "forgive . . . forgive." After several weeks of hearing the same message from above, I snapped, "Easy for You to say 'forgive'! He didn't rip off Your $32,500! It was mine!" The moment I said this, I realized my ignorance. God had given His Son for me—and for that man. Everything I had was His. I fell on my knees in the bedroom and prayed, "I forgive Ray, Lord. Help him to make things right with You."

I felt strongly that because I had forgiven Ray, our nest egg would be returned. A scripture in Proverbs flooded my spirit: "Yet when he [the thief] is found, he must restore sevenfold." That night I wrote the word *Return* on a piece of paper. As I held it up before God, I felt impressed to write a book and call it *The Return*. Within ninety days the book was a reality and in the next twelve months became a bestseller. The royalty from sales was exactly seven times what had been stolen from us! Radical Forgiveness opened the door for the Favor of God.

One of the accounts the Old Testament has to offer on Radical Forgiveness is the one of Jacob and Esau, the twin sons of Isaac and Rebecca. It could be said that those two boys were born fighting. They struggled in their mother's womb, and when born, Jacob's tiny hand grasped Esau's heel. So the boys were named—Esau, meaning "hairy" because he was born covered with red hair; and Jacob, meaning "he who supplants" or usurps another's place.

The Bible tells us little of their childhood other than that Esau grew to be a hunter and Jacob a dweller in tents. There is one other important detail about their lives that plays an important role in the story of the two brothers:

> Isaac loved Esau because he enjoyed eating the
> wild game Esau brought home, but Rebekah loved
> Jacob. [132]

Perhaps it was Isaac and Rebecca's very acts of partiality—favoring one son over the other—that fostered the spirit of rivalry, contention, and bitterness between the twins. Like the discord between Isaac and Ishmael, it created a feud that has lasted nearly four thousand years.

Esau was the eldest (by minutes, probably), the child charged with carrying on the family business. Instead he was *ish-sadeh*, which is translated "a man of the open fields." He was a man who shirked his responsibilities for the joy and thrill of hunting. Esau was impulsive, headstrong, disobedient, and hedonistic—he thought first of his own desires and their fulfillment instead of home and hearth. Jacob, though often thought of as wily and deceptive, was *ish-tam*, which translates to "a man who ultimately went whole-heartedly after God."

After a long day of hunting, Esau arrived home to the smell of a pot of lentil stew hanging over Jacob's fire. Esau's first thought was of his own belly. "I'm starving to death," he cried. "Jacob, give me some of your stew."

Jacob offered to exchange a bowl of soup for his brother's birthright—the exclusive right of the oldest son to a double portion of his father's wealth. Esau apparently had no qualms about trading his inheritance for a bowl of beans and quickly devoured the meal. Just as swiftly as his hunger was satiated, he apparently forgot about the deal with his brother.

Sometime later Rebecca overheard Isaac's plan to bless Esau as his firstborn and began to plot how she could advance God's promised plan:

> "Two nations are in your womb, and two peoples from within you will be separated; one people will be stronger than the other, and the older [Esau] will serve the younger [Jacob]."[133]

Isaac was aware that he was near death and knew it was time to impart blessings upon his sons. He called Esau to his tent and asked him to kill a dear and make the savory stew that he loved. Isaac promised that after he had eaten, he would bestow a blessing upon Esau. Rebecca, who had overheard Isaac's request of Esau, hatched a scheme to deceive Isaac. She explained the ruse to Jacob, and he eagerly jumped onboard. Rebecca dressed Jacob in his brother's smelly clothing in order to fool his nearly-blind father into believing he was Esau. Was Isaac actually fooled by the trickery? Perhaps—perhaps not. He did, however, bestow the double portion belonging to the eldest son upon Jacob:

> "May many nations become your servants, and may they bow down to you. May you be the master over your brothers, and may your mother's sons bow down to you. All who curse you will be cursed, and all who bless you will be blessed."[134]

When Esau found out what had happened, he was livid:

Esau hated Jacob because their father had given Jacob the blessing. And Esau began to scheme: "I will soon be mourning my father's death. Then I will kill my brother, Jacob." [135]

Esau went to his father, bowed before him, and pleaded for a blessing. With a heavy heart, Isaac responded:

> "Your dwelling will be away from the earth's richness, away from the dew of heaven above. You will live by the sword and you will serve your brother. But when you grow restless, you will throw his yoke from off your neck."

Simply stated, the words were less a blessing, more like a curse. While Jacob would enjoy God's covenant blessings, Esau and his descendants would make their home in a dry, arid land, live under the threat of constant battles, and would be servants to Jacob except for rare periods of rebellion. His spirit was crushed and his anger overwhelming.

Knowing that Esau was exceedingly angry with Jacob, Isaac again called for his youngest son and gave yet another blessing—the covenant inheritance of Abraham:

> "May God Almighty bless you, and make you fruitful and multiply you, that you may be an assembly of peoples; and give you the blessing of Abraham, to you and your descendants with you, that you may inherit the land in which you are a stranger, which God gave to Abraham." [136]

Jacob fled Canaan to the land of his mother's brother, Laban. It would be years before he returned home. While working for Laban, Jacob married two wives, Leah and Rachel, sired twelve sons and one daughter, and became a very wealthy man. The day finally came when Jacob was so homesick he gathered his family and flocks, folded his tents, and set out for Canaan. As they neared the land, Jacob sent word to his brother, Esau, that he was coming home. When the messengers returned, their news was disturbing:

> "We came to your brother Esau, and he also is coming to meet you, and four hundred men are with him." So Jacob was greatly afraid and distressed. [137]

As you might imagine, Jacob's knees must have knocked together in fear. It didn't look good for the brother who had deceived his twin out of a blessing. Four hundred men—were they coming to greet him, or to destroy him and his family? He divided the large entourage into two camps, and then did the only thing left to do—he fell on his face before Jehovah God in prayer and supplication:

> "O God of my father Abraham, God of my father Isaac, O Lord, who said to me, 'Go back to your country and your relatives, and I will make you prosper,' I am unworthy of all the kindness and faithfulness you have shown your servant. I had only my staff when I crossed this Jordan, but now I have become two groups. Save me, I pray, from the hand of my brother Esau, for I am afraid he will come and attack me, and

also the mothers with their children. But you have said, 'I will surely make you prosper and will make your descendants like the sand of the sea, which cannot be counted.'" [138]

Alone in the camp, on his face before God, Jacob was attacked. He must have been terrified thinking that it was one of Esau's men come to kill him. All night, Jacob wrestled for his very life. As the light of dawn peeked over the horizon, Jacob realized that this was no ordinary foe; he was wrestling with the angel of God. In order to end the combat, his opponent touched Jacob's hip socket and dislocated it. The Divine wrestler shouted, "Let go of me!" Jacob refused:

> "I will not let you go unless you bless me." The man asked him, "What is your name?" "Jacob," he answered. Then the man said, "Your name will no longer be Jacob, but Israel, because you have struggled with God and with men and have overcome." Jacob said, "Please tell me your name." But [his foe] replied, "Why do you ask my name?" Then he blessed him there. So Jacob called the place Peniel, saying, "It is because I saw God face to face, and yet my life was spared." The sun rose above him as he passed Peniel, and he was limping because of his hip. [139]

God had been convinced that Jacob, now Israel, was single-minded in his resolve to hold on to Jehovah even though he had been injured. Jacob could no longer fight Esau in hand-to-hand combat. He was now the prey, totally dependent on God's mercy and Esau's grace. Jacob had been promised the Favor of God; would he also be shown favor by his brother?

Over the horizon, Jacob could see the men who accompanied his brother. He watched as a man separated himself from the rest of the company and began to walk toward him. Suddenly, the man broke into a run. It was Esau:

> But Esau ran to meet Jacob and embraced him; he threw his arms around his neck and kissed him. And they wept. [140]

Esau, who could have harbored hatred and resentment toward his brother, showed Jacob Radical Forgiveness. God's favor is poured out when Radical Forgiveness is exercised.

Forgiving someone who has wronged you is one of the great challenges of life. Those who harbor unforgiveness are burdened with misery and guilt. Those who refuse to forgive overflow with rage and resentment. Their hostility is a wall that encloses them; no one can scale that wall. Unforgiveness may go unnoticed by the individual to whom it is directed, but it defiles the one who bears it. It can, and sometimes does, literally destroy the body and the soul of the one bearing the ill will.

Releasing unforgiveness is radical. It is not something one does easily. The normal reaction is to retaliate or hold on to resentment. Forgiveness flies in the face of every natural instinct. The sad truth is that when you harbor unforgiveness—against a spouse, parent, co-worker, or anyone who wronged you—that person controls your life and it separates you from God.

God has called you to Radical Forgiveness, which sets you free from sin and death, from the past, and from separation from God. It secures the Favor of God upon your life and allows you to enjoy exceedingly abundant blessings.

WHAT I LEARNED AS A MORON

THOUGHT TO CONSIDER: When you harbor unforgiveness against someone, that person controls your life and it separates you from God.

VERSE TO CONNECT: "Bear with each other and forgive one another if any of you has a grievance against someone. Forgive as the Lord forgave you. And over all these virtues put on love, which binds them all together in perfect unity." Colossians 3:13-14, NIV

QUESTION TO CONTEMPLATE: What forgiveness can you offer than will impact the lives of others and draw you closer to God?

Mike Evans at Madrid Peace Conference.

CHAPTER

15

If you are honest and sincere, people may deceive you.
Be honest and sincere anyway. [141]

I t was october 1991, at the conclusion of Operation Desert Storm, the First Gulf War, and Israel was again being forced to the bargaining table. I sensed the Holy Spirit directing me to fly to Madrid to attend the Madrid Peace Conference. The site for the various meetings in the days to come was the richly appointed royal palace. The beautiful interior was a little like an ornately decorated Styrofoam cake—all glitter and no substance—to disguise its actual purpose; in this case, it was the place where even more land-for-peace would be demanded of the Jews.

During one of the meetings, I prayed silently as I gazed at the ceiling in the grand Hall of Columns. The magnificent hall was ornamented with the images of false gods: Apollo, Aurora, Zephyrus, Ceres, Bacchus, Diana, Pan, and Galatea. From their lofty perch, these bogus gods looked down on the official proceedings for a counterfeit peace. Like the apostle Paul at Mars Hill, I found myself praying to the one true God while under this canopy of idolatry. How ironic that Israel had been forced here, of all places, for an international peace conference—to Spain, where one-third of the Jewish population of its day had been massacred during the Inquisition. I watched sadly as representatives of nation after nation mounted the podium to insult and accuse Israel, and to demand that her leaders give up the majority of her land.

I can still hear their voices reverberating through the marble halls: *"We will accept your land in exchange for peace."* What they were really saying was: "This is a stick-up. Give me all your land and you won't get hurt—much." I tend to think of muggings happening on the streets of major cities, yet the Madrid Peace Conference, by any measure, was an international mugging. And the world was the silent witness too intimidated to report it to the police. Most of the nations represented pretended not to see the "gun" pointed at Israel's head.

As I left one of the meetings, the Syrian foreign minister stopped me. He pulled a picture of Yitzhak Shamir from his pocket and told me he intended to accuse the prime minister of being a terrorist while he was a member of the *Irgun* (an early Israeli paramilitary organization). I borrowed a cell phone and called Benjamin Netanyahu to relate to him what I had been told. The next morning before the beginning of Shabbat and in the presence of President George H.W. Bush, President Gorbachev, and other world leaders, Mr. Shamir stood and said, "I have to leave now. I am an Orthodox Jew, and I leave these proceedings to my able delegation." Thirty minutes after he departed, the Syrian foreign minister stood to speak but faced only an empty chair where Shamir had sat.

The Favor of God rested on me as I found myself virtually in every session in the royal palace, and to my knowledge I was the only minister of the Gospel present for the majority of the Middle East Peace Conference.

At the conclusion of one session, the Egyptian foreign minister and the Syrian secretary of state came up to me and asked if I was a minister. I replied, "Yes, I am."

The Egyptian asked, "What country?"

"Kingdom," I responded. "The Kingdom of God."

The Syrian minister said, "It must be a very small country."

"It is much larger than yours. It would swallow up both of your countries!"

They laughed. I looked the Egyptian foreign minister in the eye and said, "Will you obey the words of your most distinguished prime minister and secretary of state?"

He was puzzled. "We have never had a person who was both prime minister and secretary of state. If we had such a man, I would certainly obey his words."

I related the story of Joseph in the Old Testament where he had forgiven his brothers for having him imprisoned. "Joseph was prime minister and secretary of state of Egypt and embraced his brothers. Will you do the same?"

Much like the meetings in Madrid, the saga of Joseph and his half brothers opened with jealousy, hatred, callousness, and misery. The plot was filled with anxiety, fear, and confusion.

As the account begins, Joseph, Jacob's son by his beloved Rachel, had grown into a young man of seventeen. To his discredit, he flaunted his father's partiality in the faces of his older siblings.

To add fuel to the fire of discontent, Jacob had presented Joseph with a beautiful coat woven with cloth of many colors. Each of his sons had a knee-length, sleeveless tunic—plain and functional—but Joseph's coat was something special. It was not merely utilitarian; it was colorful, ankle length, and bore long sleeves. It was a symbol of a father's love for a special son, and the brothers despised both father and son because of the favoritism.

At this juncture, Joseph was not the wise elder statesman that he later became. He had dreams from God, and rather than ponder them in his heart, he shamelessly shared their contents with his disgruntled brothers. Two of Joseph's dreams depicted him as a ruler to whom his brothers must bow down. Really, now! The others were outraged with Joseph's impudence, and even his father scolded him:

> "What is this dream you had? Will your mother and
> I and your brothers actually come and bow down to
> the ground before you?" [142]

Even his father's rebuke failed to stop Joseph from being insolent. Finally the brothers had had enough of his cheekiness. The ten men—Asher, Dan, Gad, Issachar, Judah, Levi, Naphtali, Reuben, Simeon, and Zebulon—connived to rid themselves of Joseph. They saw their chance when Jacob dispatched Joseph to Shechem to inquire about the well-being of his sons who were tending the flocks. As they saw him in the distance, the first plan was to simply kill him. When Joseph arrived at the camp, the brothers grabbed him, tore his coat from him, and tossed him into a pit. Reuben, not wanting to murder his own brother, pleaded with the others to spare Joseph's life. Spotting a caravan of Ishmaelite traders on its way to Egypt, Judah suggested that they sell him as a slave. They then pulled Joseph from the hole in the ground and sold their brother. They may have thought that he would perish en route or be worked to death after he arrived—but God had other plans for that brash young man.

As the procession continued on its way across the desert, the brothers plotted to explain his son's absence to Jacob. They killed a young goat and sprinkled its blood on Joseph's colorful coat. Jacob's partiality had so hardened their hearts that they apparently had no difficulty in presenting the offending garment to their father and insinuating that Joseph had been killed. Jacob was inconsolable—he who had once deceived his own brother was now deceived by his sons. What irony!

The Bible doesn't say explicitly, but somewhere between Shechem and Egypt, Joseph must have gained some spiritual maturity. Once in the land of Pharaoh, he was sold to one of the king's military leaders, Potiphar. When the general's wife tried to seduce Joseph, he fled her presence. It is said that hell has no fury like a woman scorned, and Potiphar's wife was no exception. She contrived to have Joseph put in prison. Perhaps he wondered how his dream of being a ruler would ever come to pass in his trek from pit to prison. He may have thought he had reached his final destination and would perish in chains, but:

> The Lord was with [Joseph]; he showed him kind-
> ness and granted him favor in the eyes of the prison
> warden. So the warden put Joseph in charge of all

those held in the prison, and he was made responsible for all that was done there. The warden paid no attention to anything under Joseph's care, because the Lord was with Joseph and gave him success in whatever he did. [143]

When two of his prison mates—the king's baker and butler—had dreams, Joseph was able, with God's help, to interpret them. After three days, the butler was restored to his position of trust, but the baker was beheaded for his perceived crime. One night Pharaoh had a very disturbing dream. The butler remembered Joseph's gift for interpretation and told the king about the young man he had met in prison. Joseph was summoned from his cell to the palace. His journey from pit, to prison, to palace had been long and arduous, but Joseph was about to reap the benefits of having lived a life of integrity in Egypt.

As Joseph stood before the king, God gave him the interpretation of the dream: seven years of miraculous abundance followed by seven years of harsh austerity. So impressed was Pharaoh with Joseph that he immediately appointed him prime minister and placed him in charge of the country's agricultural program over the following fourteen years. During the feast years, Joseph preserved much of the grain in vast storehouses across the land. When famine hit the land, Joseph set regulations to disburse the grain in a manner that would safeguard the lives of the Egyptians and their surrounding neighbors.

As scarcity gripped the land of Canaan, Jacob was told that there was plenty of grain in Egypt. God was setting the stage for one of the most poignant examples of Radical Forgiveness in the Old Testament. Jacob sent his ten eldest sons to the land of Pharaoh to purchase grain:

> Now Joseph was governor over the land; and it was he who sold to all the people of the land. And Joseph's brothers came and *bowed down before him with their faces to the earth.*[144] (Emphasis mine.)

Joseph's dream was realized—and his brothers did not even recognize him. He began a prolonged game of cat and mouse. Joseph presented test after test that lasted over a period of months, and possibly years, in order to determine if his brothers were still the hateful, scheming siblings that had sold him into slavery. He was not being vindictive, as we will see, but rather viewed what his brothers meant for evil as part of God's plan to save his family. In the final challenge, Joseph demanded that the youngest brother, Benjamin, be brought to Egypt the next time the clan returned for grain. Jacob refused to allow him to go until the time came that they must buy grain or perish, but relented after his son Judah assured Benjamin's safety.

In this final test, Joseph tried to ascertain if the brothers would abandon Benjamin as they had abandoned him. Was he being unforgiving? No, he was simply trying to determine if his brothers had become more caring individuals. When the time came for the men to return to Canaan, Joseph had his steward divide the funds used to buy the grain and place a portion in each man's sack. In Benjamin's sack, Joseph instructed that the steward was to also place a silver chalice. The men had not gone far from the city when the steward with a contingent of soldiers apprehended them and accused them of stealing from the prime minister's house. Feeling they were being unjustly blamed, the brothers vowed that anyone caught in possession of stolen property would become the prime minister's (Joseph) slave.

The grain sacks were opened and Joseph's cup was discovered in Benjamin's possession. The brothers were stunned. Judah approached Joseph and said:

> "Your servant my father said to us, 'You know that my wife bore me two sons. One of them went away from me, and I said, "He has surely been torn to pieces." And I have not seen him since. If you take this one from me too and harm comes to him, you will bring my gray head down to the grave in misery.' So now, if the boy is not with us when I go back to your servant my father, and if my father, whose life is closely bound up with the boy's life, sees that the boy isn't there, he will die. Your servants will bring the gray head of our father down to the grave in sorrow. Your servant guaranteed the boy's safety to my father. I said, 'If I do not bring him back to you, I will bear the blame before you, my father, all my life!' Now then, please let your servant remain here as my lord's slave in place of the boy, and let the boy return with his brothers. How can I go back to my father if the boy is not with me? No! Do not let me see the misery that would come on my father." [145]

Joseph could no longer control his emotions. He cried to his steward to have the room cleared. His Radical Forgiveness would be offered in private, not before the Egyptian servants. As soon as the last Egyptian left the hall, Joseph revealed his identity to his brothers. They were even more terrified to discover that the brother they had threatened to kill and then sold into slavery stood before them. Not only was this their sibling, he now possessed the power to retaliate a hundredfold, but instead of chastising them, he cried:

> "I am Joseph! Is my father still living?" But his brothers were not able to answer him, because they were terrified at his presence. Then Joseph said to his brothers, "Come close to me." When they had done so, he said, "I am your brother Joseph, the one you sold into Egypt! And now, do not be distressed and do not be angry with yourselves for selling me here, because it was to save lives that God sent me ahead of you. For two years now there has been famine in the land, and for the next five years there will be no plowing and reaping. But God sent me ahead of you to preserve for you a remnant on earth and to save your lives by a great deliverance. So then, it was not you who sent me here, but God. He made me father to Pharaoh, lord of his entire household and ruler of all Egypt."[146]

Can you imagine the fear that must have gripped his brothers? They had been wary enough of the powerful Egyptian official standing before them; now they discovered it was Joseph, their own brother whom they had betrayed. The brothers must have felt their likelihood of any leniency had evaporated. Their only prayer was for mercy. As the blood drained from their faces in fear, guilt stripped them of all hope and left them standing in abject silence before Joseph. In the first fifteen verses of Genesis chapter 45, the brothers speak not one word. They stood, I imagine with heads bowed, until they were certain of Joseph's Radical Forgiveness.

Joseph did not minimize what had been done to him or the consequences, but he assured his siblings that he recognized there had been a purpose for the path his life had taken. God had been in control of his darkest nights and his brightest days. The capacity to offer Radical Forgiveness to those who had wronged him was because he could see the Favor of God upon his life. He found God in the pit, and in the prison, and God had not forsaken Him in the palace.

Forgiveness for Joseph was not without cost. He had paid the price for his brothers' jealousy; he had spent years in exile from his father; he had suffered at the hands of others. However, he chose to forgive. True forgiveness is a decision of the heart, and Joseph willingly made that choice. Joseph was able to love those who had spitefully used him because of Jehovah's grace and mercy displayed toward him. As a result of Radical Forgiveness, Joseph lived in the Favor of God.

As you read the story of Joseph, you realize that Joseph forgave his brothers proactively; they were forgiven before they ever set foot inside the palace. He took the initiative because Joseph understood that God had elevated him in order to save his family. You may see that as a real challenge—proactive forgiveness. Perhaps you think that forgiveness should only be extended when the one who has wronged you grovels for pardon. No, the answer is in preemptive forgiveness—Radical Forgiveness even if it is never sought. By canceling the debt and extending grace you are giving yourself a gift that money cannot buy. And it frees God to work in the life of the person who has harmed you. You are also moving closer to becoming the person God wants you to be. He wants to free you from anger and release your emotional ties to a hurtful past.

WHAT I LEARNED AS A MORON

THOUGHT TO CONSIDER: Preemptive forgiveness cancels the debt and extends grace, giving yourself a gift that money cannot buy.

VERSE TO CONNECT: "You intended to harm me, but God intended it for good to accomplish what is now being done, the saving of many lives." Genesis 50:20, NIV

QUESTION TO CONTEMPLATE: How would forgiving someone who has hurt you become a gift to you as well as to the one you forgive?

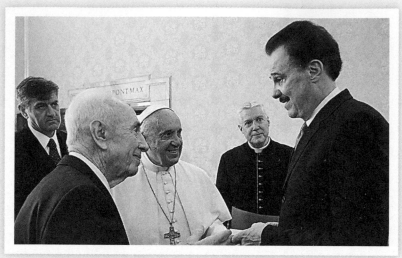

Mike Evans sharing his personal testimony with Pope Francis
and President Shimon Peres.

Mike Evans with Israeli
President Isaac Herzog.

Mike Evans with former Israeli
Prime Minister Ehud Olmert.

CHAPTER

16

To love means loving the unlovable.
To forgive means pardoning the unpardonable.
Faith means believing the unbelievable.
Hope means hoping when everything seems hopeless. [147]

Many people today are spiritual prisoners, and are hurting. My mother was like that. When she died, I joined my family for her funeral. I got to the old home place only to find that one of my siblings had tried to have her buried before my arrival. They didn't stop there; they took what money they could find and spent it on booze and drugs. One had even purchased a car. As I walked into my mother's house, I encountered a group of drugged people, having a beer party.

My mother's body was at the funeral home awaiting burial. Rather than having a quick funeral, the decision had been made to delay her burial indefinitely; no one wanted to spend the money. I was furious.

Leaving my siblings in the living room, I walked upstairs to the room where, at the age of eleven, I had seen Jesus. I knelt down and prayed, "Jesus, in this room You appeared to me. You told me You loved me. God, my mother is dead, now what are You going to do?"

Instantly He brought two scriptures to mind. The first was Timothy 1:7:

"I have not given you a spirit of fear, but of power, love and a sound mind."

Then He reminded me of the verse that says:

The Lord directs the steps of the godly. He delights in every detail of their lives. [148]

The Spirit of God whispered, "Who really killed your mother? Who is causing all the problems?"

Instantly, everything came into focus. I knew who the Enemy was, and I knew what had to be done. When I walked into the room downstairs, I could have fought with my brothers; I could have cursed them for their selfishness and insensitivity. I could have taken the opposite path and joined them in their revelry. I could have turned my back on God—but I didn't.

Now, kneeling in prayer, I chose to believe that I did not have to operate in the spirit of fear, but could wholly rely on God's power, and love, and His provision for a sound mind.

As I arose and descended the stairs to stand in the midst of my family, I said "You will be saved! I am coming for you."

I love my siblings, and it grieved my spirit that they refused to commit their lives to the living God. As I watched them stagger around the room, I felt in a sense what the father must have felt when the prodigal son asked for his inheritance—a feeling of frustration and loss. The parable told by Jesus is a perfect picture of a father's love and Radical Forgiveness for a thankless and lost child.

We are told little about the prodigal son, but much can be surmised from the experiences of those who have walked away from God and chosen a life of debauchery. In Luke chapter 15, Jesus first told the story of the lost sheep, then the lost coin. He ended the chapter with the parable of the prodigal, or lost, son. We read of a father who had two sons. The eldest was the practical plodder. He lived at home, labored in his father's business, and was sensible and levelheaded.

The younger son was the playboy. He sought pleasure, wanted to party, and catered to his friends. He shirked his responsibilities for a life of self-indulgence. He longed to answer to no one—especially his straightlaced father and dull older brother. Seeing nothing before him but a slow, tedious life, the profligate approached his father. He saw gaining his inheritance as the answer to all his problems in life. The love of money was a seed that had taken deep root in his soul and had grown into a tree overshadowing all he did.

Heartlessly, the younger son went to his father and said, (paraphrased), "Old man, it's taking you way too long to die. I don't want to wait until you're in the ground to get my inheritance. I want it now."

With great sorrow the father agreed to the request of his beloved son. He gathered sums equal to one-third of his estate—the share of the younger son. The older son would have two-thirds as his birthright. The grieving parent presented the inheritance to his demanding child, and not long after that, the younger son got together all he had, set off for a distant country and there squandered his wealth in wild living. [149]

I believe that the son had heard of a country where everything he could imagine would be available, where every wish was granted, every restriction imposed by his conservative parent would be laid aside. He would be free to do as he wished—with no restraints. Having undertaken the journey in his mind, he then set out to fulfill that dream.

All went well initially. He was replete with treasure. He may have wined and dined his friends, indulged in drunken revelry and any other activity after which he lusted. Aristotle described a prodigal thus: "A prodigal means a man who has a single evil quality, that of wasting his substance." [150] When he had spent his last farthing, hocked his last plush garment, he found himself without a friend in the world. He had eaten his fill; he had drunk with abandon. There was nothing left for him to do but clothe himself in sackcloth and find a way to survive.

Bowed and broken, he made his way to the local pig merchant and pled for any menial task available. He was soon put to work doing the most demeaning task any Jew could have been given—working in a pigsty among the unclean animals. How the playboy had fallen! He was so hungry that even the husks he fed the swine looked like a feast, but no one offered him a bite.

Meanwhile, the desolate father was watching for and praying for his wayward son. The faithful elder son was taking care of the family business. As the father paced the rooftop each evening, he longingly looked down the road hoping to catch a glimpse of his beloved younger son. The father had long ago extended Radical

Forgiveness to his child; he yearned to see the face of his son, to have him home, safe and sound.

One day, the father's prayers were answered. The prodigal realized how foolish he had been:

> When he came to his senses, he said, "How many of my father's hired men have food to spare, and here I am starving to death! I will set out and go back to my father and say to him: Father, I have sinned against heaven and against you." [151]

The light of love finally penetrated his profligate mind and the prodigal finally realized that what he had done was unforgivable. He could no longer consider himself a son, but perhaps his father would allow him to work as a laborer in the family business. Crawling home wouldn't be an easy task, but it would, if his father acquiesced, save his life. I can almost see him as he stopped by the watering trough and tried to wash some of the mud and pig stench out of his ragged clothes before he turned his face toward home.

The vigilant father, always watching for his prodigal son, spotted someone in the distance. Did he recognize his son's gait? Could he see the way his shoulders drooped? Whatever sparked the knowledge that the figure was likely his son, the father dropped everything. Tucking up his robe to make running easier, he sped down the road toward the lonely traveler.

In that day it was unheard of for a man to bare his legs. So why did the father humiliate himself? It was Jewish custom that if a son wasted his birthright among the Gentiles and then made his way home, he would undergo *kezazah*—a cutting-off ceremony. A large pot would be smashed before the prodigal while those gathered would shout, "You are now cut off from your people!" It was a sign of total rejection. To spare his son the shame, his long-suffering father wanted to reach him before the prodigal entered the village. As he ran down the street, he would have amassed a throng of curious followers that would have observed the father's actions. He fell upon his son, and despite the absence, the father would have expressed his joy and thanksgiving before the entire town.

The son had his speech ready:

> "Father, I have sinned against heaven and against you. I am no longer worthy to be called your son."[152]

The returning son barely stammered out the words, when the overjoyed father grabbed his son and embraced him tightly. He yelled for the servants to bring the best robe—likely one of the father's own. It was a sign of worth and of devotion. The son was loved and had been accepted by his father. The servants were told to bring a ring for the long-lost child's hand—a sign of influence and relationship. Sandals were placed on his feet—an indication that he was not to be a servant but a son!

The father goes even further:

> "Bring the fattened calf and kill it. Let's have a feast and celebrate. For this son of mine was dead and is alive again; he was lost and is found."

In biblical times, the fatted calf was kept back for special occasions—like the Day of Atonement. It was not designated for an everyday occasion or party. In the father's eyes, this was no ordinary celebration. The son he thought lost to him had returned. It was a time for commemoration of Jehovah's goodness. The father's Radical Forgiveness paved the way, not for what should have been a funeral under the law, but a celebration. He may well have been reminded of one of the psalms of David as the preparations were made:

> [The Lord] does not treat us as our sins deserve or repay us according to our iniquities. For as high as the heavens are above the earth, so great is his love for those who fear him; as far as the east is from the west, so far has he removed our transgressions from us. As a father has compassion on his children, so the Lord has compassion on those who fear him. [153]

The father's Radical Forgiveness activated the Favor of God. His son who he thought lost to him had been found. The lessons he had learned in the far country would color his future. He would long remember the grace—the unmerited favor and mercy—the unparalleled generosity—shown to him by his loving father. The prodigal returned with nothing—no money, ragged and tattered clothes, and no hope. But by his father's grace, he was restored to his place as a son.

Jesus used the parable of the prodigal son to impress on His followers the depth of His heavenly Father's love and the all-encompassing power of Radical Forgiveness. If you have, as an act of the will, separated from your heavenly Father, turn and run toward home. Avail yourself of the salvation and Radical Forgiveness that is so freely offered, and activate the Favor of God in your life.

WHAT I LEARNED AS A MORON

THOUGHT TO CONSIDER: Experiencing God's forgiveness activates His power in our lives to forgive others and experience supernatural joy.

VERSE TO CONNECT: "For God has not given us a spirit of fear, but of power and of love and of a sound mind." 2 Timothy 1:7, NKJV

QUESTION TO CONTEMPLATE: What confessions may you need to make to more fully experience His power of forgiveness within you?

Mike Evans with President Donald Trump in the White House.

Mike Evans with Franklin Graham, CEO of
Samaritan's Purse and son of evangelist Billy Graham.

Mike Evans having dinner with NBA legend
Michael Jordan and his daughter Rachel.

Mike Evans with dear friends Pastor
Jack Graham and Pastor Robert
Jeffress at the White House.

President Donald Trump in the Oval Office congratulating Mike Evans.

CHAPTER

17

The measure of a life, after all,
is not its duration, but its donation. [154]

M y dear friend Prime Minister Yitzhak Rabin was the target of a man filled with hate and seeking revenge. On November 4, 1995, Yigal Amir, an Orthodox Jew and right-wing radical—angry that Rabin had signed the Oslo Accords—shot the prime minister in the arm and back. He suffered a punctured lung and died forty minutes after reaching the hospital. I had been out on an errand, and Carolyn met me with the news as I walked in the house.

My heart was broken. I had prayed with him in Jerusalem and knew him to be a great man. Funerals in Israel take place very quickly. His was to be a state funeral, and I didn't have an invitation. I walked into my study and began to pray about what to do. *"Go,"* the Lord instructed.

So I went. As the plane was landing, I couldn't believe my eyes. Representatives of most of the nations of the world were there.

Their planes were parked everywhere, and there were more than 18,000 people in security details.

Queen Beatrice of the Netherlands, Prince Charles of England, Chancellor Helmut Kohl of Germany, British Prime Minister John Majors, presidents Jimmy Carter, Bill Clinton, and George H. W. Bush were there. . .eighty-six world leaders.

When I flagged down a cab, I was told we would not be able to get anywhere near the funeral.

I smiled at the driver, "You just drive, and I'll pray."

He was right. Miles from the funeral, the streets were blocked. The military was everywhere. I didn't have clearance for my cab, and neither did the driver. Normally, security forces would have turned us around very quickly.

Suddenly from outside the window I heard a loud voice. "Get this cab out of here, now!"

I rolled down my window. The Israeli colonel whom I knew looked at me and smiled. "Mike Evans, it's you. Oh well, you don't believe in 'No,' do you?"

"Not when God sent me, I don't."

"Okay, go, but you'll never get through the security checkpoints."

We drove several miles through empty streets. I got out and went past two different checkpoints. No one said a word. As I was walking up the hill to the funeral, security guards were eyeing me, but no one spoke. I had no credentials except a pass from heaven. As I stood a short distance from a world leader, an official from the prime minister's office rushed up to me. I heard him say, "Mike, did you not go to the Hyatt Regency Hotel? Your state invitation and pass are there." Through prayer, God miraculously opened every door to get me where He wanted me to be.

In news stories today we can find numerous instances of people responding out of hatred, just as the assassin did who killed Mr. Rabin. We hear fewer stories of those who make the decision to choose to forgive.

Kinneret was 23 years old, a ballerina, a student of alternative medicine, and exceptionally beautiful. She earned extra money for school tuition as a photographic model, and worked as a waitress in a small coffee shop in Tel Aviv. One evening, a young man walked into the shop, and Kinneret walked toward him to take his order. As she neared him, he exploded a bomb wrapped around his body, killing himself, and creating havoc and gore around him. The coffee shop was a terrible mess, but few people were injured since it was nearly empty. When the ambulances arrived, paramedic Itsik Kohav saw a leg sticking out from underneath the overturned bar. Flames engulfed the area fueled by the alcohol ignited when the bomb exploded.

Kohav lifted the bar and found a girl underneath. She seemed unaware of her injuries, but Itsik knew she had little chance of survival. Kinneret never uttered a word of complaint. . .not once on the ride to Ichilov Hospital emergency room. In the ER, she was given a two percent chance of living through the night.

It was eighty-eight days before Kinneret breathed on her own, longer till she ate, bathed, stood, walked, or dressed alone, but Kinneret is an incredible miracle. When she awoke from her ordeal, Kinneret changed her name to Kinneret Chaya—Kinneret lives. Even today, she has the use of only one lung, sees through only one eye, and hears in only one ear, but she is an articulate and wonderful young woman. To see her is to understand that even a terrorist's hatred could not dim the beauty of her smile.

When Kinneret first came home from the recuperation unit, I went to visit her. She was encased in a body cast, yet I could see the joy in her eyes. Being sensitive to the fact that Kinneret Chaya and her family are Jewish, I asked her parents for permission to pray for her. As I knelt before this wonderful girl, the only place I could touch her was on her feet. I told her two things: 1) She could take her experience and learn from it; that in life, such tragedies teach us to be either bitter or better, and always to choose the better; and 2) that she had an angel on her shoulder. Someone was watching over her that terrifying night, and had big plans for her future.

Kinneret Chaya married the dedicated young man who stood by her through her struggles and recuperation. She never gave up on life; never gave up on her recovery, never stopped fighting the pronouncements of those who said she would be crippled. . .physically and emotionally. Kinneret's belief in God strengthened as her body recovered from the near-catastrophic terrorist attack. Today, she celebrates the miraculous—Kinneret Chaya is the mother of a beautiful little girl. She chose to forgive and move forward, not to allow her shattered body to define her life. In her own words, "Kinneret died that night in the flames, but Kinneret Chaya was born."

Another of those stories was played out in the public eye in 2006. An Amish community in Nickel Mines, Pennsylvania, was invaded by Charles Roberts IV, a mentally ill pedophile. He cold-bloodedly shot five young female students in the head before turning the gun on himself. The reaction of the Amish community was astounding; a total departure from what many would have done. First, they refused to be described as victims. Then, staggering under their own grief, Amish men and women reached out in love to the gunman's survivors—his dazed and confused wife and children. On the day Roberts took the lives of the five innocents, the grieving grandfather of one of the girls visited the home of the murderer's father to comfort him. The Amish delivered no tirades, no reproach, no signs of hatred toward the innocent family. They offered only compassion and forgiveness, the same comfort they delivered to the bereaved within their own group. At Roberts' funeral, more than half the mourners were Amish.

The community understood that the killer was sick, tormented, and crazed. It was understood that there could never be an excuse for the terror and heartache Robert's actions had caused. Despite that, he and his family were offered the Radical Forgiveness that comes only as a result of grace and mercy, and yields the Favor of God.

The testimony I shared at the beginning of this book is a picture of how such forgiveness can work in your life. What is Radical Forgiveness? It is a gift. When we choose to forgive, we are giving an unearned and undeserved gift. It is the gift given to us by Jesus at Calvary. Earlier I wrote of the old song that says, "He paid a debt He did not owe; I owed a debt I could not pay." [155] Jesus did not owe Mankind salvation; He gave His life freely for all. We only have to accept His gift!

The Bible gives us many examples of Radical Forgiveness, and we have just explored three instances. It can be a difficult thing to do—a personal challenge akin to Jacob wrestling with the angel of the Lord. Long nights are spent, sometimes in prayer and supplication, sometimes in worry, oft times in imagining scenarios where we confront the one who harmed, insulted, embarrassed, or betrayed us. It's not an easy process; in fact, it's hard!

Radical Forgiveness can give us the spiritual, physical, emotional, and financial prosperity we seek. It magnifies the image of God, activates the Word of God, and brings the Favor of God.

In Matthew, Peter approached Jesus with what he thought was a difficult question:

> "Lord, how many times shall I forgive my brother when he sins against me? Up to seven times?" Jesus answered, "I tell you, not seven times, but seventy-seven times." [156]

Such Radical Forgiveness will heal broken hearts, mend lives, and unlock the doors of blame. It will set the captive free to a life of light and the unmerited Favor of God—a life filled with love and peace.

In 2012, a Texas newspaper published the story of a young Christian woman in Pakistan who was horribly disfigured because of religious persecution. As 16-year-old Julie sat in her small office in Pakistan, a man entered. He saw a tiny silver cross on a chain around her neck and asked three times if she was a Christian. She answered that she was. The man turned and stalked out of the office. He returned about a half hour later with a turquoise bottle in his hand.

Realizing what he was about to do, Julie tried to block the flow of battery acid as it arced toward her face. The right side of her face melted under the impact of the burning chemical. The liquid etched its way into her chest and arms bone-deep. She tried to run from the building when a second man grabbed her by the hair and held her as the first man poured acid down her throat. Finally freeing herself from the two assailants, she ran screaming down the street. As she did, her teeth fell from her mouth. A woman took pity on her, covered Julie with a scarf, and took her home. She poured water on the burns and eventually got the young victim to a hospital.

The two men were detained but accused Julie of insulting Islam. The hospital where she was taken was threatened with arson and she was turned out into the street. A second medical facility refused to treat her, and only with much pleading by her family did a third doctor finally agree to see her. According to the newspaper report:

> [Julie] could not speak or move her arms. Doctors said 67 percent of Julie's esophagus was burned. She was missing an eye and eyelids. Her remaining teeth could be seen through her missing cheek. The doctors predicted she would die any day. [157]

After a year in the hospital, Julie's family pleaded with a bishop in Pakistan for help. He contacted a hospital in Houston, Texas, and arranged for her to be treated. There he gave her some valuable advice before she departed for the United States:

> "If you forgive them, your wound will heal without medication. You can heal from the inside out." [158]

A family in the Houston suburbs gave Julie a loving home, a

caring church congregation, and taught her so speak English. They sat by her side as she underwent and recovered from one surgery after another. She credits the doctors with giving her back her life. And she credits God with teaching her to forgive. She said:

"Those people [her attackers] they think they did a bad thing to me, but they brought me closer to God. They helped me fulfill my dreams. I never imagined I could be the person I am today." [159]

Julie learned Radical Forgiveness after a vicious attack, and God has poured His favor out on her life. She completed high school and is now enrolled in college. Her dream is to someday be a pastor. Julie lives with the precious Christian couple who welcomed her into their home and made her part of their family. In July 2012, she celebrated becoming a naturalized US citizen. Today Julie lives and thrives in the Favor of God because of Radical Forgiveness.

These precious people have learned the miracle of forgiveness. It is not in forgetting what has been done to you. No, it is remembering the hurt and the pain and making a conscious choice to forgive. Those memories become a tribute to the grace of God, which frees you to be the person God has ordained you to be.

If you have been wounded, seek the Lord. Ask Him to heal your heart and help you to forgive. Then reach out in love to the one who offended you! Allow God to restore you both and establish peace once again.

Are you holding a grudge against someone? Why not stop right now and ask God to give you a heart of forgiveness and restoration. Ask Him to give you an attitude of gratitude.

WHAT I LEARNED AS A MORON

THOUGHT TO CONSIDER: Forgiving someone who has offended you replaces a grudge with gratitude and offers restoration to show God's love to others.

VERSE TO CONNECT: "He heals the brokenhearted And binds up their wounds." Psalm 147:3, NKJV

QUESTION TO CONTEMPLATE: Is there a grudge you need to release to the Lord to more fully experience restoration in your life?

Mike Evans with Guatemalan security team.

Mike Evans, hosting Trump Evangelical Advisers
with the Mayor of Jerusalem Nir Barkat.

Glenn Beck and David Barton listening to Mike Evans in Israel.

Mike Evans with Former Secretary of Housing and Urban
Development Dr. Ben Carson at the White House.

Mike Evans with Vice President Mike Pence.

PART THREE:
WHAT I LEARNED
AS A MORON

PUT ALL
YOUR FAITH
IN GOD

Mike Evans with his dear friend Tom Winters at the White House.

Mike Evans with the former ambassador
from Iran to the U.S.

Mike Evans with Pastor Jack Graham
and Donald Trump attorney Jay Sekulow
in Washington, D.C.

CHAPTER

18

People are often unreasonable, irrational,
and self-centered. Forgive them anyway.[160]

My 1978 trip to the Sinai with Jamie Buckingham that I wrote about earlier was to be, ultimately, a turning point in my life. As we followed in Moses' footsteps, the day came when it was my turn to do the dishes. In the desert there are no dishwashers, no farmhouse sinks, no dish soap, none of the modern conveniences to which we are accustomed. There I was, squatting down under the night sky, tired, hot, and sweaty, all the while dodging scorpions and scrubbing the pots with sand. Yes, sand! The universal Brillo Pad. Water in the desert is too precious to waste on dirty pots.

Earlier in the day we had made plans to climb Mount Sinai to visit the spot where Aaron and Hur had held Moses' hands up for victory in the battle against the Amalekites (Exodus 17:12).

I decided there was no way I was going to spend hours trudging up the side of that mountain. I was a jogger; I could make it in much less time. Leaving my extra gear behind (including my water bottle) and taking off my shirt, I ran straight up the mountain. When I reached the summit, instead of celebrating my feat, I collapsed in a heap. By the time the team arrived, I was in the full throes of heat exhaustion. My pulse was racing; my head was pounding; I was weak as a kitten, white as a sheet, and dizzy as a kid on a merry-go-round.

As soon as the team gathered at the top, Bill Nelson, an astronaut[161], delivered a devotional on being one with Christ. Finally humbling myself, I gained enough strength to croak, "Bill, I'm sick. I think I'm dehydrated and may have heatstroke." He kindly gave me his extra shirt and hat, and controlled sips of water until he was able to help me down off the mountain. Unfortunately, I had overstepped the bounds of God's law that says if I overextend myself in the middle of the desert without proper preparation, I will suffer the consequences—and with heatstroke, they can be fatal.

As we continued to cross the desert sands, we stumbled upon a Bedouin tent and stopped to visit with its inhabitants. An Arab woman came out to offer food and drink. When one of our guides told her there was a doctor in our midst, Dr. Angus Sargeant, she ran into her tent and returned carrying her little six-year-old daughter. We were appalled at the appearance of the child. Flies covered her head, obscuring a vile infection. The youngster's hair was matted with a green substance, and pus was oozing from the wound.

One of the family members had tried to cauterize the wound by taking a hot knife to the little one's head, consequently scarring her scalp. I couldn't conceive of the horror and pain the child must have endured. Angus was stunned but finally stuttered, "I can't help. She needs surgery. We have no way to do that here. I'm sorry."

Suddenly my heart filled to overflowing with compassion for this child and her mother. The Lord gave me a scripture from Isaiah, "But He was wounded for our transgressions, He was bruised for our iniquities; the chastisement for our peace was upon Him, and by His stripes we are healed." [162] When I looked at her, I thought of my three girls, and without thinking, I reached out and laid my big hand over the little girl's head, and I prayed! I implored God to heal the child as tears rained down my face. Since Hebrew and Arabic are similar, I hoped the mom would understand at least some of my prayer. In that moment I realized God had done it again—I had been supernaturally affirmed by God's Word just as I was at the age of eleven.

When we arose the next morning, Angus said, "I've got to try to set up a makeshift operating room and operate on that little girl. Otherwise she may not survive the infection." He got up and strode across the common area to the Arab mother's tent. He went inside while we waited for him. After about three or four minutes, we heard him crying. I was certain he was mourning a dead baby. I eased the flap open and stepped inside the tent to console him. Angus held a rusty cup filled with tea. The mother had given it to him in gratitude, offering the best she had.

As he lifted it to drink, he said, "Lord, this is the greatest physical miracle I've ever seen."

I stepped around Angus and looked at the little girl lying on a pile of rugs. She was totally healed! Praise began to flow from the doctor as he placed the cup to his lips.

What a time of rejoicing we had! God's wonderful plan for

my life included being in the middle of Moses' desert in a time of trouble and being used as an instrument for healing. I stepped back outside the tent and in Radical Humility raised my hands and eyes heavenward to "Praise God from whom all blessings flow." [163]

Moses, in whose footsteps we followed crossing the desert, personified the utter standard for a life of humility. We need only look in the Old Testament to read a parenthetical statement about him:

> Now Moses was a very humble man, more humble
> than anyone else on the face of the earth. [164]

God would have of necessity selected the most meek and humble man to lead His people through the wilderness. God wanted someone who was teachable; someone who would follow His directives without question; someone with no ego to hinder His plan. Moses was a commanding and authoritative leader but one with self-discipline and an utterly unselfish desire to please Jehovah.

There are numerous scriptures in the Bible to strengthen God's desire for men of humility who would serve Him with a whole heart. God directed Isaiah the prophet to write:

> I live in a high and holy place, but also with him who
> is contrite and lowly in spirit, to revive the spirit of
> the lowly and to revive the heart of the contrite. [165]

Isaiah later wrote:

> This is the one I esteem: he who is humble and con-
> trite in spirit, and trembles at my word. [166]

What is the opposite of "humility"? It is arrogance, conceit, self-importance, pride. In the book of I Peter chapter 5, verse 5, God shows us how He deals with pride:

> Be clothed with humility, for God resists the proud,
> but gives grace to the humble.

God resists—fights, confronts, and disregards—those who are proud, who have an exaggerated view of their own importance. He opposes those who attribute their successes to their own labors and fail to admit that everything they possess comes directly from the benevolent hand of a loving heavenly Father. We can summarize God's message on humility in five little words: "I'm God and you're not!"

Author Phillip Keller wrote of the fruits of humility in his book *A Gardener Looks at the Fruit of the Spirit*:

1. "Humility is the only seedbed from which faith can spring. . .In brokenness and contrition the humble person cries out to God for help. He reaches out to Christ for restoration and healing. He exercises faith in another because he knows he must touch someone greater than himself.

2. It is to such souls that God gives Himself gladly, freely. He draws near to those that draw near to Him. He delights to dwell with those of a broken and contrite spirit. 'The Lord is nigh unto them that are of a broken and contrite heart; and saves such as be of a contrite (meek) spirit' (Ps. 34:18). . .In vivid and shattering

contrast we are warned explicitly that God actually RESISTS the PROUD. He does not just tolerate or indulge arrogant souls. He actually opposes them actively. This is a terrifying truth that should make any self-centered, individual tremble (James 4:4-10).

3. In contrast to this, the third amazing reality about humility is the impact it makes on our fellowman. It is the genuinely humble, gentle soul who wins friends and draws around him a circle of loving associates. This quality of life draws others as surely as nectar in a blossom draws bees. The gentle genial person is the recipient of affection. People bestow on him their blessings. He is lavished with love and surrounded with compassion. The proud, arrogant, person has few friends, if any. He stands upon his little pedestal of pride in grim and gaunt loneliness. Others leave him alone. They ignore him deliberately. If he is so independent, let him live his own Life; let him go his own way; let him suffer the agony of his own selfishness." [167]

The Apostle Peter wrote: Humble yourselves, therefore, under God's mighty hand, that he may lift you up in due time. [168]

Moses' power stemmed from the fact that he trusted God. He recognized how small he was and how big his God was. He acknowledged that his reputation and integrity were based not on his own efforts, but on God's love and mercy. Moses exhibited three of the most important characteristics of humility: 1) he accepted wise counsel; 2) he placed himself under God's authority, and 3) he was teachable.

Solomon wrote in Proverbs:

> Plans fail for lack of counsel, but with many advisers they succeed. [169]

Humble people do not think it beneath them to seek wise counsel. We do not enter this world with the Wisdom of Solomon. Often we don't know how to handle those trying circumstances in life. God made provision for us by placing wise counselors, pastors, teachers, and friends in our lives. However, as one writer penned:

> God's wisdom can't bring hope to those who don't think they need it, or those who know they need it but won't seek it, or those who know they need it and seek it, but then ignore it. Unfortunately a lot of people look for their counsel in the current sages of today like Oprah Winfrey, or Dr. Phil, or Judge Judy, or Warren Buffett. These are influential people, but if we want true counsel we need to look to God for it. [170]

When Moses became overburdened with the task of advising and judging the Children of Israel in the desert, his father-in-law, Jethro, realized how desperate Moses was for assistance, and asked:

> "What is this you are doing for the people? Why do you alone sit as judge, while all these people stand

around you from morning till evening?. . .What you are doing is not good. . . . Listen now to me and I will give you some advice, and may God be with you. You must be the people's representative before God and bring their disputes to him. Teach them his decrees and instructions, and show them the way they are to live and how they are to behave. But select capable men from all the people—men who fear God, trustworthy men who hate dishonest gain—and appoint them as officials over thousands, hundreds, fifties and tens. Have them serve as judges for the people at all times, but have them bring every difficult case to you; the simple cases they can decide themselves. That will make your load lighter, because they will share it with you. If you do this and God so commands, you will be able to stand the strain, and all these people will go home satisfied." [171]

Moses could very well have been angered by Jethro's seeming interference. He could have ranted and raved to his wife, Zipporah, that her father didn't think he had enough sense to lead the people. He could have stomped off angrily, tearing through the camp and glaring at anyone who got in his way. Instead, this radically humble man did just the opposite:

Moses listened to his father-in-law and did everything he said. He chose capable men from all Israel and made them leaders of the people, officials over thousands, hundreds, fifties and tens. They served as judges for the people at all times. The difficult cases they brought to Moses, but the simple ones they decided themselves.[172]

The advice of his father-in-law lessened the burden for Moses. He realized that he had a desperate need for help, and that God revealed the answer through wise counsel.

Secondly, Moses was willing to place himself under God's authority. He had lived in a palace where everyone was at his beck and call, subject to his whims and desires. Yet Moses had chosen the road that led him from Pharaoh's palace to God's throne room. He turned his back on wealth and power; he followed God's leading. Moses recognized that he served only at God's pleasure. He had seen firsthand what happened to Korah, Dathan, and Abiram, the rebels who defied heavenly directives. The three men, great leaders among their own tribes, rebelled against God's authority and Moses, His representative. They conspired to challenge the law that had been given to Moses based simply on the premise that because of their tribal leadership, they should be making the laws. Their kinsmen supported the three rebellious leaders during the confrontation.

Moses could have summoned men from the camp to execute judgment on the three men and their followers, but he chose not to do so. Why? He was well aware that it was not he who had freed the Children of Israel from bondage. Moses knew that God would fight his battles, and he need do nothing but hold his peace.[173] The rebels in the camp, and those who may have been tempted to follow after them, needed to know that the gods left behind in Egypt were powerless gods. The God who led them out was a living God clearly able to administer His own laws and effect judgment when required.

Moses called the entire congregation together and admonished them:

> "Move back from the tents of these wicked men! Do not touch anything belonging to them, or you will be swept away because of all their sins." [174]

As the congregation murmured and stumbled back from the tents of Korah, Dathan, and Abiram, Moses said:

> "But if the Lord brings about something totally new, and the earth opens its mouth and swallows them, with everything that belongs to them, and they go down alive into the grave, then you will know that these men have treated the Lord with contempt." [175]

Moses' Radical Humility sprang from the Divine assurance that Yahweh was in control. It assured him protection from his enemies, and the Favor of God. Obedience to God's will and calling is not an easy choice, but Moses chose that pathway. Like Moses, you can choose to obey, or choose to walk away from God's plan and purpose for your life.

Thirdly, Moses was eminently teachable. He realized that as a servant of Jehovah, it was his role to listen and learn, to open his heart to God's instruction, and benefit from His counsel. So profound was Moses' humility that God invited him to the mountaintop to personally receive the law. Later, God met him in the

Tabernacle "as a man speaks with his friend." [176]

The day finally came when Moses was instructed to choose his replacement:

> So the Lord said to Moses, "Take Joshua son of Nun, a man in whom is the spirit of leadership, and lay your hand on him. Have him stand before Eleazar the priest and the entire assembly and commission him in their presence. Give him some of your authority so the whole Israelite community will obey him. He is to stand before Eleazar the priest, who will obtain decisions for him by inquiring of the Urim [177] before the Lord. At his command he and the entire community of the Israelites will go out, and at his command they will come in." Moses did as the Lord commanded him. He took Joshua and had him stand before Eleazar the priest and the whole assembly. Then he laid his hands on him and commissioned him, as the Lord instructed through Moses. [178]

A less humble man might have argued with God that Joshua, at the age of 80, was too young to take on the task of shepherding the Children of Israel into the Promised Land. After all, Moses was now 120 years old. He had more experience; he was a friend of God. He might have rehearsed all God had done through him. He might have supposed he knew it all. He might have—but he didn't. He accepted God's choice of the man who was to follow in his footsteps and humbly anointed Joshua for the task ahead. Moses' Radical Humility had produced a teachable spirit in a man who recognized

God's sovereignty and valued the Favor of God above all else.

Moses was applauded by God for his Radical Humility. He could have wallowed in pride, in his accomplishments as the leader of a willful and rebellious tribe of people. He could have tooted his own horn, believing himself to be more important than any other Israelite, but in doing so, he would have lost the Favor of God.

Radical Humility is the knowledge that you are not above others in your gifts, appearance, achievements, intelligence, or fortune. Humility flies out the window when you think that you are better than others, that they are beneath you and do not deserve either your courtesy or respect.

You exhibit Radical Humility when you rejoice in the successes of others, and refuse to pout when a friend or neighbor is exalted and you are not. When you are content to labor in the background for Christ without accolades or appreciation, that is Radical Humility. When everything you do becomes about Him, not about you, men can say of you as they did of Moses, there goes "a very humble man [or woman]."

WHAT I LEARNED AS A MORON

THOUGHT TO CONSIDER: Humility includes the ability to serve without expecting accolades, rejoicing in the impact of God through your life even when no one else notices.

VERSE TO CONNECT: "But I will look to this one, At one who is humble and contrite in spirit, and who trembles at My word." Isaiah 66:2, NKJV

QUESTION TO CONTEMPLATE: How can you be better known as a person of humility, like Moses, who places the will of God before the approval of others?

Mike Evans with White House Press Secretary Sarah Huckabee Sanders and her father Gov. Mike Huckabee at the Friends of Zion Museum in Jerusalem.

Mike Evans with Tony Perkins, President of the Family Research Council, and former Minnesota Republican Congresswoman Michele Bachmann.

Mike Evans and Shimon Peres.

Mike Evans with President Ronald Reagan.

CHAPTER

19

Faith, as Paul saw it, was a living, flaming thing leading to surrender and obedience to the commandments of Christ. [179]

In the 1980s I was invited to the White House during Ronald Reagan's presidency. As we stood in the Oval Office, Mr. Reagan pointed out his mother's Bible, which was open to II Chronicles 7:14 in the NIV:

> If my people, who are called by my name, will humble themselves and pray and seek my face and turn from their wicked ways, then I will hear from heaven, and I will forgive their sin and will heal their land.

The president noted where his mother had written in the margin, *"Son, this scripture is for the healing of the nations."* We walked to his magnificent desk that had been a gift to President Rutherford B. Hayes from Queen Victoria. The heavily carved treasure had been built with timbers from the *Resolute*, a vessel used in British Arctic Exploration. Sitting on the desk was a sign that read:

"A man can become too big in his own eyes to be used by God, but never too small."

The apostle Paul proved the truth of that statement. He was one who served Christ with Radical Humility—after his conversion. Before he met Christ on the road to Damascus, his character was quite different.

Paul was on the fringe of the crowd that had mortally stoned Stephen. Stephen had been chosen by the early Church to minister to the widows in the congregation. He was arrested for preaching about Jesus and taken before the Sanhedrin—the early Jewish court. During his trial, he angered the men who were sitting in judgment because of his testimony. So incensed were the men with Stephen that they dragged him outside the city and murdered him. Paul, a devout Pharisee, had by that time acquired the name of one who wanted to rid the known world of Christians. He had been mentored by Gamaliel, one of the greatest teachers in the history of the Jews. Paul, however, did not agree with his instructor on the question of how to deal with the Christians. Gamaliel had advised:

> "Men of Israel, take care what you are planning to do to these men! Some time ago there was that fellow Theudas, who pretended to be someone great. About 400 others joined him, but he was killed, and all his followers went their various ways. The whole movement came to nothing. After him, at the time of the census, there was Judas of Galilee. He got people to follow him, but he was killed, too, and all his followers were scattered. So my advice is, leave these men

alone. Let them go. If they are planning and doing these things merely on their own, it will soon be overthrown. But if it is from God, you will not be able to overthrow them. You may even find yourselves fighting against God!"[180]

Paul was much harsher in his ideas about how to halt the Christian invasion: He thought men and women alike should be seized, tried, convicted, and punished swiftly and harshly. His aim was to ferret out every Believer in the region and destroy their faith in Jesus Christ.

In Saul's day, before his conversion and name change, there was no word for "humility" in either the language of the Greeks or the Romans. The very idea of a man being humble was totally alien. It was a derogatory term often used to describe Christians—one that signified weakness of character, or one to be pitied. The Greek word for humility is *tapeinophrosune*. Greek literature is devoid of that word until the second century when it was borrowed from Christian literature. It is likely that Saul used the term like a curse when apprehending his hated foes. His fervent opposition reached the stage of fanaticism as he traveled from city to city hunting for followers of Christ. Saul went to the high priest:

> He requested letters addressed to the synagogues in Damascus, asking for their cooperation in the arrest of any followers of the Way he found there. He wanted to bring them—both men and women—back to Jerusalem in chains.[181]

Before his conversion, Saul was: radical, fanatical, egotistical, determined, uncompromising, and arrogant—the exact opposite of the humble servant of Christ. What a change was wrought in Saul as he stalked toward Damascus on his mission. He lost Self in the light of God's love and grace, changed his name to Paul, and his entire demeanor was transformed:

> "I became a servant of this gospel by the gift of God's grace given me through the working of his power. Although I am less than the least of all the Lord's people, this grace was given me: to preach to the Gentiles the boundless riches of Christ." [182]

Paul turned from being a fearsome adversary to the cause of Christ to becoming "less than the least." This phrase truly portrays Paul's sincere and Radical Humility; it was not a garment that he put on when convenient in order to impress others. In his own judgment, Paul was on a lower level than all the saints who were serving Christ in their daily and dangerous determination to walk in His light.

There is no reason to question Paul's genuineness in his own assessment. He had, after his encounter on the road to Damascus, become a deeply, profoundly humble man. He acknowledged that all his years prior to conversion were meaningless:

> "If someone else thinks they have reasons to put confidence in the flesh, I have more: circumcised on the eighth day, of the people of Israel, of the tribe of Benjamin, a Hebrew of Hebrews; in regard to the law,

a Pharisee; as for zeal, persecuting the church; as for righteousness based on the law, faultless. But whatever were gains to me I now consider loss for the sake of Christ. What is more, I consider everything a loss because of the surpassing worth of knowing Christ Jesus my Lord, for whose sake I have lost all things. I consider them garbage, that I may gain Christ and be found in him, not having a righteousness of my own that comes from the law, but that which is through faith in Christ—the righteousness that comes from God on the basis of faith. [183]

Paul's humility resounds in this passage. Everything on which he had based his prior existence, his education, his wealth, his devoutness, his lineage, his zeal against Christians, he now counts as garbage—as excrement—when compared to his new life in Christ. Paul willingly stepped off the pedestal; he gladly gave it all up; and in so doing, he was abundantly blessed with the Favor of God. He could convincingly profess:

"That's why I take pleasure in my weaknesses and in the insults, hardships, persecutions, and troubles that I suffer for Christ. For when I am weak, then I am strong." [184]

Paul knew he had nothing to boast about—except his own weakness. His life paled in comparison to God's strength. Paul was completely aware that the only good to be seen in him, the only power to be manifested through him came from God. He had no other explanation for the things he was able to accomplish. Jehovah was his source.

Only when Paul, through prayer and fasting, had brought Self under complete control did he freely, humbly, and gladly bow his knee to the will and purpose of God. The Father's response was to spread His abundant grace on Paul—and it was much needed. The apostle's life was one of extreme adversity and distress. Everywhere Paul turned there was degradation, suffering, rebuke, and danger. It would have been natural for Paul to become disheartened, discouraged, and depressed. Instead, he cried:

> "I have been crucified with Christ; it is no longer I who live, but Christ lives in me; and the life which I now live in the flesh I live by faith in the Son of God, who loved me and gave Himself for me." [185]

Paul's trials and tribulations led him through valleys deep and dark. Through it all, the illustrious apostle remained humble, pliable, and useful in the Kingdom. He knew that God's grace was sufficient to keep him. When Paul was under a great weight, he fell on his face and poured his heart out to the One who could lift the load. The secret of his powerful walk with God was his Radical Humility. Like John the Baptist in John 3:30, Paul knew that:

> "He [Jesus] must increase, but I *must* decrease."

Humility is never easy for one distinctly and individually called by God. Few, if any, of us could testify of being struck down and blinded by God at our conversion, as was Paul. He could have boasted of how he was THE called-out one. He could have worn his superiority like a mantle—demanding the choice seat at banquets, commandeering the best chariot for his travels, claiming the only first-class cabin on the ship. He could have, modestly of course, boasted of his superiority. Paul could have certainly bragged about his accomplishments. Instead, he remained honorable, principled, and humble in the sight of God and man. His ministry was that of a true apostle, characterized by meekness, truth, and love.

In return for that Radical Humility, God blessed Paul's ministry. Unlike the false prophets that flourished in his day, Paul did not draw huge crowds, nor was he welcomed as a hero. Rather, Paul lived a life of physical danger:

> "Five times I received from the Jews the forty lashes minus one. Three times I was beaten with rods, once I was pelted with stones, three times I was shipwrecked, I spent a night and a day in the open sea, I have been constantly on the move. I have been in danger from rivers, in danger from bandits, in danger from my fellow Jews, in danger from Gentiles; in danger in the city, in danger in the country, in danger at sea; and in danger from false believers. I have labored and toiled and have often gone without sleep; I have known hunger and thirst and have often gone without food; I have been cold and naked." [186]

Despite the hardships, Paul could still say with great love and confidence:

> "For when I am weak, then I am strong." [187]

At any time, Paul could have taken the easy path, but he chose Radical Humility. When you labor to be a genuine child of God, strive for humility. It comes when you honestly assess yourself in light of God's Word. When you do, you will live your life in God's life-changing favor.

WHAT I LEARNED AS A MORON

THOUGHT TO CONSIDER: Faith involves obeying the eternal facts of God over the temporary feelings of self.

VERSE TO CONNECT: "By faith Abraham, when called to go to a place he would later receive as his inheritance, obeyed and went, even though he did not know where he was going." Hebrews 11:8, NIV

QUESTION TO CONTEMPLATE: Will you choose faith over feelings when tested to choose the way that is most comfortable today?

Mike Evans at the Vatican.

Prince Albert of Monaco at the presidential palace
with Mike Evans and President Shimon Peres.

President of Bulgaria Rosen
Plevneliev receiving the Friends
of Zion award with Mike Evans.

Empress of Iran Farah Pahlavi and Mike Evans.

Mike Evans and President of
Honduras receiving the Friends
of Zion award in Jerusalem.

Mike Evans and former New York
City Mayor Rudy Giuliani.

CHAPTER

20

Nothing sets a person so much out of the
devil's reach as humility.[188]

There are times in a man's life when he must come face-to-face with his enemy and trust solely in God to see him through the encounter. When I was thirteen, I had circled a scripture in my Bible:

> "Fear thou not; for I am with thee: be not dismayed; for I am thy God: I will strengthen thee; yea, I will help thee; yea, I will uphold thee with the right hand of my righteousness. Behold, all they that were incensed against thee shall be ashamed and confounded: they shall be as nothing; and they that strive with thee shall perish."[189]

When I heard that Ronald Reagan had refused to allow Yasser Arafat, the pistol-waving terrorist, to attend the General Assembly in New York, and because of that restriction the United Nations would convene a special session in Geneva, the Spirit of God spoke to me through this scripture. The voice of God was speaking again as clearly as He had spoken to me when I was eleven.

I flew to Geneva, Switzerland, on December 9 and checked in to the Hilton Hotel, all the time believing that somehow God would cause me to ride upon the high places of the earth. He would open doors to leaders of nations because I was delighting in Him. I knew if it came to pass, truly supernatural affirmation from the Father would come with it.

To my amazement, I was allowed into the facility where the General Assembly meetings were being held, but would only be allowed upstairs in the nosebleed section. During the breaks I shared the Gospel with dozens of ambassadors and foreign ministers. After Arafat had delivered his speech, it was concluded that he had not clearly stated that he would denounce terrorism as expected. He was then forced to hold a press conference, which was predominantly peopled by the executive council and members of the Palestine Liberation Organization. The location had not been divulged to the general public.

The moment I heard of the meeting, I walked the halls of the building in prayer. The Spirit of God spoke to me and directed me to go to room 401. Once inside, He sent me to the second row of seats next to a long table. There I was instructed to put my locked briefcase on the center chair and then leave the room.

Hours later, Arafat's cronies filled the room where strict security was in place to keep out those who were unwanted. When the room was completely filled, I approached one of the terrorists guarding the door.

"Excuse me, sir, I need to go to my seat."

"You have no seat here. You cannot enter," he snapped.

"But I have already been inside," I said. "Go to the front row of chairs. You will see my briefcase on the second row, middle seat. Open it; the combination is 0001. Inside you will see my passport and several other things."

He turned and stalked up the aisle. Shortly he came back and reluctantly escorted me to the chair that held my briefcase. Minutes later, Arafat came in. I was directly in front of him in the middle seat. The camera crews had been assigned row three—just behind me. Not even the PLO executive council had been permitted to sit in rows one and two. The cameramen were protesting because my head was in the way.

Before me was a table where Arafat and the few men who would accompany him were to sit. They entered the room, and the PLO chairman delivered his speech.

After his speech, he said, "I shall allow three of you to speak. You may choose among yourselves."

I knew they would not choose me, so I instantly grabbed my Bible and stood to my feet, secure in the scripture that God had activated in my life. Also in my hand was a copy of the PLO covenant, which calls for the destruction of the State of Israel.

I said, "Mr. Arafat, if you denounce terrorism, then you must condemn this covenant that calls for the destruction of Israel." Then, while holding up my Bible, I began to recount the biblical position of the Jewish people.

When I finished speaking, I turned; not only was Arafat livid but I was surrounded by men whose eyes were filled with murderous hatred because of what I had said. *Lord, You divided the sea for*

Moses. I only need about six inches to get out of this room. Suddenly it was as if a carpet had been rolled out. I saw a path I could navigate. I walked quickly through the midst of the gathering into the dark hallway. The voice of the Enemy taunted me with *"You'll never make it out of here alive. They will stab you in the back."* I had no idea where I was going but went in the direction I felt prompted by the Spirit to go. *"A cab will be waiting with the door open,"* the Lord said to me. *"Get in and go to your hotel. No man will harm you."*

Just as I was directed to stand before Yasser Arafat and challenge him, so Elijah was challenged to face his enemy—another very dangerous man. Elijah was another, like Moses, who had a teachable spirit. The day came when, despite all the miracles he had performed at God's bidding, Elijah was told that his role as prophet to Israel would be handed to another. But before we assign Elijah to a fiery chariot and the balcony of heaven, let's take a look at his life as humble prophet. He first appears on the scene in I Kings 17:1 (NKJV):

> And Elijah the Tishbite, of the inhabitants of Gilead, said to Ahab, "As the Lord God of Israel lives, before whom I stand, there shall not be dew nor rain these years, except at my word."

Now, that's definitely out of left field! Elijah gets right in the king's face and says, "Hey, Ahab, no rain—not even dew for the next three years. God said so!"

All we know about Elijah at this point is that he was an inhabitant of Tishbeh (reputedly in the Upper Galilee region). Some Bible scholars think he had migrated from there to Gilead. It was, as we say in Texas, in the "boondocks." Before Elijah, whose name means "my God is the Lord," burst on the scene, the northern kingdom, Israel, had been ruled by a succession of wicked men. When we first meet Elijah, Ahab had ascended to the throne after the death of his father, Omri. The Bible says he had "done worse than all that were before him," and that was bad! Ahab entered into an arranged marriage with Jezebel, the daughter of King Ethbaal, a Phoenician.[190] The kingdom had come under the thumb of a man and his wife, and that, according to Charles Swindoll, was "a little like going from Jesse James to Bonnie and Clyde,"[191] or from the frying pan into the fires of hell.

Some historians record that Jezebel's parents were a high priest and priestess who worshipped Baal (one of the seven princes of hell). She, too, was likely a priestess. For the first time in the books of Kings and Chronicles, we are introduced to the wife of a king of either Judah or Israel. There is, therefore, some biblical significance associated with Jezebel. It is for a very good reason that her name has come to mean an impudent, shameless, or morally unrestrained woman.[192] She was a ruthless and pagan queen.

Ahab was apparently what we today would call a "henpecked husband," one who resorted to pouting and grumbling to get his own way. He frequently acquiesced to Jezebel's wishes and leadership in ruling the kingdom. He apparently knew that if he wanted something badly enough, Jezebel would make it happen. In I Kings 16, we begin to see why God called Elijah as a prophet to Israel:

> He [Ahab] set up an altar for Baal in the temple of
> Baal that he built in Samaria. Ahab also made an
> Asherah pole and did more to arouse the anger of the

Lord, the God of Israel, than did all the kings of Israel before him. [193]

Ahab had not been the first king over the northern kingdom to promote idol worship. His ancestor, Jeroboam, was the first to plant the seeds of idolatry in the region:

> Jeroboam did not change his evil ways, but once more appointed priests for the high places from all sorts of people. Anyone who wanted to become a priest he consecrated for the high places. [194]

The words "high places" were used to describe the pagan altars where the Israelites worshipped idols of wood and stone, and where they sacrificed their children to the gods of the Canaanites. The murderous and deceptive Jeroboam laid the foundation for his successors, including Ahab. This is the atmosphere into which Elijah would be sent to proclaim the Word of God.

First, God commanded Elijah to go to the Brook Cherith, where he would have water during the terrible drought that had gripped both Israel and Judah. God promised to supply the prophet with food delivered daily by ravens. The big, black birds are omnivorous—they dine on both plant and animal matter. How many would be humble enough to eat what the ravens dropped on the driveway daily? Yet Elijah trusted God and depended on Him for survival.

Faith? Yes! Humility? Definitely! The man of Radical Humility obeyed God whether in the glare of the spotlight or hidden in a cave by a stream; whether eating filet mignon or bird food. Elijah placed his very life in God's hands. He submitted to the command immediately without question or hesitation. When the drought worsened and the brook dried up, God sent the prophet on a long, dangerous walk from his cave all the way to the Mediterranean coast. His destination was Zarephath; his next hiding place, the home of a widow and her only son. Elijah asked her for bread and water. Her answer must have stunned the prophet:

> "As surely as the Lord your God lives," she replied, "I don't have any bread—only a handful of flour in a jar and a little olive oil in a jug. I am gathering a few sticks to take home and make a meal for myself and my son, that we may eat it—and die." [195]

Jehovah breathed the solution into Elijah's spirit, and Elijah said to her:

> "Don't be afraid. Go home and do as you have said. But first make a small loaf of bread for me from what you have and bring it to me, and then make something for yourself and your son." [196]

That instruction must have been radically humbling—the great prophet of God sent to eat a piece of flatbread from the last smidgen of flour and oil the widow possessed. Elijah was not to give; he was to take. As a prophet of God accustomed to the miraculous, he surely must have wanted to be the one to provide an abundant supply for this widow—a room filled with oil, flour, lentils, vegetables—but no. Like the Children of Israel who received manna sufficient for the day, God supplied a daily quantity of flour and oil for the widow, her son, and her houseguest. She had trusted God for provision; Jehovah-Jireh, the God who provides, answered.

Because the widow offered Elijah the last of her food, God miraculously supplied her needs:

> The bin of flour was not used up, nor did the jar of oil run dry, according to the word of the Lord which He spoke by Elijah. [197]

During his stay in Zarephath Elijah would have an opportunity to repay the widow a thousandfold. Her child died. She lifted his still, little body and carried him to the prophet. Elijah took the boy. There was no wailing, no gnashing of teeth, and no questioning of God's power or ability. God had proved faithful to meet the prophet's needs. He didn't chide the grieving mother. He responded with kindness.

With Radical Humility, Elijah turned to Jehovah-Rophi, the God who heals, and He answered. Elijah was able to present the young child, in perfect health, to his grieving mother!

For nearly three years, Elijah had hidden from Ahab and Jezebel, first by the brook and then in Zarephath. Why? Because the queen had spent those three years diligently trying to massacre God's prophets. She had succeeded in killing all but 101—Elijah and one hundred prophets hidden in caves by Obadiah, Ahab's palace administrator, who fed them from his own food supply. In actuality, Ahab was unknowingly feeding the very men Jezebel was trying to slaughter.

Suddenly, God told Elijah it was time for him to make his presence known to Ahab and Jezebel. As he went on his way, he met

Obadiah who ironically was out with Ahab "looking" for the hidden prophets. Elijah's first words were, "Take me to Ahab." Obadiah was stunned—not to mention in fear for his life. He was concerned that if he went to tell Ahab Elijah had surfaced, then "as soon as I leave you, the Spirit of the Lord will carry you away to who knows where. When Ahab comes and cannot find you, he will kill me." [198]

Elijah assured the king's administrator that he would hold his ground until he saw Ahab.

"I swear by the Lord Almighty, in whose presence I stand, that I will present myself to Ahab this very day." So Obadiah went to tell Ahab that Elijah had come, and Ahab went out to meet Elijah. When Ahab saw him, he exclaimed, "So, is it really you, you trouble-maker of Israel?" [199]

Standing before the king was a tired, dusty, humble man—a picture of both heroism and humility—waiting to deliver God's message. Ahab had not seen his nemesis for three years, during which time the country was gripped by drought and famine. On his trek from the widow's modest dwelling to the royal palace, Elijah must have encountered the dead and the dying. He must have been confronted with hopelessness at every turn, but he knew that God was about to move, the situation about to change. El Elyon, the Most High God, had a plan, and no king, no evil dictator, no worldly queen, or circumstances could foil His plans or change His mind.

Into the presence of the earthly ruler of Israel walked the man deemed responsible for the whole problem—Elijah. Ahab tried to lay the blame at the feet of the prophet, but the humble prophet was not alarmed. He simply turned the tables on the king and leveled the charge:

"You and your family are the troublemakers, for you have refused to obey the commands of the Lord and have worshiped the images of Baal instead."[200]

Ahab had shamelessly flaunted the first two commandments and had not only placed Baal before Jehovah, he had set up groves in honor of the deadly deity. According to author Matt Barber:

The principal pillars of Baalism were child sacrifice, sexual immorality (both heterosexual and homo-sexual) and pantheism (reverence of creation over the Creator). Ritualistic Baal worship, in sum, looked a little like this: Adults would gather around the altar of Baal. Infants would then be burned alive as a sacri-ficial offering to the deity. Amid horrific screams and the stench of charred human flesh, congregants—men and women alike—would engage in bisexual orgies. The ritual of convenience was intended to produce economic prosperity by prompting Baal to bring rain for the fertility of "mother earth."[201]

The United States today is following the same path, but it is strewn with politically correct words such as "same-sex marriage," or "pro-choice." The terrible truth is that our children are being sacrificed on the altar of Self to the god of "Me."

Elijah boldly stood before Ahab and said something like, "Hey, king, you can't blame me for this mess. It's all your fault! You made the choice to disobey God's laws. If you want to know why we haven't had rain, Ahab, look in the mirror. It is *you* who has forsaken Yahweh to go after false gods."

The prophet's next directive was a call to action:

> "Now summon all Israel to join me at Mount Carmel,
> along with the 450 prophets of Baal and the 400
> prophets of Asherah who are supported by Jezebel." [202]

The call went out and the crowd gathered. Elijah had his instructions from God and was ready to face the 850 false prophets. Of course, he had the advantage: he knew the winner before the first side of beef hit the altar of Baal. However, he had a point to prove to a vacillating nation. He defined the question:

> "How much longer will you waver, hobbling between
> two opinions? If the Lord is God, follow him! But if
> Baal is God, then follow him!" [203]

Too often meekness and humility are equated with weakness. Not true of Moses, and certainly not true of Elijah! He unwaveringly faced an indecisive congregation. God had anointed him for that time and place, for that day and hour. When the flames died, he would exhibit incontrovertible evidence that Jehovah alone was the one true God.

The priests of Baal presented their offerings to their god. With much dancing and shouting, they tried vigorously to call down fire from heaven to consume the gift. Standing over to the side, leaning on a pile of stones that had once been an altar to Jehovah, Elijah chided the worshippers of Baal and Asherah:

> "Shout louder!" he said. "Surely he is a god! Perhaps
> he is deep in thought, or busy, or traveling. Maybe he
> is sleeping and must be awakened." [204]

The activity around the altar to Baal only grew more frenzied. The priests jumped about like a pile of frogs just released from a gunnysack. They howled like long-tailed cats in a room full of rocking chairs. They cut themselves until the blood ran down their arms—and their god remained silent. It was absolute bedlam, total idiocy. All day, Elijah watched as the priests and prophets of Baal descended into hysteria, followed by incapacitating exhaustion. Finally they dropped into the dust surrounding the altar—bloody, spent, and disgraced.

At last, God's time had come. Elijah gathered twelve stones, one each to represent the twelve tribes. He then erected an altar to Jehovah. Not satisfied, he dug a trench around the structure deep enough to hold approximately fifty pounds of wheat. He arranged layers of wood on top of which he laid the offering. Then he said:

> "Fill four large jars with water and pour it on the offering and on the wood. Do it again," he said, and they did it again. "Do it a third time," he ordered, and they did it the third time. The water ran down around the altar and even filled the trench. [205]

After the offering and the wood were soaked and the trench was filled with water, Elijah prayed a twenty-four-word prayer:

> "Answer me, Lord, answer me, so these people will know that you, Lord, are God, and that you are turning their hearts back again." [206]

No fanfare. No shouting. No frenzy. No self-mutilation. Just a quiet, confident trust in the God of Israel. Suddenly, without warning, fire fell from heaven, consumed the offering, the wood, the stones, the soil beneath the stones, and the water in the trenches! The Children of Israel fell on their faces before God and acknowledged His sovereignty.

Elijah's showdown on top of Mount Carmel is reminiscent of another showdown on top of Mount Calvary. Each was a battle between light and darkness, a battle between good and evil, a challenge between Jehovah and Satan. Elijah was a man of great faith and Radical Humility; Jesus Christ was the epitome of faith and humility. No wonder His disciples responded, "Elijah," when Jesus asked, "Who do men say that I, the Son of Man, am?"[207]

Near the top of any list of men of Radical Humility would be the name Elijah. The prophet's life is a prototype of Christ before His journey to the cross. The comparisons are many: Both were humble, tender, kind, and patient. Yet upon occasion, both uttered scorching words of judgment and retribution. Both enjoyed the unending Favor of God during their journey on earth.

Elijah learned Radical Humility during a devastating famine in the land. Is there a famine in your land today? Perhaps it is a financial famine, and the job that provided food and drink has dried up. How are you thinking about your circumstances? Consider that God is your source—He is the One who can meet your every need, daily. He knows what you need and how to provide for you, His child.

Is your famine found in a crumbling relationship that you thought would endure "until death do us part"? Your hope is fading; your tears soak your pillow at night. Is it time to return with Elijah to Zerephath and learn of Radical Humility? If we could interview

Elijah today, he would assure that it was Jehovah's lesson in Radical Humility that prepared him for the challenge atop Mount Carmel.

As you meditate on the life of Elijah, his Radical Humility, and his walk of faith, look heavenward to the Author and Finisher of your faith for the grace to walk humbly before Him and thus live in the Divine Favor of God!

WHAT I LEARNED AS A MORON

THOUGHT TO CONSIDER: Humility provides strength, not weakness, in the spiritual battles we face in life.

VERSE TO CONNECT: "Fear not, for I am with you; Be not dismayed, for I am your God. I will strengthen you, Yes, I will help you, I will uphold you with My righteous right hand. Behold, all those who were incensed against you Shall be ashamed and disgraced; They shall be as nothing, And those who strive with you shall perish." Isaiah 41:10-11, NKJV

QUESTION TO CONTEMPLATE: How could choosing humility strengthen my spiritual battle against the attacks of the enemy?

Mike Evans, the first evangelical to speak at the Kremlin Palace, broadcast live primetime to the former Soviet Union.

Mike Evans presenting his first book to Israel Prime Minister Menachem Begin.

Former President of Israel and Mike Evans.

CHAPTER

21

A man can no more diminish God's glory
by refusing to worship Him than a lunatic can
put out the sun by scribbling the word,
'darkness' on the walls of his cell. [208]

"I*'ve seen your ministry; now I'll show you Mine.*" Those were the words Jesus spoke into my spirit. As I humbled myself and lay on my face praying and weeping, He said, *"Son, I'm going to open up Russia and you will be a part of it."*

I had traveled to Russia several times to bring "soap"—large bars and small ones—to the underground church. No, it wasn't Dove or Irish Spring; it was what Russian Believers called Bibles. On one occasion, when I was smuggling Bibles in, a soldier in customs asked me to open my five suitcases. Each was filled with Bibles. He said, "What is inside these suitcases?" I was aware that if caught with the Bibles, I would go to prison. He repeated, "Open all the suitcases." As I did, I prayed, *"Jesus, help me."* As I opened the suitcases, the soldier just stared at the contents. I had three suitcases filled with large Bibles and two filled with small Bibles.

He said to me, "Are these the large soap?"

"Yes," I said.

"Are these the small soap?"

Again I said, "Yes."

"Okay," he said. "Close your suitcases; you can go."

I walked out of there with a skip, a shout, and tears of joy. Several of the pastors to whom I was bringing the "soap" were not there. Instead, their congregations met me and I ministered to them in the woods. I was told that the pastors were in "Bible School." I rejoiced that they were able to meet and learn more about God's Word. Much to my dismay, I discovered later that "Bible School" meant prison—the pastors had been arrested and imprisoned.

As I lay in prayer before the throne of God, the Holy Spirit ministered to me that because Russia had not let God's people go back to the land of Israel, judgment would come. But because of God's sentence upon the Communist leaders, a million Russian Jews would pour out of the Soviet Union. Shortly after the revelation from the Holy Spirit, I produced a television special and a book, *Let My People Go*. One man who was being held in a Russian gulag was featured; he was Anatole (Natan) Sharanski—one of almost 400 Russian Jews being held. As God began to move, the 400 were released, and more than a million Jews found freedom from repression. As foretold, God's judgment had come as the old Soviet Union collapsed during the presidency of Ronald Reagan.

In Revelation 4:10–11 (NKJV), you see another picture of Man meeting His Maker:

> The twenty-four elders fall down before Him who sits

on the throne and worship Him who lives forever and ever, and cast their crowns before the throne, saying: "You are worthy, O Lord, to receive glory and honor and power; for You created all things, and by Your will they exist and were created."

That must have been only a taste of how Isaiah felt when he encountered the King of Kings and Lord of Lords. Isaiah, whose name means "Yahweh saves," was the son of Amoz. Apparently the members of his family were a part of the upper class in Israel—or at least that could be assumed from his close relationship with King Uzziah. Some historians believe he was the king's cousin, and because of that connection was appointed pastor of the court.

Uzziah had been crowned king of Judah at the tender age of sixteen. His reign lasted for fifty-two years. Under the tutelage of a prophet named Zechariah, the king remained true to Jehovah. Perhaps his mentor died or the king's instruction came to an end. For whatever reason, Uzziah's eyes were blinded by his success. (He had raised a well-trained army and developed tactical weapons.) It was then that he turned from God and began to follow his own egotistical thoughts and desires. The king began to believe himself to be above the laws of God. From II Chronicles we can follow Uzziah's descent into rebellion:

> But after Uzziah became powerful, his pride led to his downfall. He was unfaithful to the Lord his God, and entered the temple of the Lord to burn incense on the altar of incense [also called the Golden Altar]. Azariah the priest with eighty other courageous

priests of the Lord followed him in. They confronted King Uzziah and said, "It is not right for you, Uzziah, to burn incense to the Lord. That is for the priests, the descendants of Aaron, who have been consecrated to burn incense. Leave the sanctuary, for you have been unfaithful; and you will not be honored by the Lord God." Uzziah, who had a censer in his hand ready to burn incense, became angry. While he was raging at the priests in their presence before the incense altar in the Lord's temple, leprosy broke out on his forehead. When Azariah the chief priest and all the other priests looked at him, they saw that he had leprosy on his forehead, so they hurried him out. Indeed, he himself was eager to leave, because the Lord had afflicted him. King Uzziah had leprosy until the day he died. He lived in a separate house—leprous, and banned from the temple of the Lord. [209]

What a sad ending for a young man with such promise. It is little wonder that in the first chapters of the book of Isaiah we find the prophet pleading with the people of Judah to repent and turn back to God. Chapter five of Isaiah resounds with the word *Woe*. The prophet was warning the nation to repent and return. He cautions them in verse 20:

> "Woe to those who call evil good and good evil, who put darkness for light and light for darkness, who put bitter for sweet and sweet for bitter."

In chapter six, we find Isaiah prostrate in the Temple. He had humbled himself, and Jehovah responded with a vision for the prophet's eyes only. Isaiah was transported from the confines of the Temple into the very throne room of God. His attention was not captured by the beauty of his surroundings—oh no! His awareness was immediately centered on the One whose Presence was overwhelming. God was reassuring Isaiah that a nation which had just lost its beloved king was not without a Ruler. He was still on the throne for all to follow. Uzziah was not Judah's Supreme King; he led only at the will of the Sovereign Lord. Isaiah described God's appearance:

> In the year that King Uzziah died, I saw the Lord, high and exalted, seated on a throne; and the train of his robe filled the temple. Above him were seraphim, each with six wings: With two wings they covered their faces, with two they covered their feet, and with two they were flying. And they were calling to one another: "Holy, holy, holy is the Lord Almighty; the whole earth is full of His glory." At the sound of their voices the doorposts and thresholds shook and the temple was filled with smoke. [210]

No matter whose name follows "King," "President," or "Prime Minister," God is ultimately in control. No one ascends to office or holds it without God having allowed them to be placed there. You and I need not despair if a beloved ruler dies or a favored candidate loses an election; God is still on His throne and in total control.

In Isaiah's vision, the throne room of heaven is filled with smoke. It is reminiscent of the Temple dedication in II Chronicles 7:

When Solomon finished praying, fire came down from heaven and consumed the burnt offering and the sacrifices, and the glory of the Lord filled the temple. The priests could not enter the temple of the Lord because the glory of the Lord filled it. When all the Israelites saw the fire coming down and the glory of the Lord above the temple, they knelt on the pavement with their faces to the ground, and they worshiped and gave thanks to the Lord. [211]

When Moses was summoned to the top of Mount Sinai for the giving of the Ten Commandments:

. . .the cloud covered it, and the glory of the Lord settled on Mount Sinai. For six days the cloud covered the mountain, and on the seventh day the Lord called to Moses from within the cloud. To the Israelites the glory of the Lord looked like a consuming fire on top of the mountain. Then Moses entered the cloud as he went on up the mountain. [212]

Isaiah suddenly found himself in the same position of men such as Moses and John—in a smoke-filled, heavenly temple. He was surrounded by the seraphim or "burning ones" of heaven who, though angelic beings, did not fail to cover themselves in the presence of Almighty God. Day and night these creatures cried loudly, "Holy, holy, holy is the Lord Almighty; the whole earth is full of His glory." [213] So thunderous was the noise that the very foundation of the temple shook. It is interesting to note that one of Isaiah's favorite titles for Jehovah was "the Holy One of Israel." He had entered the Presence of God and had come away with a renewed conviction of the holiness of God. It was not to be trivialized or marginalized. God is holy!

Perhaps Lewis A. Drummond, former president of Southeastern Baptist Theological Seminary, was thinking of Isaiah's encounter with God when he said:

> "A spiritual awakening is no more than God's people seeing God in His holiness, turning from their wicked ways, and being transformed into His likeness." [214]

God is love! God is holy! God is righteous! That doesn't mean God meets the standard for those qualities; God *is* the standard by which all else is measured. Isaiah had entered into the presence of the epitome of holiness—Jehovah God. It is the character of the great I AM!

Isaiah's response was immediate:

> "Woe to me! . . . I am ruined! For I am a man of unclean lips, and I live among a people of unclean lips, and my eyes have seen the King, the Lord Almighty." [215]

The prophet was in the presence of holiness, and with Radical Humility he realized his position. He had been concerned with the sinfulness of Judah; now he was concerned with his own impurity when seen under the microscope of God. Isaiah realized he was ruined. He had no place to hide. The smoke of God's holiness was seeping into every pore of his body, into the core of his being—and he was doomed. Humility should be the basis for every Christian life. To come to Christ, you must recognize that you are a sinner in desperate need of a Savior. That realization then requires the humility to lay aside your own pride and ego and lie prostrate at the foot of the cross of Christ. It means acknowledging that no matter how you might have failed, God is greater than your sin.

As Isaiah lay on his face before the Lord God Almighty, he became more and more aware of how holy his God is and how sinful *he* was. He cried that he was a man of unclean lips and he dwelled in the midst of a people whose lips were unclean. James the apostle wrote:

> Likewise, the tongue is a small part of the body, but it makes great boasts. Consider what a great forest is set on fire by a small spark. The tongue also is a fire, a world of evil among the parts of the body. It corrupts the whole body, sets the whole course of one's life on fire, and is itself set on fire by hell. [216]

Isaiah was struck by his own guilt in the presence of utter Holiness. And he realized the entire nation was equally unworthy to stand before God. However, Jehovah did not abandon Isaiah to his woeful status:

> Then one of the seraphim flew to me with a live coal in his hand, which he had taken with tongs from the altar. With it he touched my mouth and said, "See, this has touched your lips; your guilt is taken away and your sin atoned for." [217]

John wrote:

> If we confess our sins, he is faithful and just and will forgive us our sins and purify us from all unrighteousness. [218]

Isaiah prostrated himself in Radical Humility in the awesome presence of Jehovah-El Elyon, the Lord, the Most High God. In the midst of the smoke, Isaiah was called to a new pursuit and responded to the summons:

> Then I heard the voice of the Lord saying, "Whom shall I send? And who will go for us?" And I said, "Here am I. Send me!" [219]

An encounter with God always brings inevitable change. Either your commitment to Him grows deeper and you become more like your heavenly Father, or you harden your heart and die spiritually. The Bible is filled with stories of men who met God and went away with a new mission: Noah, Abraham, Moses, David, Daniel, Peter, and, of course, Isaiah.

God calls the humble to fulfill His mission. His power is made perfect in your weakness. Only with the realization that you can do nothing without Jehovah are you then ready to be used by Him. Only then can you say with Radical Humility, as did Isaiah, "Send me." At that point of surrender, you will be showered with the Favor of God.

WHAT I LEARNED AS A MORON

THOUGHT TO CONSIDER: God calls the humble and the most unlikely to fulfill His most significant missions.

VERSE TO CONNECT: "Then I heard the voice of the Lord saying, 'Whom shall I send? And who will go for us?' And I said, 'Here am I. Send me!'" Isaiah 6:8, NIV

QUESTION TO CONTEMPLATE: What mission could God be calling you to prepare for through humbling yourself before Him?

Mike Evans with former Mayor of Jerusalem Nir Barkat.

President of Israel Reuven Rivlin
and Mike Evans.

Mike Evans in the Vatican on his
way to meet with Pope Francis.

Mike Evans with the Crown Prince of the UAE Sheikh Mohamed bin Zayed bin Sultan Al Nahyan.

Mike Evans honoring Guatemalan President
Jimmy Morales at Friends of Zion in Jerusalem.

Mike Evans, President George W. Bush,
and President Shimon Peres.

PART FOUR

WHAT I LEARNED AS A MORON

CELEBRATE SUFFERING AND SACRIFICE

Mike Evans hosting Prime Minister Begin at the Waldorf Astoria
in Jerusalem with the owner of the Dallas Cowboys, Ann Murchison,
and First Lady of Alabama Bobbie James.

Mike Evans with Natan
Sharansky who he helped
get out of prison.

Mike and Carolyn Evans.

Carolyn and Mike Evans, Sara and Prime Minister
Benjamin Netanyahu, and Ambassador David Friedman.

CHAPTER

22

"...and a little child will lead them."[220]

My beautiful wife, Carolyn, was raised in a loving Christian home. When she first learned of the abuse I had suffered at the hands of my father, she said she likely would not have married me had she met my family first. She had been taught as a child to marry a person of the same faith and who was from a godly home. In no way did that describe my childhood home; it had been utterly chaotic.

When we first felt led to begin our ministry to Israel, our car was about our only possession of any worth—and it was old and rusty. We had little else, but in order to lay a foundation we sold our furniture and invested the proceeds in the ministry. We kept only one mattress. The night we sold our possessions, Carolyn and I both came down with the flu. We spent the night crawling on our hands and knees to the bathroom.

The next day, weak but determined, we climbed into our dilapidated car and made our way to a church in Columbus, Indiana, for a speaking engagement. The pastor had gone to Florida and was stranded there because of a blizzard that had descended on the city. A handful of people braved the terrible conditions to be in church.

After the service, we waded through the snow and ice to find a smoking hulk where our car had sat. A short in the wiring had caused a fire; our car was totally consumed. We had no idea that the seed we had planted was about to spring forth—yes, in the midst of a blizzard. God was about to use a man named Gene Darnell, a real intercessor. He loaded us into his car and took us home with him for the night. The next morning, as we pondered how we were going to get home, Gene handed me the keys to a brand-new Buick Electra! He told us that God had instructed him to give us the car. To say that we were overjoyed is an understatement. Gene became our first partner, and he, like Abraham, believed in the things that were not seen as though they were. We were amazed and overwhelmed at God's provision. We knew we had experienced a miracle of boundless proportions, and I have been eternally grateful.

Soon Carolyn and I began to feel led of the Holy Spirit that we were to return to Texas for one more year of schooling. Once again, we packed up our few belongings and headed south to Fort Worth.

On the way home we stopped to look at mobile homes in Little Rock, Arkansas. We would need a place to live while we pursued another year of training. As we walked the lot and discussed what would make a perfect home for our little family, we had no idea that the owner—Bill Roetzell, a member of Gideon International—was having morning devotions and was on his knees in prayer. When he arose and saw us outside, the Spirit of God spoke to him and said,

"You are to give them a new mobile home, but not off the lot. It must come from the factory."

He did just that! When he told us about the new trailer, he said we would need a car at least the size of a Buick Electra to tow it. We were able to say, "That's exactly what we have." That generous gift became our home as well as national and international headquarters for the next few years. We moved our little home into the Santa Dee Trailer Court in Fort Worth. I called it our "international headquarters to the nation of Israel." People would laugh until they cried when they heard that. Our home was thirty-two feet long by eight feet wide, and the ceilings were only six feet high. As I walked from one end to the other, I broke light bulbs with my head. The shower was so small I had to kneel down as if praying in order to shower. We had a sliding door between the bedroom and bathroom. Carolyn attached a mirror to the door in an attempt to make our space look larger. I awoke one night and saw someone staring at me. I jumped up and crashed right into the mirror. I had been looking at myself! On another night, I stepped out of bed and put my foot in the toilet. To say our quarters were small is an understatement.

Shortly after completing our year of training, David Wilkerson felt led of the Lord to give us Camp David, his property on Possum Kingdom Lake near Graham, Texas, as a training center. All we had to do was pick up the small monthly payment. When he had dedicated the facility, David prayed that God would give us cows to help feed all the kids who would pass through the doors of the Teen Challenge facility. There were a number of young Jewish people in the program. Most had come off drugs and were trying to get their lives back together. I remember our first gift of one hundred dollars.

Someone sent five twenty-dollar bills in an envelope addressed to "The Jews, Graham, Texas. The postman delivered it to me and said, "There is only one Jew besides you and he owns a salvage business. This must be your mail."

When our eldest daughter, Michelle, was five years old, I came home and said to Carolyn, "God has told me to buy a training center in New York to assist Jewish young people coming off drugs. I believe God will provide a million dollars, but I don't know how we will get the money." We had no money to invest, as our first year's income had been a mere $4,500. We barely had enough to meet necessities but were happy in our little home. Michelle said, "Daddy, I've got a million dollars in my piggy bank." She left the room and came back into the kitchen with her piggy bank. She said, "Daddy, I will give you the money. It's here in my piggy bank."

With tears in my eyes, we broke open her piggy bank and counted out $3.26. I wept as faith rose up in my heart. I took Michelle's offering, went to the bank, and opened an account for the training center. The banker asked me if I had mental problems, and I explained what we felt led of God to do. He assured me that we would not be getting the funds. "You can't pray money in, Reverend Evans. You need to see a counselor."

Every day, I went to the retreat center and shut myself in with God in prayer and fasting. Sixteen weeks later, every dime we needed for the building had been miraculously received! Dr. Pat Robertson sent us a check for $10,000. When Pat Boone and people nationwide funded the project and the million dollars was in the till, the banker apologized. Michelle's holy offering touched the heart of God and moved His hand.

It is often said, correctly, "You can't out-give God." If you live a life of Radical Generosity—whether time, treasure, talent, or tithe, God will open the windows of heaven and "pour out for you such blessing that there will not be room enough to receive it." [221]

WHAT I LEARNED AS A MORON

THOUGHT TO CONSIDER: When you live with radical generosity, expect to experience radical blessings from God.

VERSE TO CONNECT: "Each of you should give what you have decided in your heart to give, not reluctantly or under compulsion, for God loves a cheerful giver." 2 Corinthians 9:7, NIV

QUESTION TO CONTEMPLATE: In what ways could you become more radical in generosity to better experience God's blessing in your life?

Auschwitz concentration camp at March of the Living.

Getting Holocaust survivors
out of Ukraine to Israel.

Saving an elderly Ukrainian.

CHAPTER

23

*"When we realize that everything that
we have is a gift from God, it becomes possible
for us to give in a radical way."*[222]

It is staggering to realize that there are more than 200,000 Holocaust survivors still living in Israel today. They are aged and frail, and most have no immediate family members still living—these are the survivors of Adolf Hitler's horrendous attempt to destroy the Jewish people. When you meet these precious people and hug them, you can still see the Nazi concentration camp identification numbers that were tattooed on their arms when they were very young. The war that brought such devastation followed on the heels of what was often called the "war to end all wars."

I had the privilege in late 2012 to join more than one hundred ministry partners as we met with a number of Holocaust survivors in the Holy City. We gathered in a beautiful community center that will double as a bomb shelter when necessary. It was made available to them by loving friends, Jerusalem Prayer Team Partners, and Radical Generosity. It was the first outreach project handled through the Jerusalem World Center, another JPT ministry project. The shelter has air-conditioning, heat, a kitchen, television, Internet, an air filtration system, beautiful bathrooms, and much more.

Earlier in the day, our group had visited Yad Vashem—the Holocaust Memorial in Jerusalem. As we ministered to and prayed for these precious people who had suffered so much, many eyes filled with tears. We were seeing before us people for whom those horrible days were not just stories but memories. Still, war has continued to threaten the Jewish people as tyrant and fanatic threaten to "wipe Israel off the map."

The first war recorded in the Bible is found in Genesis chapter 14. Chedorlaomer, the king of Elam, had joined forces with five other kings in the region. They attacked the kings of Sodom and Gomorrah and after having put them to flight, sacked the cities and carried off the inhabitants. Among the captives were Abraham's nephew, Lot, and his family. Abraham might well have decided that Lot had made his own bed, and would therefore have to lie in it. After all, Lot had chosen to live in the city known for its deviant residents. He might have decided that he and his followers could never compete against such a vast army. Abraham did neither; instead, he summoned 318 of his trained servants and set out to rescue his family members.

Later, when Jesus related the parable of the house built on the rock and the one built on the sand, He may well have been thinking of Abraham and his nephew. Lot had chosen to build his house on shaky ground, leaving himself vulnerable to thieves and looters. Abraham had built his house on the foundation rock of belief and faith in Jehovah, and was ready for the challenges ahead. He and his men pursued the marauders and rescued Lot, his family, and his possessions, as well as the king of Sodom and his subjects.

As Abraham was returning home, he was met by Melchizedek, who some say was Noah's son Shem, while others believe he was the preincarnate Christ. Whether he was God or simply a type, it is apparent that he is truly representative of a heavenly visitation with Abraham. The tired leader needed to be strengthened, comforted, and inspired. Often when you, child of God, have been wearied by the battle, strength comes through His Word or the tender ministries of a servant of God.

We know with certainty that Melchizedek was at the very least a foreshadow of our Lord, as that is made apparent in Hebrews 7:1-3, NIV:

> This Melchizedek was king of Salem and priest of God Most High. He met Abraham returning from the defeat of the kings and blessed him, and Abraham gave him a tenth of everything. First, the name Melchizedek means "king of righteousness"; then also, "king of Salem" means "king of peace." Without father or mother, without genealogy, without beginning of days or end of life, resembling the Son of God, he remains a priest forever.

Abraham, like Melchizedek, was also a type of Christ. He pursued Lot, rescued him from a life of bondage. Lot could not free himself; he was held captive by an evil king. Jesus Christ pursued you, who were dead in your trespasses and sin—bond slaves to Satan—and rescued you, not with troops and arms, but by His precious blood and through His unmerited grace. You were set free through the shedding of His blood and restored to the Kingdom of God.

As we have seen, the writer of Hebrews has described Melchizedek as having no father or mother. He seemed to come from out of nowhere, for his genealogy is unknown. Secondly, he was said to be a priest of the Most High God and yet he was born before either Aaron or Levi. He asked Abraham for nothing. The Scriptures declare that it was Melchizedek who offered bread and wine—symbols of Christ's perfect sacrifice and obedience—to the weary warrior.

Humbled by the presence of the unassuming king of Salem, Abraham was constrained to offer him one-tenth of all that he had—not what had been taken from the King of Sodom and recaptured by Abraham's men. The King had offered Abraham all of the wealth that had been retrieved from the enemy. Abraham declined the offer from the wicked ruler with one exception: from that bounty, he took enough to feed his hungry troops and a portion to reward them for their labors.

Abraham chose to break bread with the King of Righteousness, Melchizedek, and honor him with an offering. He allied himself with the one who worshipped El Elyon, God Most High—the one who followed after the Supreme Ruler of the Universe. Along with the bread and wine, he offered a blessing:

"Blessed be Abram by God Most High, Creator of heaven and earth. And praise be to God Most High, who delivered your enemies into your hand." [223]

Abraham practiced Radical Generosity and was rewarded with the blessings and Favor of God. He gave from the abundance of his gratitude. Abraham knew that all he had was by the hand of Yahweh. He gave not because it was a law or commandment; he gave voluntarily and with confidence in God's abundant supply. It was an act of obedience and trust. The Creator responds to your gifts freely given. He welcomes your deliberate act of worship and consecration to Him. He blesses your Radical Generosity by bestowing His grace and favor on you.

As I have said, "You can't out-give God." I can testify to the truth of that statement. Too often it is thought to be just monetary giving, but that is not the case. First and foremost, God wants the gift of *you*—your time, your knowledge, your gifts, your expertise. The most Radical Givers have given their lives for the cause of the Gospel; others serve on mission fields at home and abroad. Many have given their time and talents to the Lord—preaching, singing, encouraging, baking cookies, ministering to the homeless, spending time daily in prayer and intercession.

Ten of Jesus' disciples gave their lives as martyrs to spread the Good News of His birth, death, and resurrection. Of the other two, Judas took his own life, and John died on the Isle of Patmos after having been beaten and abused for his faith. There is no more Radical Gift than that of making the ultimate sacrifice. Unfortunately, as fanatic Islam spreads around the world today, rights of Christians have declined exponentially, and more are giving their lives. In a 2010 ABC news story, the reporters opined:

> In many countries through the Muslim world, religion has gained influence over governmental policy in the last two decades. The militant Islamist group Hamas controls the Gaza Strip, while Islamist militias are fighting the governments of Nigeria and the Philippines. Somalia, Afghanistan, Pakistan and Yemen have fallen to a large extent into the hands of Islamists. And where Islamists are not yet in power, secular governing parties are trying to outstrip the more religious groups in a rush to the Right.

This can be seen in Egypt, Algeria, Sudan, Indonesia to some extent, and also Malaysia. Even though this Islamization often has more to do with politics than with religion, and even though it doesn't necessarily lead to the persecution of Christians, it can still be said that where Islam gains importance, freedoms for members of other faiths shrink. [224]

To the world, Radical Generosity is a senseless act: "What? Give abundant offerings? How are you going to pay your bills?" Let me encourage you today. Giving opens the windows of heaven and brings God's blessings. They may not just be monetary blessings. . .bargains come your way, unexpected gifts, or perhaps a better job.

The entire New Testament is filled with instances of Radical Generosity:

For God so loved the world that He *gave* His only begotten Son, that whoever believes in Him should not perish but have everlasting life (John 3:16, NKJV).

Follow God's example, therefore, as dearly loved children and walk in the way of love, just as Christ loved us and *gave* himself up for us as a fragrant offering and sacrifice to God (Ephesians 5:1–2, NIV).

I have shown you in every way, by laboring like this, that you must support the weak. And remember the words of the Lord Jesus, that He said, "It is more blessed to *give* than to receive" (Acts 20:35, NKJV).

The Bible records God's promises concerning giving. It is not mere coincidence that the word *give* is found 880 times. The farmer sows extravagantly so that he can harvest abundantly. When he deposits one seed into the ground, he expects a plentiful return. When you practice Radical Generosity, you reap the rich, unmerited Favor of God. When you return to God a portion of your material blessings, you will recognize that "it is he who gives you the ability to produce wealth, and so confirms his covenant." [225]

As Abraham received a blessing from Melchizedek, so those who practice Radical Generosity know how to receive from God. The spirit of giving releases a flood of blessing and you can, in turn, give of your time and your abilities. You can actually alter the effects of adversity and live in the Favor of God by releasing a spirit of Radical Generosity giving in every area of your life.

WHAT I LEARNED AS A MORON

THOUGHT TO CONSIDER: Everything we have been given is a gift from God to use in service to Him and to others.

VERSE TO CONNECT: "I have shown you in every way, by laboring like this, that you must support the weak. And remember the words of the Lord Jesus, that He said, 'It is more blessed to give than to receive.'" Acts 20:35, NKJV

QUESTION TO CONTEMPLATE: Why do you think God has given you the gifts He has chosen to share with you, and how could you express them to help others?

Mike Evans praying with Prime Minister Shimon Peres.

Michael Evans with actor Pat Boone.

Mike Evans with President of
France Giscard d'Estaing.

Mike Evans with Israeli Prime Minister
Yitzhak Rubin.

Mike Evans with the President of Kurdistan Masoud Barzani.

CHAPTER

24

*If you are kind, people may
accuse you of selfish, ulterior motives.
Be kind anyway.* [226]

Terrorists are not blinded by hatred; their targets have been fully identified—whether men, women, or children. It matters little to them who dies.

Such was the case in 2002 when an attack was launched against a busload of teachers and students during Yasser Arafat's intifada. Three of the Cohens' children—Yisrael, Orit, and Tehila—were onboard. Three massive explosive charges were laid on the road that led from Kfar Darom. They were discharged just as the bus drove over that spot in the roadway.

Two adults on the bus were killed, and five children were seriously injured. Seven-year-old Yisrael Cohen lost his right leg just below the knee; Orit (12) lost a portion of her foot, and eight-year-old Tehila lost both legs. The attack marked the third time the bus carrying children had been targeted. As rescue workers arrived on the scene, Yisrael directed them to his sister, Tehila. She was taken from the bus directly to the ICU, where Israeli doctors worked desperately to save her legs—to no avail.

When we at the Jerusalem Prayer Team heard of Tehila's plight, we asked the Partners to make it possible for her to have a motorized wheelchair that would allow her to have greater access. When the funds arrived and the chair was purchased, no press releases were issued and no one from JPT accompanied the chair to the Cohen family home.

It would be months later before I traveled to Israel to meet this extraordinary young lady, Tehila Cohen. She had endured such tragedy but never lost her spirit. She traded bitterness for joy and tears for a beautiful smile filled with hope for the future.

The aid for the young terror victim was a visual picture of what Jesus so often taught allegorically, through the use of parables. He painted word pictures based on the issues of the day. He taught of love, grace, mercy, compassion, forgiveness, and generosity. Jesus also answered with parables to counterpointed questions—the kind intended to test and/or humiliate this Teacher from Galilee. Luke wrote of such an encounter in chapter 10—the tale of the Good Samaritan. It began with Jesus having been questioned by a young expert in the law, one who taught or interpreted the Mosaic Law. He issued a challenge:

"Teacher, what shall I do to inherit eternal life?"

Far from being stumped, Jesus responded in a way the questioner would certainly understand. He answered the question based on scripture:

"You shall love the Lord your God with all your heart, with all your soul, and with all your strength." [227]

Then Jesus added a phrase from Leviticus, "love your neighbor as yourself." [228]

Perhaps the examiner asked out of curiosity to test Jesus' knowledge of the Torah; perhaps it was to contrast his own intellectual superiority compared to the simplicity of Jesus' teachings. Apparently the well-used ploy of answering a question with a question was practiced as early as the days of Christ, for the young man asked, "And who is my neighbor?" [229] It may have been an attempt to shirk his responsibility, to sidestep the law, or at least to free himself from aiding anyone outside his own community or race. Let me assure you that the response did not catch Jesus by surprise; he was prepared with the illustration of the Good Samaritan:

"A man was going down from Jerusalem to Jericho, when he was attacked by robbers. They stripped him of his clothes, beat him and went away, leaving him half dead. A priest happened to be going down the same road, and when he saw the man, he passed by on the other side. So too, a Levite, when he came to the place and saw him, passed by on the other side. But a Samaritan, as he traveled, came where the man was; and when he saw him, he took pity on him. He went to him and bandaged his wounds, pouring on oil and wine. Then he put the man on his own donkey, brought him to an inn and took care of him. The next day he took out two denarii [the equivalent of two days' wages] and gave them to the innkeeper. 'Look after him,' he said, 'and when I return, I will reimburse you for any extra expense you may have.'" [230]

Jerusalem sat on a mountain ridge in Palestine 2,500 feet above sea level. Jericho, located in the Jordan River plain, was 853 feet below sea level. The seventeen-mile journey from the crest to the valley was a downward trek of over 3,300 feet through rocky ridges and desert places. There were sufficient places for robbers to hide and pounce on unsuspecting travelers, as they did to one sojourner. Not only was he robbed but also beaten, stripped, and left for dead.

Then Jesus began to patiently explain to the cocky young man just who his neighbor was. He indicated that the first rubbernecker on the scene was a priest, soon followed by a Levite. Both represented the influential religious community. Because of their elevated position in society, apparently each thought himself above stopping to give aid to one of a lower class. It may have been that both men pondered only long enough to ascertain that the wounded man was not a friend or neighbor—one from their own social strata. Maybe one or both could think of an appropriate passage from the Torah that would have prevented their ministering to the man. Whatever the reason, it was a heartless and selfish act, and was certainly not confined to an illustration in a parable, as you can see from today's news stories:

> On June 16, 2008, on a country road outside Turlock, California, friends, family and strangers, including a volunteer fire chief, stood by as a man methodically

stomped his two-year-old son to death, while explaining in a calm voice that he "had to get the demons out" of the boy. He stopped at one point to turn on the hazard lights on his truck. [Even then], No one moved to take the child. [231]

In April 2010, a man was stabbed to death in New York City after coming to the aid of a woman who was being attacked by a robber. The body lay on the sidewalk for more than an hour before firefighters arrived. Approximately twenty-five people walked by while he lay dying. . .one of them took pictures, however none of them helped or called emergency services. [232]

In June 2008, a 49-year-old woman collapsed in the waiting room of a hospital in Brooklyn after waiting nearly 24 hours for treatment. She was ignored by other people present in the room, including two security guards. People tried to help her only after another hour had passed; she died. [233]

Some of those who refused to provide assistance noted fear as the basic reason for not stopping to help. Maybe that applies to the two clerics who passed the wounded man on their way to Jericho—fear that the attackers were still waiting in ambush. Could it be that the "I don't want to get involved" attitude of this modern age began long ago in the hearts of those two men? Whatever the excuse, they gathered their cloaks about them and gave a wide berth to the victim. They saw a need and looked the other way.

Then Jesus introduced the hero of the parable—a lowly Samaritan, a half-breed. Riding on his donkey, he traversed the barren places alone until he spotted the bloody and naked man on the roadside. His heart seized with compassion, and I can picture him running forward and dropping to the ground to offer help. This religious outcast didn't hesitate; he saw the need and he acted. He was not concerned with fulfilling the letter of the law, as had been the priest and Levite. No, he immediately went to work. He did not reach for a mere vial of water to pour over the wounds of the sufferer; instead, he took oil and wine from his pouch. The two, stirred together, were used as a both a cleanser and a balm. They were not inexpensive choices for the Samaritan. He offered his best. After cleaning the injuries, he took garments from his supply and tore them into strips to bandage the cuts and abrasions.

The Samaritan didn't stop there; he didn't abandon the man to the elements. He placed the unfortunate traveler on the back of his donkey and supported him until they came to an inn. There he took care of the man at his own expense until it was safe to leave him in the care of the innkeeper. The Samaritan left the equivalent of what would have been two days' wages for a worker to take care of any needs that might arise. He assured the business owner that when he returned, he would gladly reimburse him for any additional charges.

Compassion can be costly. Loving one's neighbor as oneself can be more involved than a casual wave when paths cross. The priest and Levite were motivated by the law. As Christians, the motivation must be one of love, mercy, and kindness. Micah 6:8 reads:

> He has showed you, O man, what is good. And what
> does the Lord require of you? To act justly and to love
> mercy and to walk humbly with your God.

Those were the traits of Radical Generosity exhibited in abundance by the Samaritan. He was yet another type of Christ who saves, not by the law, but by grace. He does not bypass anyone in need of salvation by grace. The balm applied to the wounds of the injured man were a type of the blood of Christ, which, when applied to your life, provides salvation and healing. The Radical Generosity of the Samaritan mirrors the Radical Generosity by which Christ gave Himself to provide for a lost Mankind. His sacrifice provided the Favor of God for you and me. Radical Generosity is sparked by genuine love.

WHAT I LEARNED AS A MORON

THOUGHT TO CONSIDER: Radical generosity is sparked by genuine love that overflows from a deep, abiding relationship with God.

VERSE TO CONNECT: "He has shown you, O man, what is good; And what does the LORD require of you But to do justly, To love mercy, And to walk humbly with your God?" Micah 6:8, NKJV

QUESTION TO CONTEMPLATE: What could you do today to "love mercy" and impact the lives of another person or group of people through your generosity?

Former Israeli Prime Minister Shimon Peres visits
the Friends of Zion Museum in Jerusalem.

Mike Evans with family members in Jerusalem.

Mike Evans meeting with President Reuven Rivlin
in Jerusalem.

Mike Evans and Rick Warren,
Pastor of Saddleback Church.

Mike Evans giving this newest book
to his old friend Pat Robertson.

Mike Evans and Reuben Hecht (L),
Mike's mentor.

Mike Evans with the Russian ambassador to Israel honoring Russia
for saving Jews during the Holocaust.

CHAPTER

25

You must make your choice. Either this man was, and is,
the Son of God, or else a madman or something worse.
You can shut him up for a fool; you can spit at him and kill him
for a demon; or you can fall at his feet and call him Lord and God.
But let us not come with any patronizing nonsense about
his being a great human teacher. [234]

In previous chapters, we explored the lives of biblical men and women who exhibited Radical Obedience, Radical Forgiveness, Radical Humility, and Radical Generosity, but there is One who is greater than all—the perfect Pattern—our Lord Jesus Christ. There are many examples of His life from which to choose, but we are going to focus on just four: Christ's obedience to the Father in offering His life; the humility with which He laid aside his robes and washed the feet of the disciples; His forgiveness to those who crucified Him; and the most exceptional gift of all—the generosity of His selfless sacrifice.

Christ was the image of Radical Obedience. From the moment He left the throne room until the day He was nailed to the cross,

His obedience was evident. The very fact that He came to earth was a work of obedience. His thirty-three years were focused on doing the Father's will. Love begets obedience. Jesus said:

> "But the world must learn that I love the Father and that I do exactly what my Father has commanded me." [235]

Not only did Jesus do the Father's will, He spoke the Word:

> "For I did not speak of my own accord, but the Father who sent me commanded me what to say and how to say it."[236]

For many, the desire for things that satisfy the natural man—power, praise, wealth, gluttony, sexual exploits, drugs—take precedence over obedience. Christ battled temptation through the power of the Word, and He was victorious over the Enemy. You and I have the same sword of the Spirit—the Word of God—to brandish against attacks from Satan.

Obedience is not always easy, as we learn from Jesus when He was in the Garden of Gethsemane. When He walked away from His disciples, it was to wrestle in solitude about that which was to come. He fell on His face before the Father and in torment, agony, and desolation, He began to petition for his release:

> "Abba, Father, all things are possible for you. Remove this cup from me."[237]

And yet He ended the cry with a plea for an obedient spirit:

> "Yet not what I will, but what you will." [238]

This is the prayer that never fails. Words fail and grief over-whelms to the point that all you can do is cry out to God. That was the place where Jesus found himself in the garden—grief-stricken, facing the horrors of an unspeakable death, so heartbroken that He sweat drops of blood—but He uttered the words that He knew would capture the ear of the Father: "Thy will be done." He sur-rendered in absolute compliance with the Father's will.

The picture of Jesus staggering through the streets of Jerusa-lem under the weight of the cross is a picture of Radical Obedience. He quietly and humbly submitted to death on the cross. He knew that it was the Father's will that He lay down His life. He accepted His role in the plan of salvation. In the Garden of Gethsemane, He said "yes" to God and humbly submitted Himself to do the work He had been called to do.

Jesus left heaven in order to become the Lamb of God, the perfect sacrifice for the sins of all. He was obedient to the Father's commands, to His call, and to His will:

> "I can do nothing on my own. As I hear, I judge, and
> my judgment is just, because I seek not my own will
> but the will of him who sent me." [239]

His ordeal from arrest to death demonstrated obedience. Song-writer Carl Overholt wrote:

> He could have called ten thousand angels
> To destroy the world and set Him free
> He could have called ten thousand angels
> But He died alone for you and me. [240]

Paul wrote to the Philippians of Christ's obedience:

> And being found in appearance as a man, he humbled himself and became obedient to death— even death on a cross!

Our Lord was the ultimate example of Radical Obedience, and thus lived, and died, in the Favor of God:

> Because of the joy awaiting him, he endured the cross, disregarding its shame. Now he is seated in the place of honor beside God's throne. [241]

✦ ✦ ✦

Our Lord was an example of Radical Obedience, but also an example of Radical Humility. One incident comes to mind immediately: the washing of the disciples' feet. While Jesus was all God and all man, His disciples were completely human with all man's frailties and failures. Peter's faith was strong when he stepped out of the boat, but one look at the waves and fear foiled faith. Thomas doubted; James and John jockeyed for the best seat in the Kingdom that was to come—humanity on display.

In Mark chapter 9, Jesus and the disciples were on the road to Capernaum. The twelve were engaged in a heated discussion on the subject of who was the greatest, unaware that Jesus had been listening to the argument. He asked them what they had been debating. A guilty silence was His only response. Seizing on their reluctance, Jesus used the opportunity for a lesson in true greatness:

Sitting down, Jesus called the Twelve and said, "If anyone wants to be first, he must be the very last, and the servant of all." [242]

Apparently, His lesson fell on stony ground because in chapter 10, Jesus is approached by James and John:

"Teacher," they said, "we want you to do for us whatever we ask."

"What do you want me to do for you?" he asked.

They replied, "Let one of us sit at your right and the other at your left in your glory." [243]

Did I mention that the disciples could be a little sneaky when it suited their purpose? First, the two made a very flexible request: Just give us whatever we ask. This seems a little self-centered, does it not? Jesus, knowing what His future held, tried to gently dissuade them:

"You don't know what you are asking," Jesus said. "Can you drink the cup I drink or be baptized with the baptism I am baptized with?" [244]

In other words, could they withstand the trials and tribulations He would endure at the hands of those who hated Him? This was reminiscent of His question to Phillip, "Have I been with you so long, and yet you have not known Me. . .?" [245] The two disciples seemed not to understand His question, for they, too, readily agreed that they were prepared for anything. Some think this was a prophecy of how they would die—as martyrs.

The ten remaining disciples were happy to know that James and John had requested the most prominent roles in Jesus' coming kingdom. Certainly not! They were angry. Egos got in the way of humility. Self took the central role. Personalities clashed. The "sons of thunder" had clashed with the lightning temperament of Peter, and storm clouds were on the horizon. But just as Jesus had calmed the storm on the Sea of Galilee, He spoke peace into the midst of His rumbling disciples:

> Jesus called them together and said, "You know that those who are regarded as rulers of the Gentiles lord it over them, and their high officials exercise authority over them. Not so with you. Instead, whoever wants to become great among you must be your servant, and whoever wants to be first must be slave of all. For even the Son of Man did not come to be served, but to serve, and to give his life as a ransom for many." [246]

Generally, while on earth Jesus met questions regarding religious issues head on, and this was no exception. Here He spoke freely about what He called in Mark chapter 8 "the yeast of the Pharisees and that of Herod." He was trying to make them understand that in the world everything was—and is—about control and influence, and that was, and still is, especially true in political circles. Followers of Christ, however, should be more concerned with service and ministering to others than with argumentative religionists.

Jesus was to give His disciples a powerful lesson on the role of a servant as He neared the end of His earthly ministry: The scene is the upper room; the occasion is Passover; the meal was at an end. Jesus, the Son of God, the Darling of Heaven, the Messiah, the Savior of the World, rose from the table and laid aside His robe. He took a towel and girded it about His waist, picked up a basin and a pitcher of water, and began to make His way around the room. As He did so, He knelt on the floor in front of each disciple and gently washed and dried their feet.

It was a dirty task relegated to the lowest of servants. Those feet had trod the dusty streets of Jerusalem. They had followed in the steps of goats and sheep, of cattle and horses. The sandals on their feet provided little in the way of protection from the filth. What a picture of humility! What a portrait of servanthood. The Creator ministering to the creation! Gently He reminded them:

> "You call Me Teacher and Lord, and you say well, for so I am. If I then, your Lord and Teacher, have washed your feet, you also ought to wash one another's feet. For I have given you an example, that you should do as I have done to you. Most assuredly, I say to you, a servant is not greater than his master; nor is he who is sent greater than he who sent him." [247]

By His act of humility, Jesus made it very obvious that the role of His followers was one of service, not of infighting to determine who was the greatest. He performed the lowliest of tasks as an example for us to follow. Christ's Radical Humility was the ultimate lesson in how to gain the Favor of God.

WHAT I LEARNED AS A MORON

THOUGHT TO CONSIDER: Living according to God's will is the ultimate act of radical generosity.

VERSE TO CONNECT: "'Abba, Father,' he cried out, 'everything is possible for you. Please take this cup of suffering away from me. Yet I want your will to be done, not mine.'" Mark 14:36, NLT

QUESTION TO CONTEMPLATE: How is God leading you to follow His will and more deeply commit your life to serving Him and other people?

Mike Evans and Jehan Sadat,
former First Lady of Egypt.

Mike Evans with Guatemalan
President Jimmy Morales.

Mike Evans with former Secretary
of State Henry Kissinger.

Michael Evans II delivering food to starving jews and Christian's in Ukraine.

CHAPTER

26

He left the splendor of heaven knowing
His destiny was the lonely hill of Golgotha
there to lay down His life for me. [248]

In an earlier chapter, we read of Isaiah's vision of heaven's throne room and the majesty of Him who sits on the throne. In Revelation, John describes how what we consider costly goods on earth become building materials in heaven. Jewels become supplies for gates, and gold paves the streets. Despite the magnificence of heaven, Jesus Christ laid aside all of that to become a living sacrifice.

Since before the beginning of time, Jesus sat at the right hand of the Father, active in creation, ruling over everything—stars, planets, galaxies, all He surveyed. The angels adored Him. All heaven bowed before Him. John, the Revelator, described the scene for us:

> And every creature which is in Heaven and on the
> earth and under the earth and such as are in the sea,

and all that are in them, I heard saying: "Blessing and honor and glory and power be to Him who sits on the throne, and to the Lamb, forever and ever!" [249]

It would be impossible to define the infinite treasures that are at the fingertips of our Lord. They are immeasurable, uncontainable. The psalmist wrote of God's bounty:

"I have no need of a bull from your stall or of goats from your pens, for every animal of the forest is mine, and the cattle on a thousand hills. I know every bird in the mountains, and the insects in the fields are mine. If I were hungry I would not tell you, for the world is mine, and all that is in it." [250]

He gave it all up in order to become Man! The Lamb of God, Bread of Life, the Holy One of God, the Prince of Peace, the King of Kings laid aside His glory, His robes and scepter, clothed Himself in flesh, took on the frailties of mankind and became the sacrifice for sin. It is incomprehensible, a profound truth. Even more overwhelming. . .He died for you and me so that we may enjoy the glorious beauty of heaven:

For you know the grace of our Lord Jesus Christ, that though he was rich, yet for your sake he became poor, so that you by his poverty might become rich. [251]

Christ relinquished His rights. He surrendered His omniscience, His omnipotence, and His omnipresence. He became dependent on His mother for food and clothing. He took on scorn, rebuke, unbelief, anger, and hatred. He was arrayed not in splendor but in homespun cloth. His feet walked not on streets of gold but on the rocky and dusty roads of Palestine. He was subject to the authority of His parents, Mary and Joseph. He worked alongside His earthly father and studied in the synagogues along with other children His age. And all the while, He continued to be submissive to His heavenly Father. As He grew "in favor with God and man," He submitted to the rite of baptism by His cousin, John the Baptist.

Jesus Christ was the epitome of Radical Generosity. None will ever be able to exceed His giving. He gave up heaven. He gave His life for all. He was the Perfect Example:

> Very rarely will anyone die for a righteous man, though for a good man someone might possibly dare to die. But God demonstrates his own love for us in this: While we were still sinners, Christ died for us. [252]

And no one will ever be able to adequately set to paper the wondrous gift He has given us. As hymnist Frederick M. Lehman penned:

> Could we with ink the ocean fill, and were the skies of parchment made; were every stalk on earth a quill, and every man a scribe by trade; To write the love of God above would drain the ocean dry; nor could the scroll contain the whole, though stretched from sky to sky. [253]

Jesus gave us access to God the Father. When He uttered the words, "It is finished," and breathed His last breath on the cross, the veil in the Temple was torn from the top to the bottom. It became possible for Man, covered by the blood of Christ, to enter into the Holy of Holies—the very presence of God—and offer his prayers and petitions directly to God. What a magnificent gift! No longer was it necessary to wait for a specific day or festival to present an offering. You can now offer your body as a living sacrifice, holy and acceptable to God through His beloved Son. [254]

Because of Christ's Radical Generosity, you can now have the Favor of God in your life. While on earth, He taught of the benefits of giving extravagantly.

In Malachi, God challenged the Israelites to give abundantly:

> "Test me in this," says the Lord Almighty, "and see
> if I will not throw open the floodgates of heaven and
> pour out so much blessing that you will not have
> room enough for it. [255]

He said, "Give extravagantly, and see how I respond." Do you want God's blessings on your life? Well, who doesn't? When you practice Radical Generosity from a heart filled with love and compassion, God responds—financially, physically, spiritually.

God acts in good measure, in great abundance. Have you ever tried to fill a bag with fall leaves or grass clippings? When the bag looks full, you shake it down, and mash it with a foot so you can get another armload or two inside the bag. That is what God says He will do for you—He will pour your bag full of blessings, then shake it down, then compress it just so He can get another armload of blessings into your bag. But He doesn't stop there, He adds even more—so that it's full and running over.

Jesus brought us salvation and crowned His work with the promise of eternal life:

> Just as Moses lifted up the snake in the wilderness, so the Son of Man must be lifted up, that everyone who believes may have eternal life in him. For God so loved the world that he gave his one and only Son, that whoever believes in him shall not perish but have eternal life. For God did not send his Son into the world to condemn the world, but to save the world through him. [256]

Paul wrote to the Galatians and cautioned them that whatever they sowed, they would also reap.[257] If you sow Radical Gifts into the lives of others, you will reap the Favor of God and the blessings of God.

✦ ✦ ✦

Jesus' words of forgiveness directed at those who crucified Him constitute the most powerful message ever spoken. It was nine o'clock in the morning on an ordinary day in Jerusalem. The sun was shining; the streets were filled with people going about their daily business. There was an underlying element of excitement. Word had spread that the Teacher had been arrested the night before and tried for blasphemy. Mobs had gathered to shout, "Crucify Him! Crucify Him!"

He had been dragged before Pontius Pilate, convicted, and stripped of His outer garments. Roman soldiers had placed a wicked crown made of thorns on His head and proclaimed Him "King of the Jews." Mocking laughter reverberated through the palace halls as Jesus, the Galilean, was ridiculed. His tired body bore the stripes that had been laid upon His back, and blood oozed from the cuts inflicted by the cat-o'-nine-tails used during the lashing.

As shopkeepers opened their doors and raised their curtains, the sounds of marching feet and the noise of something heavy being dragged through the streets could be heard in the distance. Closer and closer they came until the curious could at last see the soldiers who were driving a bloody and exhausted man toward the Damascus Gate. Across the road from the gate near the plot where Jeremiah, the prophet, was buried, is a flat ledge atop a hill that resembles a skull. Golgotha, they call it—the Hill of the Skull. This was the Roman killing ground. Here criminals died, and the time had come. Three men were to be crucified that day. Two of them were thieves; the third was the Son of God.

The soldiers waiting on the hillside had likely been chosen at random. It was just another day's work for them. They were on the crucifixion squad; not a pleasant job, but someone had to do it. The executioners were ready for the task at hand. Guilty—they didn't know or care. Innocent—maybe, maybe not; it was only a job.

Soon the mob exited the gate and crossed the road. Dragging the cross was a brawny man, a Cyrene by the looks of him. A man could be seen following him, trudging a few steps forward and then falling, only to be hauled upright and shoved another few steps along. He was totally unrecognizable. Isaiah the prophet had written:

He has no form or comeliness; and when we see Him,
there is no beauty that we should desire Him. [258]

That was certainly true of the man struggling to make His way to where they stood. His back looked like shredded meat; His swollen face a series of bleeding holes where the crown of thorns had pierced His flesh; His beard had been torn out by its roots. He appeared to be more dead than alive. Accustomed to criminals fighting their destiny, the executioners rejoiced, as it meant the man now lying on the ground would be more easily subdued for the task at hand.

With a thud, Simon, the Cyrene, dropped the cross to the ground. Shuddering, he covered his face, turned away, and stumbled to the sidelines. As he turned, he was horrified to see that the body of Jesus had been laid on the cross. His arms were stretched to their limits and ropes were wrapped around them to secure them to the crossbeam. Deftly, one of the executioners placed a spike on Jesus' wrist, and then the hammer rang out, each stroke securing the arm to the cross. The process was repeated on the opposite arm, and then one through the feet that rested on a small platform.

With the spikes and ropes in place, the cross was raised against the sky, and then, with a thud, slid into the hole that would hold it upright. Some in the crowd looked upon Jesus—naked before the world, beaten to within an inch of His life, bruised and bloody— with satisfaction. Their purpose had been accomplished. I can easily imagine that Satan and all the demons in hell were dancing with glee. The Son of God was near death. The Enemy was certain he had won!

Other bystanders bowed their heads in shame and compassion. Their beloved friend and companion hung exposed to the world. Tears rolled down those faces, and sobs could be heard echoing from the hill. As they watched in agony, the indifferent soldiers gathered in a circle at the foot of the cross. "Got any dice?" one called. "Let's cast them for His clothes."

As they began to gamble, a whisper loud enough to ring through eternity issued from the mouth of Jesus, His first words spoken from the cross:

> "Father, forgive them, for they do not know what they
> are doing." [259]

Astonished, the soldiers halted their grisly game and looked heavenward. They were accustomed to hearing screams and curses, pleas of innocence, entreaties for mercy, appeals for water, but a prayer for forgiveness—unimaginable. The Man on the cross had prayed for them, pleading for God's forgiveness for their actions!

The Son knew the Father in all of His mercy and His richly abounding love. He knew the words penned in Exodus:

> "The Lord, the Lord, the compassionate and gracious
> God, slow to anger, abounding in love and faithful-
> ness, maintaining love to thousands, and forgiving
> wickedness, rebellion and sin." [260]

Did those men even know the name of the Man they had nailed to the cross—whose side they would pierce? Did they know His name was Jesus and that He was the Lamb of God, the One God had loved before the foundations of the world were even laid? It is likely none knew just how much they would need the forgiveness offered by the One hanging above them. They simply heard:

> "Father, forgive them, for they do not know what they are doing." [261]

None understood that Jesus had taken on the role of advocate, defending the actions of those who had wronged Him. His teachings, "Love your enemies, bless those who curse you, do good to those who hate you, and pray for those who spitefully use you and persecute you," [262] were more than mere words; they were a lifestyle. It was an act of the will. It was Radical Forgiveness at work.

Jesus taught that there was a relationship between forgiving and receiving God's forgiveness:

> "And whenever you stand praying, if you have anything against anyone, forgive him, that your Father in heaven may also forgive you your trespasses. But if you do not forgive, neither will your Father in heaven forgive your trespasses." [263]

The prayer for forgiveness on the cross was not meant to be the last act of a dying man; it was an example for His followers. As they had been forgiven, so were they to forgive those who sinned against them. [264] This is Radical Forgiveness. Of course, it is often more readily talked about than practiced. It takes extreme courage to exercise that kind of forgiveness. But doing so will bring the Favor of God into your life, and will free you to be healed emotionally and physically.

WHAT I LEARNED AS A MORON

THOUGHT TO CONSIDER: Jesus served as the ultimate example of forgiveness and sacrifice through His words and His actions.

VERSE TO CONNECT: "Jesus said, 'Father, forgive them, for they do not know what they are doing.'" Luke 23:34, NIV

QUESTION TO CONTEMPLATE: What is an aspect of the life of Christ you feel led to more closely follow in your own life today?

Mike Evans and his son Michael Evans delivering 19 tons of food to feed more than 40,000 Holocaust survivors, Jews, and Christians in Ukraine during Mike's second trip to the war zone.

**Mike Evans with Ukrainian refugees
at his Friends of Zion museum in Israel.**

CHAPTER

27

In the final analysis, it is between you and God.
It was never between you and them anyway. [265]

God's favor can guard against attacks even while God's plan
is being revealed. In 1983, I had been divinely instructed
to go to Beirut, Lebanon, to deliver Bibles, food, medical supplies,
and minister to the US troops stationed there. After the horror of
the attack on the barracks that took the lives of 241 Marines, our
group headed for Nahariya, Israel, on the border. I had followed
the sea to Beirut, but it would be dark soon. As the sun set, that
would no longer be an option. Driving south, I made several wrong
turns that took us into Tyre and into the midst of the funeral of
a Hezbollah operative. Our vehicle was a rental car from Jerusalem with the distinctive Israeli license plate—not a good thing
to have when you're surrounded by raging, grieving terrorists.
Somehow God blinded their eyes and we were able to get through
the city.

Once we reached the outskirts, I made another wrong turn. Instead of going to Nahariya, I headed down a dirt road toward Damascus. Soon our vehicle was spotlighted and tracer bullets raced overhead, then 33-millimeter shells began to explode in the desert near us.

We had been on God's business, and now we were being targeted! To add to the gravity of the situation, our car's engine sputtered and died. We had left Beirut so quickly I had forgotten to check the tank. Now we were lost on a desert road, amid hostile fighters, and out of fuel. What else could happen? There seemed no way to survive. It would only be a matter of minutes before our vehicle would be blown to shreds.

As I began to petition heaven for our safety, I was startled by a knock on the car window. Despite my bravado, I jumped at the sound. I thought, *This is it! We're going to meet our Maker on the backside of nowhere. God help us!* Standing there was a young Arab man with his head covered by a *kaffiyeh*—the traditional Arab head covering. He was hefting not a weapon but a fuel can. I wondered how he could possibly have known we were out of diesel.

He walked to the back of the car, removed the fuel cap, and poured the diesel into the tank. He then came back around to the passenger door and pointed at the lock. I hesitated only briefly before pulling up the lock. He opened the door and climbed inside.

"Drive," he ordered. I had no idea where he was taking us. I looked in the rearview mirror at my passengers, shrugged, and complied. For more than thirty kilometers the young man did not speak another word, only pointed in the direction he wished the car to go. After what seemed like hours, he barked, "Stop." The young man opened the door and climbed from the car. He slammed the door, stuck his head back inside, and said, "Safe."

I turned to look at my friends in the back seat—when I turned back, the man was gone! We were out in the open. There was no place for him to disappear as quickly as he had. No one spoke a word until we drove over the border into Israel. One of my friends looked at me in awe and asked, "Can you explain what just happened?" I couldn't, other than that God had answered our prayers for safety. We were basking in the Favor of God.

Merriam-Webster defines favor as "regard shown toward another especially by gracious kindness; a special privilege or right granted." [266] As children of God, we receive forgiveness and favor—His gracious kindness. As I hope you have seen throughout the pages of this book, that favor comes as a result of Radical Obedience, Radical Forgiveness, Radical Humility, and Radical Generosity.

Jesus *humbled* Himself in *obedience* to the Father. He *gave* His life so that you and I could experience *forgiveness* for sin. God's favor rests upon Him, and is released abundantly in our lives when we follow in Jesus' footsteps. One important lesson to be learned: God bestows His favor so that you may be transformed and produce the fruits of His blessing. When that happens, God is glorified and you are blessed beyond measure.

The psalmist wrote:

> For the Lord God is a sun and shield; the Lord will give grace and glory; no good thing will He withhold from those who walk uprightly. [267]

When the children of God grasp this essential principle, they become more assured as followers of Christ. As they are released to walk in the blessings of God—they are then free to bless others.

Walking in God's favor does not mean you will not face adversity. Mary, the mother of Jesus, was "blessed and highly favored," [268] and yet she faced the scorn of her neighbors. She and Joseph undertook a trek from Nazareth to Bethlehem—Mary on the back of a donkey while nine months pregnant. She had no place to give birth to her Son except in a cave where animals were kept, yet she enjoyed the unheralded Favor of God.

That favor is the contrast between losing and winning. It does not mean that you will not face challenges from the Enemy. Jesus was tested numerous times, but He persevered and was not defeated. Not one of the men and women spotlighted in this book was perfect; each failed at some point in their lives. But because of God's unfailing favor and unmerited grace, they were ultimately successful. All were champions, and many were listed in the book of Hebrews' Hall of Faith.

Joseph, the son of Jacob, certainly enjoyed the Favor of God. It brought him to a place of favor in a foreign country—an honor received by few. My life has been blessed with this same favor.

✦ ✦ ✦

As you know from my testimony, Jesus Christ appeared to me face to face when I didn't even believe in Him. I was shaking my fist at God in anger. He's never appeared to me again, but He is more real to me than anyone or anything.

I would like to invite you to know my precious Savior. We all need to know my precious Savior. The following verses explain our need for God, His gift, how we can believe, and the peace God provides.

> **Romans 3:23** teaches, "For all have sinned, and come short of the glory of God." We all fall short and stand in the need of God's forgiveness.

> **Romans 6:23** encourages us, "For the wages of sin is death; but the gift of God is eternal life through Jesus Christ our Lord." When we believe, we receive eternal life as a free gift from the Lord.

> **Romans 10:9** explains how we can receive this gift. "If you confess with your mouth Jesus as Lord, and believe in your heart that God raised Him from the dead, you will be saved."

> **Romans 5:1** teaches that this gift brings peace to our lives. "Therefore, since we have been justified through faith, we have peace with God through our Lord Jesus Christ."

I can tell you for sure that God loves you and has a great plan for your life. I'm not talking to you about changing religions. I'm talking to you about a personal relationship with Jesus Christ. I would like to invite you right now to pray this prayer with me:

"Lord Jesus, I acknowledge that I am a sinner, and I cannot save myself. Thank You for giving Your very life on the cross for my sins. I put my faith in God right now and I make you the Lord of my life. Come into my heart, Lord Jesus. Forgive me and be my

Lord and Savior and take control of my life. I believe that You love me and have a great plan for my life."

If you prayed this prayer, I want you to send me a personal letter. I promise you that I will read it and I will write you back. I will also send you a gift to help you grow in your faith.

Write to:

Jerusalem Prayer Team

Attn: Mike Evans

P.O. BOX 30000

Phoenix, AZ 85046

Or send a message online at:

https://www.jerusalemprayerteam.org/about/contact-us

✦ ✦ ✦

My first meeting with my dear friend Benjamin Netanyahu took place during an early trip to Israel. The Holy Spirit had led me to the home of his father, Benzion. I went to offer my condolences on the anniversary of the death of his son, Jonathan, who was killed during the rescue of Jewish hostages in Entebbe, Uganda. I had no idea what might happen when I arrived, but God had paved the way before me. The elder Mr. Netanyahu was a considerate host. He greeted me graciously and invited me into his home. A few minutes later, a young man walked into the room. About thirty years old, he was dressed in a suit and carried himself with confidence. He glanced at me and smiled shyly.

I told him of the purpose of my visit, and as I looked in Benjamin's eyes, his pain at the loss of his brother was palpable. In an instant I felt the anointing of the Holy Spirit rising within me. I stood slowly, put my hand on Benjamin's shoulder, and said, "You loved your brother Jonathan as Jonathan of old loved his friend David. From the ashes of your despair will come strength from God.

"Yet unlike Jonathan, who died in battle defending his country, you will accede to the seat of power. One day you will become the prime minister of Israel, not once but twice. And the second time will be the most crucial in Israel's history." Then I asked if I could pray with him. Benjamin acquiesced, and I reached in my pocket for a small vial of oil I had purchased earlier that day at the Garden Tomb. I anointed his head with oil and prayed for the Favor of God upon his life. Netanyahu has been a more than capable leader of Israel during two terms in office, and has been compared by some to British statesman Winston Churchill.

At the 1991 Madrid Peace Conference mentioned earlier, I found myself in the midst of Israel's first press conference in the city. I was astonished to see Deputy Foreign Minister Benjamin Netanyahu presiding. The young man I had anointed all those years before was now a polished speaker and an effective representative of his homeland. Only sixty observers were allowed inside, and I was sitting in the first seat on the first row. When Benjamin finished speaking, he asked for questions and I asked several that pointed to the critical issue of Jerusalem. Granting me favor to speak, Netanyahu handed me the microphone. My questions and statements affirming the plan and purpose of God for Jerusalem as documented in the Bible were covered by the world press!

Because of Radical Obedience, the Favor of God rested on me as I found myself in virtually every session at the Royal Palace. Throughout the Madrid Conference, scriptures rolled through my spirit, especially the prophetic ones, indicating that in the last days, Israel would become the center of world attention, her problems unable to be resolved through various peace attempts. I thought of Zechariah's prophecy about Jerusalem being an "immovable rock" when besieged by all the nations of the world in the final moments of history. Surely I was seeing the precursor of these events.

Walking in Radical Obedience, Radical Forgiveness, Radical Humility, and Radical Generosity has produced the Favor of God upon my life—as it will in your life. God honors unswerving obedience. He delights in the kind of humility that is not afraid to be thought weak for the Kingdom's sake:

> But God chose the foolish things of the world to shame the wise; God chose the weak things of the world to shame the strong. [269] [And] For when I am weak, then I am strong. [270]

Radical Obedience can be achieved even when being obedient to God's Word seems illogical. It means submitting to God's plan even when your own strategy seems more logical. Radical Obedience defies conformity and marches on regardless of what others may think. It means stepping outside your comfort zone to fulfill the call of God on your life.

Radical Humility mandates that you do what God has called you to do even when those on the sidelines laugh and point their fingers in derision. Radical Humility will destroy your ego and turn you into a genuine follower of Jesus Christ. Someone wrote a book about the kingdom of self[271] and how it robbed us of a close relationship with God. Like little kids, we defiantly yell, "I can do it myself." Then we wonder why we can't get anything done. God won't go around us or over us; He will work through us—but only if we let Him, and only if we walk in Radical Humility.

Living a life of Radical Forgiveness simply means you relinquish the right to retaliate. It doesn't lessen the price the one who has harmed you must pay. There are consequences to the choices people make. Radical Forgiveness, however, sets you free to move forward, to live your life in God's grace and peace. Radical Forgiveness is an astounding magnet for the Favor of God.

Radical Generosity is generated by an intimate relationship with a profoundly giving heavenly Father. His love for us becomes the benchmark by which we invest in the lives of others. Just as Jesus poured out Himself to provide salvation for us and rescued us from sin and death, so Radical Generosity prompts us to reach out to better the lives both of those close to us and those far removed.

God's favor is not limited to this life. The best is yet to come, and how we live our lives *here* has a direct relationship to what we find awaiting us in heaven. In I Corinthians 2:9 (NKJV), Paul the apostle quotes Isaiah the prophet:

> But as it is written: "Eye has not seen, nor ear heard, nor have entered into the heart of man the things which God has prepared for those who love Him."
> (Isaiah 64:4)

Artists who have tried to paint the splendor of heaven have come up short simply because it is impossible for the human mind to conceive the grandeur of God's house. Paul was lifted all the way up to the third heaven, but failed to write a book that would give us a true picture of the tree of life, those gates of pearl, streets of gold, and walls of jasper. John the Revelator wrote of heaven, but gave us only a scant description of its beauty. One reason it may be impossible to do justice to the majesty of heaven is that it is totally overshadowed by the presence of God Almighty.

When you have lived a life of Radical Obedience, Radical Forgiveness, Radical Humility, and Radical Generosity, you will be greeted with the words:

> "Well *done,* good and faithful servant; you were faithful over a few things, I will make you ruler over many things. Enter into the joy of your lord." [272]

Living in the Favor of God is based on relationships—first with God, then with others. When disobedience, unforgiveness, haughtiness, and selfishness control your life, chaos rules. But as you practice Radical Obedience, Radical Forgiveness, Radical Humility, and Radical Generosity, God rains down favor and His peace follows. When you read the Word, pray diligently, and exercise those four principles, the image of God is magnified and His Word is activated in you.

If you want to increase in favor with God and Man as Jesus did, then open yourself up to Radical Obedience, Radical Forgiveness, Radical Humility, and Radical Generosity. Just as Jesus was affirmed by His Father, "This is My Beloved Son in whom I am well pleased," so will you be as you live in the unsearchable richness of the Favor of God.

WHAT I LEARNED AS A MORON

THOUGHT TO CONSIDER: God's plan for your life includes facing adversity, but always leads to ultimate victory.

VERSE TO CONNECT: "For the LORD God is a sun and shield; The LORD will give grace and glory; No good thing will He withhold From those who walk uprightly." Psalm 84:11, NKJV

QUESTION TO CONTEMPLATE: What adversity are you facing that God could use to show Himself victorious in your life?

Mike Evans a leader in March of the Living with President of Poland, Andrzej Duda.

Mike Evans provides support to war victims in Ukraine.

Mike Evans provides support to war victims in Ukraine.

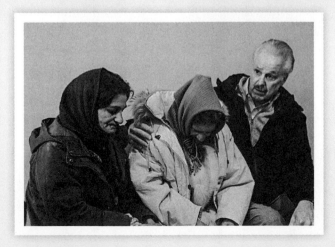

ENDNOTES

1. Corrie ten Boom Quotes, http://christian-quotes.ochristian.com/Corrie-Ten-Boom-Quotes/; accessed November 2012.

2. Ibid.

3. II Corinthians 5:17, NLT

4. Acts 17:28, KJV

5. Revelation 3:8, NKJV

6. See Endnote 165

7. John 3:30, NKJV

8. John 12:32, KJV

9. Romans 6:16, NIV

10. Mark 11:25, NKJV

11. Matthew 23:11–12, NASB

12. Luke 6:38, NIV

13. See Endnote 165.

14. I Samuel 16:1, ESV

15. Matthew 19:30, KJV

16. I Samuel 16:13, NKJV

17. Isaiah 11:1,10 RSV

18. Psalm 27:10, NIV

19. I Samuel 17:34–37, NLT

20. I Samuel 17:43–44, NIV

21. I Samuel 17:45b, NIV

22. Zechariah 4:6, paraphrased

23. II Samuel 18:33, NLT

24. Proverbs 6:31, NKJV

25. I Chronicles 22:2–4, NRSV

26. Proverbs 25:21–22, NKJV

27. Corrie ten Boom Quotes, http://christian-quotes.ochristian.com/Corrie-Ten-Boom-Quotes/; accessed November 2012

28. I Samuel 15:22, NKJV

29. C. S. Lewis, Christian Post, http://iquoteit.christianpost.com/tag/obedience/; accessed November 2012.

30. James 4:14, NLT

31. Genesis 4:5–6, NLT

32. Genesis 4:7, NLT

33. Song of Solomon 8:6, RSV

34. Genesis 4:9 (paraphrased)

35. Genesis 4:15, NKJV

36. Genesis 4:13, NKJV

37. John MacArthur, Jr., *The MacArthur New Testament Commentary* (Chicago: Moody Publishers, 1983–2007). Quoted from a sermon by Rev. Dave Schmidt, Southside Church of Christ, Fort Myer, FL; http://www.southsidechurchofchrist.com/sermons/the-faith-of-abel.html; accessed June 2012.

38. Hebrews 11:4, NIV

39. See Endnote 165.

40. Acts 16:9, NKJV

41. Genesis 6:5–6, NIV1984

42. "Noah Found Grace in the Eyes of the Lord": http://artists.letssingit.com/statler-brothers-lyrics-noah-found-grace-in-the-eyes-of-the-lord-sv36796#ixzz1zCNJs7Nv; accessed June 2012.

43. Genesis 15:6, KJV

44. Hebrews 11:7, NASB

45. John 10:9, NKJV

46. John 14:6, NKJV

47. Genesis 7:16

48. Greg Pratt, "Noah, Man of Obedience," SermonCentral.com, November 2006, http://www.sermoncentral.com/sermons/noah--man-of-obedience-greg-pratt-sermon-on-faith-97649.asp; accessed June 2012.

49. Genesis 9:9–15, NKJV

50. Genesis 9:16, NLT (italics and bold added)

51. D. L. Moody, Christian Post, http://iquoteit.christianpost.com/tag/obedience/; accessed November 2012.

52. Abraham, Jewish Virtual Library, accessed July 2012.

53. Genesis 12:1–3, NIV

54. Genesis 15:2–6, NKJV

55. Genesis 17:5, 15, NKJV

56. Genesis 22:2, NKJV

57. Genesis 22:3, NKJV

58. Genesis 22:5, NKJV

59. Genesis 22:6–7, NKJV

60. Genesis 22:12, NKJV

61. Genesis 22:15–18, NKJV

62. James 2:23, NKJV (See also Isaiah 41:8)

63. C. H. Spurgeon, "The Obedience of Faith," August 2, 1890, at the Metropolitan Tabernacle, Newington.

64. John 19:17

65. D. L. Moody, Christian Post, http://iquoteit.christianpost.com/tag/humility/; accessed November 2012.

66. Isaiah 43:1819, NKJV

67. Exodus 2:10, NKJV

68. Exodus 2:14, NKJV

69. Exodus 3:5–10, NIV

70. Exodus 7:2, 5, NKJV

71. Exodus 33:21–23, NIV

72. Psalm 115:4–8, NIV

73. Exodus 32:19–20, NIV

74. Exodus 32: 26–28, NLT

75. Romans 6:23, KJV

76. I Samuel 15:22, NLT

77. Deuteronomy 6:7, NKJV

78. Exodus 20:3–5a, NIV

79. Deuteronomy 34:5–6

80. Jeremiah 29:11b, NKJV

81. See Endnote 165.

82. Isaiah 40:31, NKJV

83. Esther 2:2, NKJV

84. Esther 3:8, NIV1984

85. Esther 4:14, NIV

86. Esther 4:16, NIV

87. Esther 6:6, NKJV

88. Ibid.

89. Esther 6:7–9, NLT

90. Esther 6:10, NLT

91. Esther 7:3–4, NIV

92. Esther 7:6, NIV

93. Esther 7:8b, NIV

94. Oswald Chambers, Christian Post, http://christian-quotes. ochristian.com/; accessed November 2012.

95. Philippians 4:19, NKJV

96. Genesis 25:1–2, KJV

97. Judges 6:12–13, NKJV

98. Judges 6:15, NKJV

99. Hudson Taylor Quotes: http://christian-quotes. ochristian.com/; accessed September 2012.

100. Judges 6:20–21, NKJV

101. Judges 6:25, NLT

102. Judges 7:5–7, NKJV

103. Judges 7:12

104. Judges 7:20b, NKJV

105. Judges 8:28, NKJV

106. See Endnote 165.

107. Daniel 1:3–7, NIV

108. Daniel 3:5–6, NIV

109. Exodus 20:3–5a, NIV

110. Daniel 3:12, NIV

111. Daniel 3:16–18, NIV

112. Daniel 3:24, 25, NKJV

113. Arthur Smith, "The Fourth Man," http://artists.letssingit.com/statler-brothers-lyrics-the-fourth-man-3z8kkmf#ixzz20uloRyUR, accessed July 2012.

114. Daniel 3:26–27, NKJV

115. Daniel 3:28–30, NKJV

116. Isaiah 21:9, NKJV

117. Proverbs 21:1, NKJV

118. Daniel 6:4–5, NKJV

119. Daniel 6:6–8, NKJV

120. Daniel 6:10, NKJV

121. Daniel 6:11, 13, NKJV

122. Daniel 6:19–22, NIV

123. C. S. Lewis, http://christian-quotes.ochristian.com/; accessed September 2012.

124. Words and music by Ellis J. Crum

125. Daniel 10:9, NKJV

126. Matthew 18:7, NKJV

127. Matthew 19:26, KJV

128. Duong Sheahan, "Unforgiveness, a Deadly Virus," http://ezinearticles.com/?Unforgiveness---A-Deadly-Virus&id=784282; accessed July 2012.

129. Philippians 3:13, NLT

130. Nehemiah 9:17, NRSV

131. Rick Warren, *The Purpose Driven Life* (Grand Rapids, MI, Zondervan, 2002), p. 356

132. Genesis 25:28, NLT

133. Genesis 25:23, NIV

134. Genesis 27:29, NLT

135. Genesis 27:41, NLT

136. Genesis 28:3–4, NKJV

137. Genesis 32:6–7, NKJV

138. Genesis 32:9–12, NIV1984

139. Genesis 32:26–31, NIV1984

140. Genesis 33:4, NIV

141. See Endnote 165

142. Genesis 37:10, NIV

143. Genesis 39:21–23, NIV

144. Genesis 42:6, NKJV

145. Genesis 44:27–34, NIV

146. Genesis 45:3–8, NIV

147. G. K. Chesterton, http://christian-quotes.ochristian.com/G.K.-Chesterton-Quotes/page-9.shtml/; accessed November 2012.

148. Psalm 37:23, NLT

149. Luke 15:13, NIV

150. Kenneth E. Bailey, *The Cross and the Prodigal: Luke 15 Through the Eyes of Middle Eastern Peasants* (Downers Grove, IL: Intervarsity Press, 2005), p. 151.

151. Luke 15:17–19, NIV

152. Luke 15:21, NIV

153. Psalm 103:10–13, NIV

154. Corrie ten Boom Quotes, http://christian-quotes.ochristian.com/Corrie-Ten-Boom-Quotes/page-2.shtml; accessed November 2012.

155. Words and music by Ellis J. Crum

156. Matthew 18:21–22, NIV1984

157. Susan Carroll, "Her Cross to Bear," *Houston Chronicle*, July 8, 2012, Section A, page 22.

158. Ibid.

159. Ibid.

160. The verses written on the wall of Mother Teresa's home for children in Calcutta, India, and are widely attributed to her. They seem to be based on a composition originally by Kent Keith, but much of the second half has been rewritten in a more spiritual way.

161. In 1986, he became the second sitting member of the United States Congress to fly in space, as a Payload Specialist on the Space Shuttle *Columbia*. http://en.wikipedia.org/wiki/Bill_Nelson; accessed June 2011.

162. Isaiah 53:5, NKJV

163. Thomas Ken, 1674, http://www.cyberhymnal.org/htm/p/r/praisegf.htm; accessed November 2012.

164. Numbers 12:3, NIV

165. Isaiah 57:15, NIV1984

166. Isaiah 66:2, NIV1984

167. Phillip Keller, *A Gardner Looks at the Fruit of the Spirit* (Nashville, TN: W Publishing Group, 1987), pp. 169–170. Quoted by Keith Hunt, "Humility: The Precious Gem of the Christian Crown, http://rogerswebsite.com/others/Humility.htm; accessed August 2012.

168. I Peter 5:6, NIV

169. Proverbs 15:22, NIV

170. Jim Keevert, "Seeking Wise Counsel," http://www.hvlcoc.org/archived%20message%20from%20shepherd/seeking%20wise%20counsel.htm; accessed August 2012.

171. Exodus 18:14, 17, 19–23, NIV

172. Exodus 18:24–26, NIV

173. Exodus 14:14, ASV

174. Numbers 16:26, NIV

175. Numbers 16:30, NIV1984

176. Exodus 33:11, NIV1984

177. "Urim" were stones kept in a pouch on the high priest's breastplate, used in determining God's decision in certain questions and issues.

178. Numbers 27:18–23, NIV

179. A. W. Tozer, Christian Post, http://iquoteit.christianpost.com/tag/obedience/; accessed November 2012.

180. Acts 5:35–39, NLT

181. Acts 9:2, NLT

182. Ephesians 3:7–8, NIV

183. Philippians 3:4–9, NIV

184. II Corinthians 12:10, NLT

185. Galatians 2:20, NKJV

186. II Corinthians 11:24–27, NIV

187. II Corinthians 12:10, NIV

188. Jonathan Edwards, http://christian-quotes.ochristian.com/; accessed November 2012.

189. Isaiah 41:10–11, KJV

190. I Kings 16:31, KJV

191. Charles Swindoll, *Elijah: A Man of Heroism and Humility* (Nashville, TN: Word Publishing, 2000), p. 9.

192. Merriam-Webster, http://www.merriam-webster.com/; accessed August 2012.

193. I Kings 16:32–33, NIV

194. I Kings 13:33, NIV

195. I Kings 17:12, NIV

196. I Kings 17:13, NIV

197. I Kings 17:16, NKJV

198. I Kings 18:12, NLT

199. I Kings 18:15–17, NLT

200. I Kings 18:18, NLT

201. Matt Barber, "Today's Baal Worshipers," *World Net Daily*, December 19, 2008, http://www.wnd.com/2008/12/83960/; accessed August 2012.

202. I Kings 18:19, NLT

203. I Kings 18:21, NLT

204. I Kings 18:27, NIV

205. I Kings 18:33–35, NIV

206. I Kings 18:37, NIV

207. Matthew 16:13, NKJV

208. C. S. Lewis, http://www.pietyhilldesign.com/gcq/quotepages/worship.html, accessed November 2012.

209. II Chronicles 26:16–21, NIV

210. Isaiah 6:1–4, NIV

211. II Chronicles 7:1–3, NIV

212. Exodus 24:15–18, NIV

213. Isaiah 6:3, NIV

214. Lewis Drummond, sermonindex.net, "Great Quotes on Holiness," http://www.sermonindex.net/modules/newbb/viewtopic.php?topic_id=32680&forum=35&9; accessed August 2012.

215. Isaiah 6:5, NIV

216. James 3:5–6, NIV

217. Isaiah 6:6–7, NIV

218. I John 1:9, NIV

219. Isaiah 6:8, NIV

220. Isaiah 11:6, NIV

221. Malachi 3:10, NKJV

222. Dr. Timothy Keller, Redeemer Presbyterian Church, New York, NY, http://sermons2.redeemer.com/sermons/radical-generosity; accessed November 2012.

223. Genesis 14:19–20, NIV

224. Juliane von Mittelstaedt, Christoph Schult, Daniel Steinvorth, Thilo Thielke, Volkhard Windfuhr, "Christianity's Modern-Day Martyrs: Victims of Radical Islam," ABC News, March 1, 2010, http://abcnews.go.com/International/christian-martyrs-victims-radical-islam/story?id=9976549; accessed September 2012.

225. Deuteronomy 8:18, NIV

226. See Endnote 165.

227. Deuteronomy 6:5, NKJV

228. Luke 10:27, NIV; Leviticus 19:18, NIV

229. Luke 10:29, NKJV

230. Luke 10:30–35, NIV

231. http://en.wikipedia.org/wiki/Sergio_Aguiar#Sergio_Aguiar

232. Ikimulisa Livingston, John Doyle, and Dan Mangan (2010-04-24). "Stabbed hero dies as more than 20 people stroll past him," April 24, 2010, NYPOST. com. http://www.nypost.com/p/news/local/queens/passers_by_let_good_sam_die_5SGkf5XDP5ooudVuEd8fbI; accessed September 2012.

233. Video Shows Woman Ignored While Dying in New York Mental Hospital," FOXNews.com, January 7, 2008, http://www.foxnews.com/story/0,2933,374321,00.html; retrieved September 2012.

234. C. S. Lewis, http://www.pietyhilldesign.com/gcq/quotepages/jesuschrist.html; accessed November 2012.

235. John 14:31, NIV1984

236. John 12:49, NIV1984

237. Mark 14:36, ESV

238. Ibid.

239. John 5:30, ESV

240. Carl Overholt, "Ten Thousand Angels," http://www.songlyrics.com/loretta-lynn/ten-thousand-angels-lyrics/; accessed September 2012.

241. Hebrews 12:2, NLT

242. Mark 9:35, NIV1984

243. Mark 10:35–37, NIV

244. Mark 10:38, NIV

245. John 14:9, NKJV

246. Mark 10:42–45, NIV

247. John 13:13–16, NKJV

248. Dottie Rambo, "If That Isn't Love," http://www.songlyrics.com/dottie-rambo/if-that-isn-t-love-lyrics/; accessed September 2012.

249. Revelation 5:13, NKJV

250. Psalm 50:9–12, NIV

251. II Corinthians 8:9, ESV

252. Romans 5:7–8, NIV1984

253. Frederick M. Lehman, "The Love of God," 1917; http://bridgetwillard.wordpress.com/2011/04/21/hymn-theology-and-were-the-skies-of-parchment-made/; accessed September 2010.

254. Romans 12:1 (paraphrased)

255. Malachi 3:10, NIV1984

256. John 3:14–17, NIV

257. Galatians 6:7, paraphrased

258. Isaiah 53:2, NKJV

259. Luke 23:34, NIV

260. Exodus 34:6–7a, NIV

261. Luke 23:34, NIV

262. Matthew 5:44, NKJV

263. Mark 11:25–26, NKJV

264. Matthew 6:9–13, KJV (The Lord's Prayer)

265. See Endnote 165.

266. Merriam-Webster Online, http://www.merriam-webster.com/dictionary/favor; accessed September 2012.

267. Psalm 84:11, NKJV

268. Luke 1:28, paraphrased

269. I Corinthians 1:27, NIV

270. II Corinthians 12:10, NKJV

271. Earl Jabay, *The Kingdom of Self,* Logos International, 1980.

272. Matthew 25:21, NKJV

SCRIPTURES

Scriptures on Obedience:

Deuteronomy 6:4-9

Colossians 3:22

1 Peter 4:16-17

1 Samuel 15:22

Galatians 5:13-14

Ephesians 6:1-3

Hebrews 13:17

Deuteronomy 4:1

John 15:14

2 John 1:6

Scriptures on Forgiveness:

Matthew 4:24

1 Corinthians 13:4-7

Galatians 6:1-2

Ephesians 4:31-32

I John 1:9

James 5:16

Luke 6:27

Matthew 6:14

2 Corinthians 2:5-8

I Corinthians 10:13

Mark 11:25

Matthew 18: 21-22

Colossians 3:13

Romans 12:20

Scriptures on Generosity (Giving):

Deuteronomy 15:10

1 Chronicles 29:9

Proverbs 21:26

Proverbs 28:27

Matthew 6:3-4

John 3:16

II Corinthians 8:2-21

Acts 20:35

Deuteronomy 16:17

Deuteronomy 16:17

Proverbs 11:24-25

Proverbs 22:9

Malachi 3:7-12

Luke 6:38

Proverbs 3:9-10

II Corinthians 9:5-15

2 Corinthians 9:6-8

Scriptures on Humility:

1 Peter 5:5-6

James 4:6

2 Chronicles 7:14

Romans 12:3

Ephesians 2:8-9

Romans 3:23

Philippians 2:3-11

Colossians 3:12

Matthew 23:12

Luke 14:11

Proverbs 22:4

Romans 12:3

Ephesians 4:2

James 4:10

Jeremiah 9:23

Proverbs 11:2

Micah 6:8

II Corinthians 12:5-12

Psalm 147:6

Proverbs 18:12

Psalm 103:1-5

> Praise the LORD, my soul;
>> all my inmost being, praise his holy name.
> Praise the LORD, my soul,
>> and forget not all his benefits—
> who forgives all your sins
>> and heals all your diseases,
> who redeems your life from the pit
>> and crowns you with love and compassion,
> who satisfies your desires with good things
>> so that your youth is renewed like the eagle's.

Psalm 90:17

> May the favor of the Lord our God rest on us;
>> establish the work of our hands for us—
>> yes, establish the work of our hands.

Proverbs 3:34

> He mocks proud mockers
>> but shows favor to the humble and oppressed.

Matthew 6:33

> But seek first his kingdom and his righteousness, and
>> all these things will be given to you as well.

BOOKS BY: MIKE EVANS

Israel: America's Key to Survival

Save Jerusalem

The Return

Jerusalem D.C.

Purity and Peace of Mind

Who Cries for the Hurting?

Living Fear Free

I Shall Not Want

Let My People Go

Jerusalem Betrayed

Seven Years of Shaking: A Vision

The Nuclear Bomb of Islam

Jerusalem Prophecies

Pray For Peace of Jerusalem

*America's War:The Beginning of
the End*

The Jerusalem Scroll

The Prayer of David

The Unanswered Prayers of Jesus

God Wrestling

The American Prophecies

Beyond Iraq: The Next Move

The Final Move beyond Iraq

Showdown with Nuclear Iran

*Jimmy Carter: The Liberal Leftand
World Chaos*

Atomic Iran

Cursed

Betrayed

The Light

Corrie's Reflections & Meditations

The Revolution

The Final Generation

Seven Days

The Locket

Persia: The Final Jihad

GAMECHANGER SERIES:

GameChanger

Samson Option

The Four Horsemen

THE PROTOCOLS SERIES:

The Protocols

The Candidate

Jerusalem

The History of Christian Zionism

Countdown

Ten Boom: Betsie, Promise of God

Commanded Blessing

BORN AGAIN SERIES:

Born Again: 1948

Born Again: 1967

Presents in Prophecy

Stand with Israel

Prayer, Power and Purpose

Turning Your Pain Into Gain

Christopher Columbus, Secret Jew

Living in the F.O.G.

Finding Favor with God

Finding Favor with Man

Unleashing God's Favor

The Jewish State: The Volunteers

See You in New York

Friends of Zion: Patterson & Wingate

The Columbus Code

The Temple

Satan, You Can't Have My Country!

Satan, You Can't Have Israel!

Lights in the Darkness

The Seven Feasts of Israel

Netanyahu (a novel)

Jew-Hatred and the Church

The Visionaries

Why Was I Born?

Son, I Love You

Jerusalem DC (David's Capital)

Israel Reborn

Prayer: A Conversation with God

Shimon Peres (a novel)

Pursuing God's Presence

Ho Feng Shan (a novel)

The Good Father

The Daniel Option (a novel)

Keep the Jews Out! (a novel)

Donald Trump and Israel

A Great Awakening Is Coming!

Finding God in the Plague

Hitler, The Muslim Brotherhood, and 9/11

Gabriel (a thriller)

What I Learned as a Moron

TO PURCHASE, CONTACT: orders@TimeWorthyBooks.com
P. O. BOX 30000, PHOENIX, AZ 85046

MICHAEL DAVID EVANS, the #1 *New York Times* bestselling author, is an award-winning journalist/Middle East analyst. Dr. Evans has appeared on hundreds of network television and radio shows including *Good Morning America, Crossfire* and *Nightline*, and *The Rush Limbaugh Show*, and on Fox Network, *CNN World News*, NBC, ABC, and CBS. His articles have been published in the *Wall Street Journal, USA Today, Washington Times, Jerusalem Post* and newspapers worldwide. More than twenty-five million copies of his books are in print, and he is the award-winning producer of nine documentaries based on his books.

Dr. Evans is considered one of the world's leading experts on Israel and the Middle East, and is one of the most sought-after speakers on that subject. He is the chairman of the board of the ten Boom Holocaust Museum in Haarlem, Holland, and is the founder of Israel's first Christian museum located in the Friends of Zion Heritage Center in Jerusalem.

Dr. Evans has authored 111 books including: *History of Christian Zionism, Showdown with Nuclear Iran, Atomic Iran, The Next Move Beyond Iraq, The Final Move Beyond Iraq,* and *Countdown.* His body of work also includes the novels *Seven Days, GameChanger, The Samson Option, The Four Horsemen, The Locket, Born Again: 1967,* and *The Columbus Code.*

✦ ✦ ✦

Michael David Evans is available to speak or for interviews. Contact: EVENTS@drmichaeldevans.com.

JERUSALEM
PRAYER TEAM
✡
INTERNATIONAL

THE JERUSALEM PRAYER TEAM'S mission is to build Frieands of Zion to guard defend and protect the Jewish people and to pray for the peace of Jerusalem. Our goal is to enlist, inform, and encourage 100 Million people worldwide to pray for the peace of Jerusalem as directed in Psalm 122:6.

The Jerusalem Prayer Team also raises funds to meet humanitarian needs of the Jewish people in Israel providing coats, blankets and shelter for those in need. The ministry has a website that includes articles about the people of Israel, the problems being faced by her leaders and other pertinent topics.

Members are also invited to post their prayers for Israel and the Jewish people on "prayer walls" that are actually web pages with hundreds of prayers uploaded by people all over the world. This unique interactive feature is bringing people together before the throne of God.

THE FRIENDS OF ZION MUSEUM

opened in 2015 in the heart of Jerusalem with the help of thousands of supporters of Israel worldwide. It presents a technologically advanced and interactive experience that tells the stories of both the dream to restore the Jewish people to their historic homeland and the brave non-Jews who assisted them in realizing this dream.

The Friends of Zion Museum serves as a platform for fighting BDS and anti-Semitism internationally. The Museum is a non-profit organization operating in Jerusalem and supported by friends from all over the world. This is the first Christian museum in Israel, and here we are sharing the true stories of Christian love for God's Chosen People.

Tours of the museum are available in more than a dozen languages, allowing guests to experience the full benefit of their visit. The thousands of visitors who fill the museum each month hail from across Israel and all around the world.

ידידי ישראל
FRIENDS OF ZION

TO KEEP UP WITH THE VERY LATEST on the work of the Jerusalem Prayer Team, and on events that impact the nation of the Israel and the Jewish people, you need to be reading *Friends of Zion* each month. This magazine is available to anyone who requests it at no charge.

In-depth articles on current and historical events and trends, Bible study and prophetic teaching, and the latest news on the ministry will come to your home each month. It will bring you the truth that goes beyond the often-slanted news our media gives us, and help you know both what is going on and how to pray more effectively for the peace of Jerusalem and the protection of God's Chosen People.

THE ONGOING WAR IN UKRAINE is perhaps the worst humanitarian crisis of our lifetimes. More than 10 million people—almost 1/4 of the entire population—have been forced to flee their homes, with just the few possessions they can carry. Those most impacted are the very elderly—precious Holocaust survivors—and the very young, including Jewish orphans. Tens of thousands are hungry because there is no food. They urgently need our help. Your generous gift today will provide food and other vital supplies to these precious people.

We have been active in Ukraine for over 10 years, and our people on the ground are purchasing bulk supplies in Poland and getting them across the border into Ukraine in a massive 50 ft trailer. We are already a vital lifeline for thousands of people, but there is so much more that needs to be done. **For just $40, we can provide a package of essential food that will feed one person for an entire week. For just $200, we can provide food for a week to a family of four.** Your gift today will help these struggling people. **THANK YOU!**

UkraineHope.com

THE CORRIE TEN BOOM MUSEUM

is located in the house where three generations of the Ten Boom family lived between 1837 and 1945 in Haarlem, Holland.

During the Second World War, the Ten Boom home became a hiding place for fugitives and those hunted by the Nazis. By protecting these people, Casper and his daughters, Betsie and Corrie, risked their lives. This non-violent resistance against the Nazi-oppressors was the Ten Boom's way of living out their Christian faith.

During 1943 and into 1944, there were usually 5-6 people illegally living in the Ten Boom home. The Ten Boom Family and their many friends and co-workers of 'the BeJe group' saved the lives of an estimated 800 Jews and other refugees.

You can contribute to this special work by supporting the activities of the Corrie ten Boom House Foundation with your prayer. Prayer is the mainstay of the work. In addition, you can also give financial support. The Foundation is entirely depended on donations and revenues from the sale of books, DVDs and other items, and rent from the shop space.

DISCOVER MORE ONLINE AT:
CorrieTenBoom.com